Technology for Students with Learning Disabilities

TECHNOLOGY FOR STUDENTS WITH LEARNING DISABILITIES

EDUCATIONAL APPLICATIONS

EDITED BY

Kyle Higgins
and
Randall Boone

8700 Shoal Creek Boulevard
Austin, Texas 78757-6897

This text has been adapted from material that appeared in the *Journal of Learning Disabilities.*

pro·ed

© 1997 by PRO-ED, Inc.
8700 Shoal Creek Boulevard
Austin, Texas 78757-6897

Library of Congress Cataloging-in-Publication Data

Technology for students with learning disabilities : educational
  applications / edited by Kyle Higgins and Randall Boone.
        p.   cm.
   Includes bibliographical references (p.   ) and indexes.
   ISBN 0-89079-716-1 (alk. paper)
     1. Learning disabled children—Education—Computer-assisted
 instruction.   2. Learning disabled—Education—Computer-assisted
 instruction.   3. Educational technology.   I. Higgins, Kyle.
   II. Boone, Randall.
LC4704.82.T43   1996
371.92'6'078—dc21   96-48422
                                                              CIP

Printed in the United States of America

1 2 3 4 5 6 7 8 9 10   01 00 99 98 97

Contents

About the CD-ROM

This monograph comes to you in two formats. The hard copy that you are holding in your hands as you read this is the most familiar to everyone. Words on pages, pages sorted into chapters, and chapters arranged in numerical order—a book. The second format, although totally unfamiliar to some, is very different. The CD-ROM that contains the digital version of this monograph provides new opportunities not only for storing and delivering the information, but, more importantly, for organizing and using it.

One might consider the digital monograph a "value-added" edition. It contains all the original text, figures, and tables, organized in the same chapter-by-chapter fashion. But that's not all: The CD-ROM version contains enhancements that can be made available only through digital editing features such as hypertext and hypermedia links. Key words and concepts in the digital monograph provide the reader with referential connections within a single chapter and between the separate chapters. For instance, a key word or concept from Chapter 2 may be linked to a corresponding section of Chapter 7. This nonlinear organization gives a reader the opportunity to navigate instantly throughout the entire monograph at any time. A powerful indexing system, much like the search function of a word processor, is also available in the digital monograph.

Additionally, whereas print-on-paper publication often restricts authors to one example, one figure, or one table of information due to the economics of production and distribution, the CD-ROM does not share this limitation. Many of the authors, therefore, have provided additional material for the digital monograph that does not appear in the hard copy.

Although it is not the first publication of its kind, this digital monograph is certainly on the leading edge of scholarly publication in the field of education. Readers are encouraged to explore and enjoy this new format for dissemination of scholarly materials.

Technical Information

The digital monograph is delivered on a "hybrid" CD-ROM for both Macintosh and Windows-based personal computers. The digital files for the monograph were created in a Portable Document Format (PDF) with Adobe Acrobat. A free copy of Acrobat Reader (version 3.0) for both the Macintosh operating system and Windows is included on the CD-ROM and must be installed before you can view the monograph PDF files. Once it is installed, you should open the StartMe.pdf file. This will lead you to a "welcome" page that has a button that takes you to a quick tutorial on using the Acrobat Reader. It also provides information about the specific enhancements available in the digital monograph. Help files for using Acrobat are also available from Acrobat itself. In the Windows version, choose HELP from the menubar; in the Mac version, select Acrobat Reader Help from the "Question Mark" icon at the top right of the Mac menubar. Directions for a successful installation and systems requirements for your computer are given below. "Sticky notes" can be found throughout the monograph. These pop-up messages give hints on using the digital monograph and also provide supplementary information about the text.

System Requirements and Installation Instructions

Macintosh

Acrobat Reader 2.1 for Macintosh. Requires a Macintosh with 68020 or greater processor or a PowerMac, Apple system software 7.0 or greater, and 2 MB of application RAM (3.5 MB of application RAM for PowerMac version). A 2X-speed or greater CD-ROM drive and 4 MB of hard disk space are required. The installer will automatically install either the PowerMac or 68K version of the program, based on your particular computer.

Installation. The Macintosh installation process requires two separate installations and a third process of moving files. The first installs Acrobat Reader 2.1 and the second installs a companion "plug-in" that activates the Indexing system in the digital monograph.

1. Double click on the ProEd_GW CD-ROM icon. Double click on the ACROMAC folder. Double click on the DISK1 folder. Finally, double click on the ACROREAD.MAC installer icon and follow the directions on your screen.

2. Double click on the PROED_GW CD-ROM icon. Double click on the MAC folder. Double click on the READER+SEARCH folder. Double click on the SEARCH folder. Finally, double click on the SEARCH installer icon and then follow the directions on your screen.

3. You now have TWO new folders on your hard drive: (a) Adobe Acrobat and (b) Adobe Acrobat 3.0. Follow these steps: Open the Adobe Acrobat 3.0 folder and then open the Plug-ins folder. Scroll the window to find the plug-in files: AUTOINDEX and ACROBAT SEARCH. Drag these files to the Adobe Acrobat folder. Open the Adobe Acrobat Folder. Drag the AUTOINDEX and ACROBAT SEARCH files into the Plug-ins folder there.

Windows-Based PC

Acrobat Reader 3.0 for Windows. Requires a 386-, 486-, or Pentium-based personal computer with Microsoft Windows 3.1, Windows 95, or Windows NT 3.5 or greater, and 4 MB RAM. A 2X-speed or greater CD-ROM drive and 4MB of hard disk space are required.

Windows 95 or NT Installation. From the Windows Program Manager, choose Run from the File menu and type: d:WIN/RDR_SRCH/32BIT/ SETUP.EXE where d: is your CD-ROM drive designation. Follow the instructions on your screen.

Windows 3.x System Installation. From the Windows Program Manager, choose Run from the File menu and type: d:WIN/RDR_SRCH/16BIT/ SETUP.EXE where d: is your CD-ROM drive designation. Follow the instructions on your screen.

An earlier version of Acrobat Reader (version 2.1) is also available. For 2.1 installation: From the Windows Program Manager, choose Run from the File menu and type: d:acrowin\disk1\setup.exe where d: is your CD-ROM drive designation. Follow the instructions on your screen.

1. Special Education Technology: Perception and Action

KYLE HIGGINS AND RANDALL BOONE

Technology in schools is a subject apt to evoke strong feelings. Many educators have embraced it, whereas others have gone to great lengths to avoid it. Still others have passively watched it become a part of their professional lives. But what exactly is this technology that is being discussed so widely? Computers that sit on a desktop or fit in one's lap? Cordless telephones the size of one's palm? Silvery media, such as videodiscs and CD-ROMs? The Internet or Information Superhighway? Remote controls that respond to a voice command? The latest video game system?

In this book, a broader definition of technology is applied, to include not only the different kinds of machines, equipment, hardware, and software, but also a view of technology as being more than just the manufactured artifacts. Technology for a particular population includes the machines and tools available to the group, but it also comprises the specific tasks to which the tools are directed. That is, technology is defined by *how we perceive it* and *what we do with it*. Exposure to good ideas for using technological tools is imperative, then, so that in one's paradigm of technology there exist strategies for use, right alongside the visions of hardware and software. These ideas, depending on one's acceptance or rejec-

Reprinted, with changes, from "Special series on technology: An introduction," by Kyle Higgins and Randall Boone, *Journal of Learning Disabilities,* Vol. 29, 1996, pp. 340–343. Copyright © 1996 by PRO-ED, Inc.

tion of them, have the power to reprogram the way we think about a technological artifact and thus become a part of the technology itself.

All too often, assessment of our success at using technology in education has focused more on the tools of technology than on their application to solving specific problems. Computer labs in schools are a good example of this: The labs provide high visibility for the concrete infrastructure of technology use but do not provide the opportunity for immediacy of use that is necessary for integrating the technology with the classroom curriculum. The key to an effective technology is finding the right match among three key issues: (a) technological tools, (b) problems, and (c) implementation; these issues are related to one another (see Figure 1.1). Adopting the tools is easy; addressing the problems and implementation is not.

Not only is adopting the tools relatively easy, but it also is probably inevitable. We are in the midst of a rapid evolution toward what many are calling the "Information Age" or the "Communication Age" (Thornburg, 1994). Negroponte (1995) preceived the format of our communication as changing from atoms (e.g., books, tapes, videos) to bits (digital information). In describing our move into what he calls "being digital" (p. 8), Negroponte expressed that change not only is irrevocable but also is occurring exponentially. This view is supported, historically, by the S-curve of technology adoption (Horn, 1989).

Viewing the S-curve as a graph of the adoption of a particular technology, the long, flat beginning at the left side indicates early adopters of the technology. The sharp rise at the middle of the graph indicates the time at which the technology became a part of the culture. The flattening of the graph as it extends to the right symbolizes the maturation of the technology. Broadcast television and automobiles are both common technologies that are currently at the far right side of the graph (see Figure 1.2). Computer technology seems to be at the midpoint (see Figure 1.3).

The Office of Technology Assessment (OTA; 1995) report on teachers and technology estimated that every year for the past 10 years, American schools have added between 300,000 and 400,000 computers to their inventories. The OTA report stated that "total public K–12 instructional technology expenditures for 1993 were estimated at $2.13 billion" (p. 1). Money has been spent on the "things" of technology, but little has been

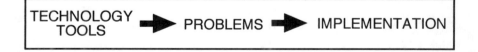

Figure 1.1.   A flow chart of the three key issues involved in effective technology.

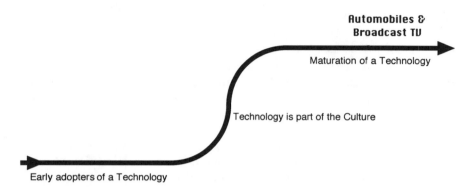

Figure 1.2. The S-curve of technology adoption for established technologies, such as broadcast television and automobiles.

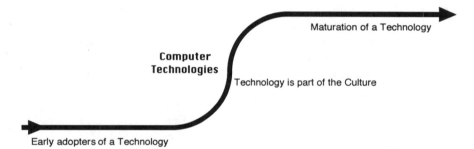

Figure 1.3. The S-curve of technology adoption for computer-related technologies.

done to foster the other, equally important element of the equation—how to use the technology. The OTA report suggested that teachers need the time and opportunity to learn what the technology can do, how to operate it, and when and how to implement and integrate it into their teaching.

Fortunately, not everyone is focusing only on the artifacts of educational technology. A recent report commissioned by the Software Publishers Association (SPA) on the effectiveness of technology in schools painted a positive image of the effects of educational technologies from 1990 to 1994 (Sivin-Kachala & Bialo, 1995). The report, based on a review of 133 research reports or reviews, suggested that current educational technologies can have a significant, positive impact on both general education students and students with learning disabilities in the areas of achievement, self-concept, and attitudes. The time has never been better to explore this impact and to seek understanding of how we can facilitate it.

This text builds on the growing body of research on the use of educational technologies for students with learning disabilities. The authors who share their findings through this book not only understand the hardware and software of educational technology, but also realize the significance of how it is used in the classroom.

Charles MacArthur, in his chapter "Using Technology to Enhance the Writing Processes of Students with Learning Disabilities," outlines computer support in writing for students with learning disabilities. He emphasizes applications that involve more than word processing, dealing instead with the fine-tuning of writing (e.g., spell checkers, grammar and style checkers) and the planning of what will be written (e.g., outlining and semantic mapping software). He concludes with a discussion of using computer networks to facilitate collaboration and communication in writing for students with disabilities.

In their chapter "The Effects of Text-Based and Graphics-Based Software Tools on Planning and Organizing Stories," Christine Bahr, Nickola Nelson, and Adelia Van Meter describe their research comparing two computer-based writing tools (computer-presented story grammar prompt vs. graphics-based writing tools). The computer-based writing tools were used by fourth- through eighth-grade students with language-related learning disabilities to write stories. The authors discuss their finding in terms of the relationship between students' learning needs and the selection of the computer-based writing tool.

"Speech-Recognizing Computers: A Written Communication Tool for Students with Learning Disabilities?" by Keith Wetzel, reports on an exploratory study using speech-recognition technology to facilitate the writing of a sixth-grade student with learning disabilities. Wetzel discusses the promise of this new technology, as well as drawbacks that may interfere with a student's use of it.

Rich Wilson, David Majsterek, and Deborah Simmons, in their chapter "The Effects of Computer-Assisted and Teacher-Directed Instruction on the Multiplication Performance of Elementary Students with Learning Disabilities," examine the learning of multiplication facts by four elementary students with learning disabilities. The authors compare the students' learning in terms of teacher-directed instruction and computer-assisted instruction, and they provide a very interesting discussion of the results.

Beatrice Babbitt and Susan Miller, in "Using Hypermedia to Improve the Mathematics Problem-Solving Skills of Students with Learning Disabilities," present and discuss several mathematical problem-solving strategies that have been found to be successful with students with learning disabilities. The authors then apply these learning strategies and direct instruction procedures to the design of a hypermedia problem-solving environment that makes use of cognitive strategy instruction and the graduated word-problem sequence.

In our chapter "Hypertext Support for Remedial Students and Students with Learning Disabilities," we and Thomas Lovitt continue an exploration of the use of hypertext for content area instruction. This study explores the use of text-only instructional support that was built into a hypermedia social studies study guide.

In "Authenticity in Learning: Multimedia Design Projects in the Social Studies for Students with Learning Disabilities," Ralph Ferretti and Cynthia Okolo present their model for the use of multimedia in project-based social studies instruction for students with learning disabilities. They discuss their current research on implementing multimedia design projects in social studies, suggest considerations regarding the implementation of multimedia design projects, and examine challenges to the implementation of multimedia design projects in a classroom environment.

Lynne Anderson-Inman, Carolyn Knox-Quinn, and Mark Horney, in their chapter "Computer-Based Study Strategies for Students with Learning Disabilities: Individual Differences Associated with Adoption Level," report the results from their recent study in which they provided laptop computers to 30 secondary students with learning disabilities to support those students' acquisition and use of effective study strategies. The authors discuss three technology user groups (power users, prompted users, and reluctant users) and discuss the learner characteristics of students within these groups.

Sheryl Day and Barbara Edwards provide an overview of recent federal legislation related to the provision of assistive technology to postsecondary students with disabilities in their chapter, titled "Assistive Technology for Postsecondary Students with Learning Disabilities." Within the postsecondary framework, they discuss the variety of assistive technologies available, the issues surrounding the provision of assistive technology, and program components found at colleges and universities around the nation.

In her chapter "Multimedia: Enhancing Instruction for Students with Learning Disabilities," Cheryl Wissick introduces the reader to multimedia terminology as well as to the different types of current multimedia technologies. She discusses the educational opportunities and challenges to be considered when using multimedia with students who have learning disabilities.

"A Federal Perspective on Special Education Technology," by Jane Hauser and David Malouf, examines how the current federal program in special education technology mirrors the patterns of change seen in technology research. They also discuss the *Technology, Educational Media, and Materials Strategic Program Agenda for Individuals with Disabilities* (Division of Innovation, 1992), the national agenda for special education technology. The four program commitments of the agenda are discussed. The authors also present a concise table describing the evolving research projects currently funded by the Office of Special Education Programs.

This text came about through discussion with Dr. Lee Wiederholt and Dr. Judy Voress concerning the importance of technology and technological applications in the education of students with learning disabilities. Dr. Wiederholt and Dr. Voress are to be commended—this book is an example of their insight (and foresight) concerning students with learning disabilities. We thank them for supporting this book, and for the support and attention they provided to each of the contributing authors.

We also offer a very special thanks to each of the authors who contributed to this book. We have known and admired the work of the authors in this book for quite some time. Over the years, these people have contributed to the literature concerning the use of technology in special education, and continue to do so today.

2. Using Technology to Enhance the Writing Processes of Students with Learning Disabilities

CHARLES A. MacARTHUR

Mark, a sixth-grade student with a severe reading disability, enjoys talking about his interests in class. However, on writing tasks, his spelling is often so unusual that even he cannot read what he has written. Consequently, Mark is extremely reluctant to write. In school, he uses a word processor that provides speech synthesis and a personalized word bank. He discusses his topic individually with the teacher, who adds key words from this discussion to his word bank. As he writes, Mark can select many of the words he needs from the word bank, rather than having to spell them. The speech synthesizer provides a check on the accuracy of his writing and supports his reading as he prepares to share his writing orally with his peers.

Each month a flurry of activity breaks out in Mrs. Adams's class as the deadline for the class magazine approaches. Students rush to complete and edit their best writing. The editors for the month collaborate on layout and production. Desktop publishing software enables them to produce a professional-looking product, with headlines, graphics, and neat columns of text. This regular publishing project has had a dramatic impact on the amount and quality of writing produced by this class. Parents and peers who read the magazine cannot tell from the product that the writers are all students with learning disabilities (LD).

Reprinted, with changes, from "Using technology to enhance the writing processes of students with learning disabilities," by Charles A. MacArthur, *Journal of Learning Disabilities*, Vol. 29, 1996, pp. 344–354. Copyright © 1996 by PRO-ED, Inc.

As these examples illustrate, computers are flexible writing tools that can enhance writing processes in many ways. They can support the basic skill of being able to produce legible text with correct mechanics, as well as the more complex cognitive processes of planning, writing, and revising text and the social processes of collaboration and communication with an audience.

The support provided by computers may be especially beneficial for students with LD, who often find writing frustrating. Students with LD perform less well than their peers on a variety of written language tasks (Englert, Raphael, Anderson, Gregg, & Anthony, 1989; Graham, Harris, MacArthur, & Schwartz, 1991). They often have difficulty with the physical demands and conventions of writing and with fluent production of sentences. Many students with LD have difficulty coordinating the complex cognitive processes of setting goals, generating content, organizing their writing, and evaluating and revising their text. However, recent research demonstrates that instructional programs that provide (a) a supportive social context for writing in the classroom, (b) meaningful writing tasks, and (c) instruction in writing processes can improve the writing achievement of students with LD (Englert, Raphael, Anderson, Anthony, & Stevens, 1991; MacArthur, Graham, & Schwartz, 1993).

The purpose of this chapter is to review specific ways in which computers can support the writing processes of, and enhance writing instruction for, students with LD. Because word processing is now quite common in schools (Becker, 1993) and published research reviews on word processing are available (Bangert-Drowns, 1993; Cochran-Smith, 1991; MacArthur, 1988), the present review starts with a brief overview of that research. The major focus of the chapter is on computer applications that go beyond word processing. Following the overview of word processing is a discussion of computer tools that can assist with the basic processes of transcription and sentence generation. Next, applications that support the cognitive processes of planning are reviewed. Finally, the use of computer networks to support collaborative writing and communication with diverse audiences is addressed. It is important to note that many of these applications, particularly the more recent advances, have little or no research support. Because development generally precedes research in this field, this chapter is not limited to research-supported techniques; however, the discussions clarify the extent to which the techniques are supported by research.

WORD PROCESSING

Word processors have several capabilities that may influence the writing process. First, the editing features of the word processor allow writers to make frequent revisions without tedious recopying. Consequently, writers may make more revisions, and it is possible that this ease of revision will encourage students to concentrate on content while writing a first draft and edit for mechanics later (Daiute, 1986a). The potential impact of word processing on revising is significant, as revision is an important aspect of the composing process that distinguishes expert writers from younger and less skilled writers (Fitzgerald, 1987). Students with LD, in particular, have a limited conception of revising as being an opportunity to correct errors, and their revisions are restricted primarily to minor changes that do not affect the overall meaning or quality of writing (MacArthur, Graham, & Schwartz, 1991).

Simply having access to word processing has little impact on the revising behaviors of students with LD; for example, MacArthur and Graham (1987) found no differences in the number or type of revisions such students made using paper and pencil compared to using word processing. Furthermore, the final drafts of papers written on a word processor did not differ from those written by hand on any of the measures used in the study, including overall quality; length; story structure; vocabulary; syntactic complexity; or errors in spelling, capitalization, and punctuation. Only two minor differences were found between handwriting and word processing: More deletions were made with the former; and word processing resulted in more revisions during writing of the first draft, whereas nearly all revisions with handwriting were made while writing the second draft.

However, instruction in revision in combination with word processing can significantly increase the amount and quality of revision by students with LD (Graham & MacArthur, 1988; MacArthur, Schwartz, & Graham, 1991; Stoddard & MacArthur, 1993). Graham and MacArthur taught elementary-school students with LD a strategy for revising opinion essays. The strategy focused on substantive revisions, such as stating the thesis clearly, giving and supporting reasons, increasing the coherence of text, and closing with a summary statement. MacArthur and his colleagues (MacArthur, Schwartz, & Graham, 1991; Stoddard & MacArthur, 1993) provided instruction in a peer revising strategy in which pairs of students with LD learned to help each other revise papers written on a word processor. In all three studies, strategy instruction in combination with word processing resulted in increases in substantive revisions and improvement in overall quality of compositions.

Second, word processors give students the power to produce neat, printed work and to correct errors without messy erasures. The literature on process approaches to writing and whole language places considerable emphasis on the value of publishing students' writing (Calkins, 1991). The motivation provided by printed published work may be especially important for students who struggle with handwriting and mechanics. Computers make it possible to publish in a wide range of professional-looking formats. Desktop publishing programs make it easy to produce newsletters, illustrated books, big books, business letters, signs and posters, and many other forms of work.

A third feature of word processors that is mentioned less often is the visibility of the text on the screen (MacArthur, 1988). This visibility, together with the use of typing rather than handwriting, can facilitate collaborative writing among peers and scaffolded interactions between teacher and student. Peers can work together, sharing responsibility for generating ideas, typing, and revising in flexible ways, as both partners can see and read the text easily and typing does not identify separate contributions. Daiute (1986b) studied pairs of low-achieving elementary-school students working on a series of collaborative writing tasks. Through careful analysis of student talk and the resulting written products, she documented ways in which the students learned writing techniques from each other.

In addition to facilitating peer collaboration, word processing can enhance scaffolded interactions between teachers and students. The visibility of the text on the screen enables teachers to more easily observe students' writing processes and intervene when appropriate (Morocco & Neuman, 1986). Teachers can scaffold students' writing by sharing writing tasks and providing appropriate coaching (Cochran-Smith, 1991). The visibility of text on the screen can also support teacher-directed group lessons. Using a large monitor or projection panel, teachers can model writing processes and discuss strategies for planning and revising. As with the other features of word processing, the impact of greater collaboration depends on the instructional program and the skill of the teacher.

Finally, typing is substantially different from handwriting. Typing is probably inherently easier than handwriting, especially for students with handwriting problems. On the other hand, typing can also be a barrier, as it is not a standard part of curricula. Students need some typing instruction if they are to use word processors regularly (MacArthur et al., 1993).

A relatively large number of studies have investigated the use of word processing with nondisabled populations. A recent meta-analysis by Bangert-Drowns (1993) found that use of word processing in writing instruction programs had a positive, though relatively modest, impact on students' writing. Cochran-Smith (1991) concluded that students have positive attitudes toward word processing but that the impact of computers on the quality of students' writing and writing processes depends on teachers' strategies for using word processing, and on the social organization of the classroom. MacArthur (1988) discussed the potential benefits and problems associated with using word processing with students with LD and reviewed the limited and inconclusive research with that population. More recent studies (MacArthur et al., 1993; Morocco,

Dalton, & Tivnan, 1990) have indicated that word processing combined with effective writing instruction can enhance the writing of students with LD.

A growing number of writing support tools are available that go beyond word processing. The next section focuses on computer tools that support the basic writing processes involved in transcription and sentence generation.

SENTENCE GENERATION AND TRANSCRIPTION

For competent adult writers, the basic processes of formulating grammatically correct sentences and transcribing them into written language are relatively automatic. In fact, evidence from studies comparing dictation and handwriting suggests that for normally achieving students, the mechanics of writing cease to be a limiting factor by the end of elementary school. The dictated stories of primary-grade children are superior to their written stories (King & Rentel, 1981), but by fifth or sixth grade, dictated compositions, although longer, are not qualitatively better than handwritten ones (Hidi & Hildyard, 1983; Scardamalia, Bereiter, & Goelman, 1982). In contrast, the dictated compositions of students with LD have been reported to be substantially longer and qualitatively superior to their compositions written via handwriting or word processing (Graham, 1990; MacArthur & Graham, 1987). The difficulties of students with LD with transcription processes—spelling, capitalization, punctuation, and usage—are well documented (Graham et al., 1991). The dictation studies suggest that these difficulties interfere with the overall composing process. This interference may take a number of forms (e.g., students may avoid using words they cannot spell). The effort devoted to mechanical issues may reduce the cognitive capacity available for planning and revising processes. Students may also write less because of the effort involved or because of low self-confidence.

These sentence-generation and transcription processes are important throughout the stages of writing. Consequently, this section discusses computer tools designed for use during both initial drafting and revising.

Spelling Checkers

The most widespread and generally useful tools to support transcription are spelling checkers. Nearly all word processors designed for adults, and most recent versions targeted at schools, include an integrated spelling checker that can be accessed without leaving the word processor. Spelling checkers perform two functions: They identify misspelled words, and they suggest correct spellings.

Although clearly useful, spelling checkers do have limitations, especially for students with serious spelling problems (Dalton, Winbury, & Morocco, 1990). Two of those limitations pertain to the identification of misspellings. First, spelling checkers flag proper nouns and special terms as errors. Second, and more important, they fail to flag misspelled words that are other words correctly spelled, including homonyms and "other correct words" (e.g., *back* for *bake* or *whet* for *went*). In two recent studies, MacArthur, Graham, and De La Paz (in press) found that about 26% to 38% of spelling errors made by fourth- through eighth-grade students with LD fit into this second category. Dalton (1988) reported that approximately 40% of spelling errors made by fourth-grade students with LD were not identified by spelling checkers. Similar results have been reported for nondisabled students (Mitton, 1987). This problem might be ameliorated by smaller or adjustable-size dictionaries having fewer uncommon words.

Two potential limitations pertain to suggesting correct spellings. First, spelling checkers fail to suggest the correct spelling for many words, especially severe misspellings. Different checkers vary in their ability to suggest the correct word; for example, MacArthur, Graham, and De La Paz (1994) reported that eight spelling checkers found the correct spelling for 46% to 66% of the words the checkers flagged as misspelled. Second, even when the spelling checker suggests the correct word, students with LD may not be able to identify the correct word from the list. Spelling checkers convert the writer's task from producing the correct spelling to recognizing it from among a list of similar words. This recognition task can be difficult for poor spellers, especially if the list is long. Of course, a trade-off exists between the length of the list and inclusion of the correct word. Two software design strategies are available to help with this issue: synthesized speech to pronounce the words in the list, and definitions of words in the list.

A recent study of middle school students with LD who had moderate to severe spelling problems provided data on the overall usefulness of spelling checkers (MacArthur, Haynes, & Graham, 1994). Twenty-six students wrote stories and revised their spelling using a spelling checker. They misspelled 4% to 35% of their words. The spelling checker flagged 63% of their errors, missing 37% that were homonyms or other correct words. The correct spelling was suggested for 58% of the flagged words, or 36% of all errors. Students were able to correct 82% of the errors with correct suggestions and 23% of the errors when the correct suggestion was not offered. Overall, students corrected 36% of their errors using the spelling checker.

A final issue about spelling checkers is whether they can be used to promote greater spelling skill as well as to directly compensate for poor spelling. One instructional technique is to have students attempt to locate misspelled words and circle them on a printout prior to using the spelling checker. Handheld spelling checkers, which require students to identify potentially misspelled words and type them on the checker, may encourage this strategy. Another approach is to teach students to use their knowledge to try alternate spellings prior to relying on the computer-generated list of suggestions. These strategies have the potential to transfer to editing spelling errors without a computer.

Speech Synthesis

Speech synthesis software (or hardware) translates text into speech. It is not as natural-sounding as digitized speech, which is recorded, but its advantage is that it can be used to speak any text. Word processors with speech synthesis enable students to hear what they have written and to read what others have written; this capability may support writing by allowing students with writing problems to use their general language sense to monitor the adequacy of their writing (Rosegrant, 1986). For example, students may notice incomplete or awkward sentences, misspelled words, or errors of meaning. In an instructional context that focuses on meaningful communication, talking word processors may help bridge the gap between what children want to express and what they have the skills to read and write. Speech synthesis can scaffold both reading and writing, for example, by helping students read language-experience stories and the writings of their peers.

Research investigating the potential of speech synthesis to improve writing among elementary-school children is limited. Borgh and Dickson (1992) compared word processing with and without speech synthesis with nondisabled second- and fifth-grade students. Both versions of the word processor incorporated a special prompting feature: Each time a period was typed, signaling the end of a sentence, a prompt appeared on the screen reminding the student to reread the sentence and consider revising it. Students did more revising after each sentence with the speech synthesis and less revising at the end of the story. No differences were found in length or quality of writing.

Research on and adoption of speech synthesis have been slowed by problems with the quality of the speech. High-quality speech synthesis, using expensive hardware (e.g., DECtalk, no date), is nearly as comprehensible as recorded speech, but less expensive hardware has been found to have serious comprehensibility problems (Mirenda & Beukelman, 1987). The quality of less expensive software-only speech synthesizers has been improving, though they still do not rival the comprehensibility of digitized (recorded) speech.

Currently, a number of word processors and related writing tools that have speech synthesis are available. The Talking Textwriter (no date) word processing software has been available for some time for both Apple II and IBM; however, it uses the relatively poor Echo speech synthesizer. My Words (1993) provides a straightforward word processor with a variety of text-to-speech options; it will read letters, words, sentences, or the full text. Write:Outloud (1993) provides speech synthesis with similar options for reading letters, words, sentences, or the full text. In addition, it provides spell checking.

Word Prediction and Word Banks

Word prediction was originally developed for individuals with physical disabilities to reduce the number of keystrokes required to type words and sentences. However, it may have potential for students with serious problems with spelling, punctuation, and syntax, as well. A brief description of one word prediction program will provide information about the basic functions (see Figure 2.1). Co:Writer (1992) is a commercially avail-

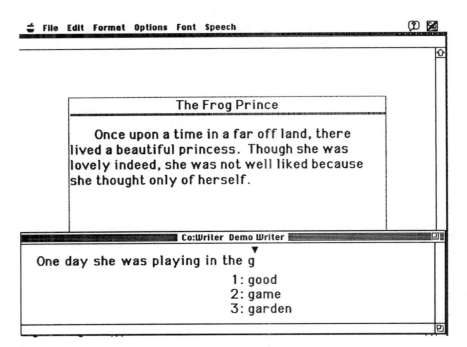

Figure 2.1. Co:Writer word prediction software with a word processor in the background. (The user has just typed "g" and the software has suggested three possible words.)

able program for Macintosh computers that supports word prediction for any word processor. The user types in a window on top of the word processor. As each letter is typed, the software predicts the intended word (offering a list of adjustable length). If the intended word is in the list, the user can type the number of the word or point and click with the mouse to insert the word in the sentence. If the correct word is not present, the user continues to type the next letter and so on. Predictions are based on spelling, syntax, and the words previously used by particular users. Speech synthesis is available to read the words in the list of suggestions, as well as the completed sentence. When the sentence is complete, it is transferred into the word processor.

A related type of software is word processors that include word banks. My Words (1993), for example, is a word processor with speech synthesis and a word bank (see Figure 2.2). In the default operation, all words typed in the word processor are collected in an alphabetized list of words at the side of the screen. This list can also be edited and locked separately from the writing. As a user types, the list automatically scrolls to find words beginning with the letters typed. For example, as the student types a *t*, the list scrolls to the first word starting with *t*. The student can

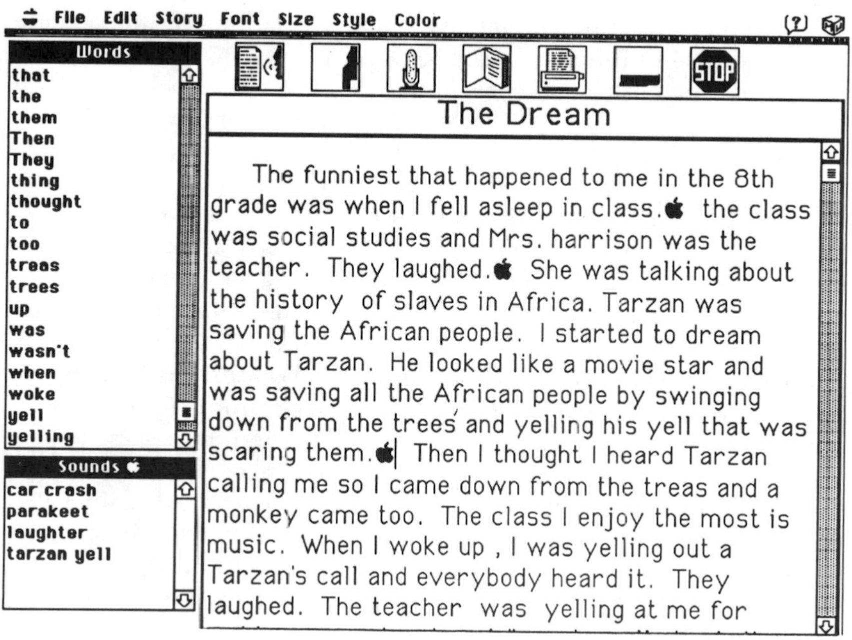

Figure 2.2. My Words, a word processor with speech synthesis and a word bank.

continue to type or select a word from the list by clicking with the mouse. Such programs provide a limited version of word prediction in a format that may be less intrusive than word prediction programs designed for individuals with physical disabilities.

Another approach to providing vocabulary support for young children is the use of word and picture banks, as in Kid Works 2 (1992). This program includes "boxes" of nouns, verbs, and adjectives. Each word is accompanied by a picture and can be pronounced by speech synthesis. Students can incorporate these words into stories as pictures to create rebus stories, or can translate them into words.

For students with LD, word prediction software and word processors with word banks assist transcription during the process of writing, rather than during revision. They have the potential to support spelling, capitalization, and sentence formation. This potential is untested; I am not aware of any empirical research on word prediction with students with LD. Our research group has conducted preliminary studies with word prediction and word bank software, but no results are available at this time.

Grammar and Style Checkers

Grammar and style checking software goes beyond spelling to check syntax, sentence structure, punctuation and capitalization, and writing style. Several sophisticated style checkers are on the market for college and adult writers, but reviewers seem to disagree on whether the advice they provide is helpful. In any case, they appear to be of limited value for elementary-school students or poor writers. They successfully identify relatively minor grammatical and stylistic problems, but often do not interpret serious grammatical and mechanical errors correctly. One program, Write This Way (Emerson & Stern Assoc., 1992), was designed specifically to meet the needs of students with LD. It consists of a basic word processor with speech synthesis, spell checking, and grammar checking. Unfortunately, the grammar checker does not appear to be successful at identifying errors in the writing of students with or without LD. In an informal review (MacArthur, 1994), the checker was used to proof 10 writing samples written by elementary-school students with LD and those same papers with spelling, punctuation, and grammatical errors corrected. It did not flag the majority of grammatical errors in the uncorrected writing versions, and it incorrectly flagged many errors in the corrected versions. When it did locate an error, its diagnoses were often difficult to comprehend. In summary, at this time I am not aware of any useful grammar-checking software for students with LD.

PLANNING PROCESSES

Experienced writers typically devote a substantial portion of writing time to planning activities. They set goals in terms of the intended audience, generate content through memory search and information gathering, and organize their material carefully (Flower & Hayes, 1981). Students with LD may have difficulty with all of these component processes (Englert et al., 1989; Graham et al., 1991). Typically, they begin writing after devoting minimal time to planning. They often have problems generating sufficient appropriate content and thus produce short compositions with limited information. They typically lack awareness of common text structures that could help them in organizing material and in generating more content. In addition, limited background knowledge may interfere with both their reading comprehension and their writing (Garner, Alexander, & Hare, 1991).

This section considers several types of software that have the potential to support these students' planning processes and facilitate their access to background knowledge. Revising processes, which also present problems for poor writers, were discussed earlier, in the sections on word processing and transcription support.

Prompting

The interactive capabilities of computers can be used to develop programs that prompt writers to engage in planning processes, by asking them a series of questions or presenting reminders. The most common prompting software presents a series of questions designed to help writers generate ideas prior to writing. These questions can be designed around particular text structures. For example, for a news article, a program might prompt students with "who, where, why, and when" questions; for a story, it might prompt them with questions about characters, problem, action, and resolution. Writer's Helper (1990) contains a large collection of interactive planning programs, including programs that support brainstorming, freewriting, and categorizing, as well as structured questions. At a somewhat lower level of interactivity, several word processors permit teachers to enter series of questions that can be locked. Students write their answers between the questions.

I am not aware of any research on the impact of using such planning programs. However, some research indicates that simple text-structure prompts may enhance the writing of students with LD (Montague, Graves, & Leavell, 1991). Prompting programs might also be used in conjunction with strategy instruction based on text structures (Graham et al., 1991).

Research has been conducted on software programs that provide prompts during the composing process to remind students to engage in planning or revising strategies. Salomon (1992) developed a special writing program that provided guidance (in the form of questions) before, during, and after writing. For example, questions before writing concerned audience, purpose, and content; questions during writing addressed elaboration, organization, explicitness; and questions after writing posed evaluation issues. Salomon reported that the quality of writing produced by students using this prompting program improved, and that those gains generalized to writing with paper and pencil. Daiute (1986a) found that a program that prompted students to revise during composing was effective in increasing the amount of revision.

Outlining and Semantic Webbing

Outlining and semantic webbing are common practices for organizing ideas prior to writing, both in school and among experienced writers. Many sophisticated adult word processors include outlining capabilities. Early programs for semantic mapping were restricted by screen size and limited graphics capabilities. A sophisticated program for semantic webbing, Inspiration (1994), is available for Macintosh computers (see Figure 2.3). The program permits the creation of semantic webs on the screen with elements that can be easily rearranged for experimentation with different arrangements of ideas. Hidden notes can be attached to the main ideas in the web. The entire web, including notes, can be automatically converted into an outline prior to writing. Most of the semantic webbing activities that teachers use on paper can be carried out on the computer using this program. For example, teachers can create blank webs that model particular text structures (e.g., compare/contrast, description). Whether the advantages of flexible rearrangement of ideas and neatness outweigh the simplicity of webbing on paper is an open question and probably depends on a number of student, task, and instructional factors. I am not aware of any research on the use of computers to support semantic webbing.

Multimedia

The potential of multimedia software to enhance writing processes is just beginning to be explored as new software tools are developed. Although multimedia can also serve as a new means of publication and help to compensate for weak basic skills, it is discussed in this section on planning processes because it has the potential to promote the generation

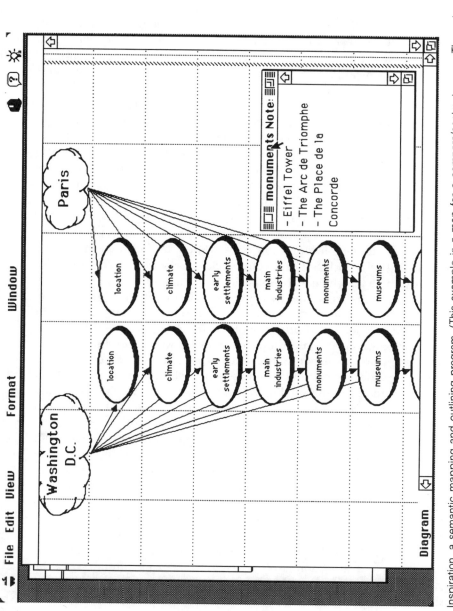

Figure 2.3. Inspiration, a semantic mapping and outlining program. (This example is a map for a compare/contrast paper. The notes for Paris monuments are shown.)

of ideas and provide background knowledge for planning. For the purposes of this review, *multimedia* includes programs that integrate drawing tools with writing as well as programs that include video and sound.

For young children, "writing" often consists primarily of drawing pictures. Children learn how to tell stories, describe their experiences, and explore what they know by drawing and talking about their drawings. Some of the most popular programs for home markets are drawing and writing programs for children, such as Kid Pix (1992) and Kid Works 2 (1992). Kid Pix has a wide variety of fanciful drawing tools but limited text capabilities; Kid Works 2 permits children to create pictures using a palette of drawing tools and to write stories to accompany their pictures; it will then play back the story, displaying the pictures and reading the story with synthesized speech. With other software, children can create visual environments that serve as backgrounds for story writing. For example, Storybook Weaver (1992) provides background scenes, objects, and animated figures for children to use in creating pictures. As they write the stories to go with the pictures, they can rely on a large picture dictionary for words they do not know how to spell. Sounds and music can be added to their stories. The Explore-a-Science series (1993) includes science topics (e.g., whales) for expository writing.

Older students are generally expected to convey their ideas via writing without the support of drawing. However, students at any age benefit from the use of visuals and other media in preparation for writing. This benefit may be especially important for students with more limited literacy skills or prior knowledge in a particular area, due to an educational disability or a different cultural and linguistic background (Daiute, 1992). Daiute reported on a multimedia project with students with poor writing skills from diverse cultural backgrounds. Students collected visuals and sounds that had personal meaning to them (e.g., snapshots, music), wrote about these images and sounds, and used simple multimedia software to combine them with their text. This descriptive study provided anecdotal evidence that multimedia can motivate students to write more and help them find new ways to express themselves.

Although multimedia has the potential to enhance writing, there are drawbacks as well. The addition of graphics and sounds to compositions may result in reduced focus on text—the text becomes relatively less important in carrying the meaning. Creating graphics and sounds also requires time and attention, which may detract from attention to the written text. Bahr, Nelson, and Van Meter (1994) investigated the effect of using graphics-based writing software on the writing of fourth- through eighth-grade students with LD. The software allowed students to create scenes and then type stories about those scenes. The authors conceptualized the graphics features as an aide to planning what to write, and compared this software to text-based planning software that presented questions based on story grammar. Students typed answers to these questions and used their responses as plans for their stories. The stories produced using the two types of software were compared on narrative maturity (a measure of overall quality) and several quantitative indicators related to length (e.g., number of words and T-units). No significant differences were found between the two conditions; however, these results should be interpreted with caution, as only 9 students participated. Clearly, further research is needed on the addition of graphics features to writing software.

Multimedia may have the potential to enhance reading and writing in content-area tasks as well. Multimedia can be used to extend background knowledge and to encourage students to explore their ideas prior to writing. Research on anchored instruction, which uses video to provide a meaningful, shared context for learning, has demonstrated the potential of multimedia materials to make information more usable for problem solving by connecting new learning to background knowledge (Cognition and Technology Group, 1993). In one project, researchers at Vanderbilt developed a multimedia composing tool that uses video to provide background information on a particular topic as a basis for writing activities for individuals with reading and writing disabilities (Hasselbring & Goin, 1991). After viewing a video segment, students receive graduated supports in reading and writing about the topic presented in the video; they can return to the video at any time to explore the content further. Another project at Vanderbilt (Kinzer, Hasselbring, Schmidt, & Meltzer, 1990) explored the use of video news reports to teach text structures and how to use the structures in reading and writing. Students learned about the typical structure of news reports (i.e., "who, what, when, where, why, and how" questions) and how to use that structure in note taking, brainstorming, and revising. Students' comprehension of television and oral news reports improved, and they included more structural elements in their written news reports.

COLLABORATIVE WRITING AND PUBLISHING WITH NETWORKS

As mentioned earlier in the section on word processing, computers can change the social context for writing by supporting publishing and collaborative writing in the classroom. Formats for publishing can be further extended with multimedia software. In addition, networks (both local area networks within a school and telecommunications networks) can offer expanded opportunities for collaborative writing and communication with diverse audiences.

In one early educational application of telecommunications, Riel (1985) developed an electronic newswire that involved students from geographically diverse cultures in collaborative production of a newspaper. Because the students from California and Alaska did not share the same cultural knowledge, they had to struggle to communicate clearly. Using a similar network with seventh-grade students from Israel, Cohen and Riel (1989) conducted a study to explore the effects of writing for authentic audiences of peers from different cultural backgrounds. They reported that essays written by students for distant peers were superior to essays written to be graded by their teachers, because the former were more explicit and detailed. Telecommunication networks for use by schools are supported by a number of state and national organizations.

Local area networks can also be used to support communication in writing. Peyton and Batson (1986) used a network within a classroom to teach writing to students with hearing impairment whereby all discussion and interaction were conducted in writing. Students viewed the ongoing conversation on their computer screens and participated by typing their remarks. For students with hearing impairment, the network provided an immersion approach to mastering English. Students with LD may also benefit from writing on such a network. The network interaction can change the social context for writing by providing a connection between conversation and formal writing.

CONCLUDING COMMENTS

As the capabilities of computers have increased in the past decade, a variety of exciting new tools have been developed that have the potential to enhance the writing of students with LD. Basic tools, such as spelling checkers, have become common even on simple word processors. Printing features and desktop publishing have become more powerful and easier to use. The quality of speech synthesis has improved, and the variety of programs providing speech has expanded. Word prediction software has become available to support access to writing and reading. Telecommunications networks are accessible to schools willing to invest in modems and a phone line. Multimedia programs that integrate drawing and writing are widely available, and programs that integrate photographs, video, and sound with writing will become increasingly available in the next few years.

The challenge for special educators is twofold: First, existing research on word processing makes it clear that simply providing technology to teachers and students will not result in improvements in students' writing. Effective instructional methods must be developed that make use of the power provided by these tools to enhance the writing of students with LD. Second, as this review reveals, research on computers and writing has been limited primarily to studies of the effects of basic word processing. Researchers need to go beyond word processing to investigate the effects of instruction using a range of technological tools to support writing. This review has attempted to provide a framework for both the development of instructional methods using technology and research on their effectiveness. Teachers, administrators, teacher educators, and researchers need to collaborate in this effort to transform the potential of technology into reality.

Author's Note

Preparation of this chapter was partially supported by a grant from the U.S. Department of Education (No. H180G30033). However, the opinions expressed are those of the author and no official endorsement is implied.

3. The Effects of Text-Based and Graphics-Based Software Tools on Planning and Organizing of Stories

CHRISTINE M. BAHR, NICKOLA W. NELSON,

AND ADELIA M. VAN METER

Untitled Story

the teacher opened the window. Then the bird came in . I got out of my chair and chased the bird. The feathers came off his wings. emily got of her seat quiet.emily ran out of classroom. tod made a loud noise. the bird flew out of the window.it went of the window.

Dinosaurs

the dinosaurs are fighting each other.there 8 triceratops. there are 10 tyrannosaurus. the triceratops won the fight. the triceratops left the place. THEY fight each other.THE t/rex fight the triceratops. THE triceratops fought the bront. THE bront fought the t/rex. 1 BRONT fought the fight. THE BRONT WON THE FIGHT. THE T/REX LOST THE FIGHT THE TRICERATOPs won the fight against the t/rex. the t/rex lost the fight.

These two stories were written by the same student using two different software programs that supported different aspects of the prewriting process.

Reprinted, with changes, from "The effects of text-based and graphics-based software tools on planning and organizing of stories," by Christine M. Bahr, Nickola W. Nelson, and Adelia M. Van Meter, *Journal of Learning Disabilities*, Vol. 29, 1996, pp. 355–370. Copyright © 1996 by PRO-ED, Inc.

The first program offered a "frozen text" feature to present a series of question prompts about story grammar components (Stein & Glenn, 1979, 1982), which the student answered as a means of planning and organizing his story. The second program presented a set of graphic choices, organized by theme, which the student used to construct a picture by clicking on labels for background scenery, people, animals, and objects, after which he wrote a corresponding story. The stories were composed over several sessions in a university-based after-school writing lab that was offered as a component of a broader research project called "Linking Text-Processing Tools to Student Needs" (Bahr & Nelson, 1993).

WRITING PROBLEMS OF STUDENTS WITH LD

Students with learning disabilities (LD) in the middle grades experience problems with multiple aspects of the writing process. Their problems extend beyond "difficulty with the physical demands and conventions of writing" and include "difficulty setting goals for communication, generating content, organizing material according to common text structures, and evaluating and revising their writing" (MacArthur, Schwartz, & Graham, 1991, p. 230). Students with learning disabilities are less likely to produce narrative compositions that qualify as stories than are peers with reading problems or no disabilities (Nodine, Barenbaum, & Newcomer, 1985). The stories they do write have less well-developed ideas (Montague, Maddux, & Dereshiwsky, 1990) and are shorter and less coherent than those of their peers (Newcomer, Barenbaum, & Nodine, 1988; Vallecorsa & Garriss, 1990). Englert (1992) summarized evidence pointing to these students' "difficulty manipulating and perceiving the relationship among ideas, monitoring their texts, and using writing strategies to produce coherent texts" (p. 153). When students with learning disabilities write stories, "they might forget to develop the story by including a problem and a plan, or the story might be finished abruptly without an ending" (Graves & Montague, 1991, p. 247). Many adopt the "What next?" strategy of beginning authors (Bereiter & Scardamalia, 1987; Scardamalia & Bereiter, 1986), simply writing whatever comes to mind (Thomas, Englert, & Gregg, 1987).

WORD PROCESSING AS AN INSTRUCTIONAL TOOL

Word processing with microcomputers has been suggested as one tool for helping such students to improve their writing. Computers have the potential to motivate reluctant writers to write; to facilitate the physical processes of writing, revising, and editing; and to result in the publication of neatly printed work (Cochran & Bull, 1991; MacArthur, 1993). Students like to use word processors (Bing, Swicegood, Delaney, & Hallum, 1993; Storeygard, Simmons, Stumpf, & Pavloglou, 1993); and Vacc (1987) found that students with mild intellectual impairments spent more time writing letters, wrote longer letters, and made more revisions in their writing when they used computers compared with writing by hand.

Some word processing programs offer special features that may be helpful to students with learning disabilities, such as synthetic-speech feedback, spelling assistance, word cueing and prediction, organizational assistance, and grammar correction and tutoring (Hunt-Berg, Rankin, & Beukelman, 1994; MacArthur, 1993). However, the impact of selected software features on students' written language development is still mostly a matter of conjecture (MacArthur, 1993).

Previous research on computer support for improving the writing skills of students with learning disabilities has yielded mixed results. In Vacc's (1987) research, students, in spite of their favorable responses to using computers, wrote more words per unit of time in the handwritten versions, and judges' holistic evaluations of letters produced under the two conditions did not differ significantly. Similarly, when MacArthur and Graham (1987) compared effects of writing by hand and using word processors on the story composition of 11 fifth- and sixth-grade students with LD, they found no discernible advantages for the computer-based versions. Stories the students produced under the two conditions did not differ in length, quality, story structure, grammatical errors, T-unit length, vocabulary, or mechanical errors. As this study and subsequent research reviews have suggested (Bangert-Drowns, 1993; Cochran-Smith, 1991; Graham, Harris, MacArthur, & Schwartz, 1991; MacArthur, 1988), simply providing a student with a microcomputer as a tool yields no special benefits in terms of written language skill.

PROCESS APPROACHES TO WRITING INSTRUCTION

MacArthur et al. (1991) showed that when computer use is combined with effective writing instruction, word processing can yield benefits for students with written-language disabilities. Their Computers and Writing Instruction Project (CWIP) was implemented by 25 elementary- and middle-school special education teachers in self-contained LD classrooms in urban, suburban, and rural districts. In addition to computers, the teachers used an instructional approach that focused on writing as a process, accompanied by explicit instruction in the use of strategies for planning and peer revision. Benefits found for the CWIP students over the controls included significant gains in the overall quality of their writing, and longer compositions with lower proportions of misspelled words (MacArthur, Graham, & Schwartz, 1993).

The writing process approach, as developed by such general educators as Atwell (1987), Calkins (1983, 1991), and Graves (1983), is widely used by many special educators at both the elementary and the secondary level (Graham & Harris, 1994). The writing process approach, like other constructivist methods, is based on a philosophy that students learn best in the process of constructing their own meanings. Students are encouraged to focus as much attention on the process of writing as on its products; to engage in recursive processes of planning, drafting, revising, and editing; to write for extended periods of time on the same piece; to gain a sense of control over the decisions they make about their writing; to write for authentic purposes and real audiences; to learn about the strategies and conventions of writing within the contexts of holistic writing experiences; and to publish what they write.

Although these features appear to offer many advantages for reluctant writers, some special educators express concern that such purely constructivist approaches as whole language and writing process instruction may not be powerful enough for students with specialized language-learning needs. Graham and Harris (1994), after reviewing their own and others' research, suggested that the benefits of a process approach to writing instruction may be weakened for writers with special needs by an overreliance on incidental learning and a lack of explicit emphasis on the mechanics of writing. Englert (1992) also noted teachers' uncertainties about how to implement such procedures. She reported that many teachers who had attended process writing workshops emphasizing social-constructivist techniques still used traditional methods based on the assumption "that students would learn to write simply by being asked to write, and by receiving instruction that emphasized writing directions and assignments" (p. 154).

SCAFFOLDING TO SUPPORT PLANNING AND ORGANIZING

Scaffolding, strategy instruction, and procedural facilitation were all designed to provide students with disabilities with additional support for learning the writing process. Although the approaches have similar goals for moving students toward independence, they also have some distinctions. Of the three, scaffolding is the least predetermined and structured. The term *scaffolding* comes from descriptions of parental verbal and nonverbal prompting of children in their early attempts to attach meaning and function to language. Bruner (1978) likened this procedure to constructing a building, whereby a scaffold is initially built to support a wall, but, as the wall becomes more structurally complete, it supports itself and the scaffold is disassembled. Scaffolding allows a "novice to carry out new tasks while learning strategies and patterns that will eventually make it possible to carry out similar tasks without support" (Applebee & Langer, 1983, p. 169).

Scaffolding Dialogues

In scaffolding dialogues, an adult or more mature peer uses questions, comments, and cues to frame, focus, and feed information back to help the student move to a higher level of understanding (Cazden, 1983; Nelson, 1995; Tharp & Gallimore, 1988). Such dialogues are fluid and cannot be effectively prescripted (Englert, 1992). Although an instructor may enter an instructional interaction with the intent to address particular needs, the dialogue is a real conversation in that its direction may be influenced by either participant. Englert and Palincsar (1991), after noting the importance of fidelity to teaching protocols in conducting research, argued that "an equally important part of the teaching equation is teachers' moment-to-moment responsiveness to their students, and their abilities to make bridges between what their students know and need to know" (p. 228).

Strategy Instruction

Whereas scaffolding is responsive to the learning demands and opportunities of the moment, strategy instruction tends to be more preplanned and structured. To some extent, strategies represent the internalized structures that scaffolding is designed to teach. For example, Englert (1992) described how she and her colleagues, in their Cognitive Strategy Instruction in Writing Project, encouraged teachers to use scaffolding dialogues to model the use of "plan think-sheets" by focusing students on prewriting questions related to audience ("Who am I writing for?"), purpose ("Why am I writing this?"), and organization ("How can I group my ideas?"). Englert emphasized the role of teachers as responsive mediators in the scaffolding process, noting that the teachers whose students achieved the best results were those who "emphasized the holistic and strategic nature of writing using dialogic and scaffolded instruction" (p. 170), and, further, that such teachers "were more effective than teachers who rigidly and rotely implemented the writing curriculum and presented think-sheets and strategies in a procedural manner" (p. 170).

Strategy instruction may also involve teaching students to use a mnemonic device for self-cuing, accompanied by practice in using the strategy. Strategy instruction aimed specifically at planning and organizing narrative writing has often focused on teaching students to include more story grammar elements (as described by Stein & Glenn, 1979, 1982). For example, Graham and Harris (1989) taught students a mnemonic device for asking themselves a series of "who, what, and how" questions (two each) related to the inclusion of story grammar elements. They reported positive effects on the students' compositions and sense of self-efficacy. MacArthur et al. (1991) suggested the mnemonic "C-SPACE" (Characters, Setting, Problem or Purpose, Action, Conclusion, Emotion) for a similar purpose (see also MacArthur et al., 1993).

Procedural Facilitation

Scardamalia and Bereiter (1986) described "procedural facilitation" as a similar approach to fostering students' acquisition of improved writing processes. An example of procedural facilitation was provided by Montague, Graves, and Leavell (1991), who helped students write more mature stories independently by providing extra planning time and a story grammar cue card. Results showed improved length and quality of dictated or handwritten stories for junior high school students with learning disabilities when the additional planning time and cue cards were provided. These results complemented those of Graves, Montague, and Wong (1990), who found that students with learning disabilities wrote stories that rated higher on both qualitative and quantitative measures when the students used a check-off sheet to monitor the inclusion of the story grammar elements (character, setting, problem, plan, and resolution) in their compositions.

Pictures as Prewriting Prompts

In addition to varied presentations of story grammar prompts, picture drawing has long been recognized as an important prewriting support for children in the early stages of learning to read and write (e.g., Calkins, 1983; Teale & Sulzby, 1986). Daiute (1992) advocated extending the use of multimedia supports for story composition into the upper grades as a bridge to composing in text-only media. She commented particularly on the needs of students with different cultural and linguistic experiences or with disabilities, noting that "when the words don't come, a picture is an acceptable substitute or prewriting activity" (p. 250).

Golub and Frederick (1970) studied the use of pictures as writing prompts, compared with writing from memory, and found that children developed ideas more fully and with more linguistic complexity when basing their writing on visual prompts, but that images had to be meaningful to the children to be helpful. Bereiter and Scardamalia (1985) also noted some unique cognitive features associated with the process of planning to write, pointing out that authors considering a potential topic must make a "meta-memorial search" to decide whether they know enough about a topic to write about it. This leads to the question about whether a visual image on a computer screen might make the memory search easier because of its relative stability during the searching process, or whether it might make the process more difficult by suggesting topics that are not sufficiently represented in the author's knowledge base.

Some distinction should be made between the strategy of using pictures to assign topics for writing and that of giving students a tool for constructing their own pictures before writing. Barenbaum, Newcomer, and Nodine (1987) compared stories written under two conditions, with pictures (but not with computers), by students who (a) had learning disabilities, (b) were normally achieving, or (c) were low achieving. In the first task, students saw a cartoon picture of a pig in a kitchen and received directions to write a complete story with a beginning, middle, and ending to go with the picture, along with the directions, "Your story could begin, 'Mama Pig is making breakfast'" (p. 177). In the second task, students received directions to draw a picture first, with reminders that "the picture should go with the story you are thinking up" (p. 177), "a good story has a beginning, middle, and ending"(pp. 177–178), and it is "best to plan a whole story before you begin"(p. 178). Finally, students were told, "Your story could begin, 'Mr. Jones likes working on a farm'" (p. 178). The students with learning disabilities wrote fewer mature stories under either condition than the other two groups; and none of the stories showed significant differences related to task. The authors concluded that "the picture-drawing task not only failed to facilitate story writing but interfered with the story production of children who knew how to write stories" (p. 183). Interpretation of these results, however, is clouded by the verbal prompts about how to begin stories, which suggested a particular topic choice.

Atwell (1987) emphasized the importance of free topic choice for preadolescent writers using a writing process approach. She acknowledged that some have trouble getting started but showed how to scaffold the planning process by modeling her own thinking, such as, "This morning when I woke up I knew we'd be writing today. So right away I started turning over different ideas in my mind while I was getting ready for school" (p. 78). It may be that particular software can provide an analogue for this form of scaffolding, helping students to turn over pictures on a computer screen as a stimulus for planning what to write.

PURPOSE OF THE STUDY

The primary purpose of the current study was to compare the effects of two prewriting software features on stories written by students with language and learning disabilities and their writing processes. The first feature was a story grammar prompt strategy, in which a computer-based scaffold presented "frozen text" questions for students to answer prior to writing. The second was a stimulus-picture construction strategy, in which students could select background and foreground elements from among several thematic choices and construct a picture prior to writing. These two features supported planning and organizing in different ways. The purpose of the study was twofold: (a) to identify group effects, in terms of measurable differences between stories produced using the two software features, and (b) to determine the extent to which individuals responded differentially to the software features.

METHOD

Subjects

Selection Criteria.   Participants were recruited from school districts in southwestern Michigan. Criteria for participation were as follows:

1. Referral by a learning disability specialist or speech–language pathologist as having learning disabilities and/or language impairments involving written-language processing;

2. Written language constituting a goal area in the student's Individualized Education Program;

3. Intelligence scores within normal limits;

4. Absence of serious emotional or behavioral disturbance;

5. Ability to complete a formal test battery (described in an upcoming section);

6. Enrollment in the fourth through eighth grade;

7. Permission from parents to participate, and transportation provided by parents to the after-school writing lab sessions twice per week.

Thirteen students began the study, which was conducted over 11 weeks at the beginning of a school year. Four students did not attend regularly so their data could not be used; thus, the analyses reported here are for 9 students.

Demographic data (see Table 3.1) were collected using procedures based on guidelines established by Entwisle and Astone (1994) for measuring youths' race/ethnicity and socioeconomic status. The 9 students who attended the lab regularly and completed all dependent measures were 7 males and 2 females ranging in age from 9 years 3 months to 13 years 9 months. Their mean age was 11 years 4 months (SD = 16.53). Parental education and employment data (provided by parents) indicated middle class socioeconomic status, with most parents having finished high school and at least some postsecondary education, and with most being employed in semiprofessional to professional occupations.

Diagnostic Written Language Assessment and Student Profiles.   Prior to participating in the writing lab, the students underwent a comprehensive diagnostic assessment of their written-language skills. Assessments were conducted in individual clinic rooms by trained graduate students in speech–language pathology enrolled in a diagnostic clinical practicum, under the supervision of a trained speech–language pathologist. The supervisor observed through a one-way mirror and double-scored all test protocols. Assessments were conducted over 2 days, requiring 2 hours on the first day and 1½ hours on the second.

The written-language assessment battery included three formal measures: (a) the Boder Test of Reading–Spelling Patterns (Boder & Jarrico, 1982), (b) the Writing Process Test (WPT; Warden & Hutchinson, 1992), and (c) the Test of Written Language-2 (TOWL-2; Hammill & Larsen, 1988). Scores for these measures are reported in Table 3.2. The scores for the Boder are shown as grade equivalents representing the grade level at which students could read single words with "flash" recognition out of context.

The scores on the WPT represent two sets of ratings, both based on compositions written in response to a prompt to write a piece for the school newspaper based on the students' most exciting experience and most boring experience. The first set yields a *development* score based on ratings of purpose/focus, audience, vocabulary, style/tone, support/ development, and organization/coherence. The second yields a *fluency* score based on ratings of sentence structure/variety, grammar/usage, capitalization/punctuation, and spelling. All ratings were assigned by examiners who had successfully completed the extensive training and calibration experiences provided by the test authors. Thus, ratings are reported as standard scores based on comparisons with normative data.

To describe individual students' relative patterns of strength and need, comparisons were made between the two sets of scores (development and fluency). This relational profile is reported as "=" if no significant difference was detected between subscores (i.e., if they were less than 1 SD apart); as " >" if students' organizational skills (development

TABLE 3.1
Demographic Characteristics of Participants

Student	Gender	CA	Grade	Ethnicity	Diagnostic label	Parental education		Parental employment	
						Mother	Father	Mother	Father
1	F	11-4	5th	Caucasian	POHI/SLI	NR	Coll.	3	3
2	M	9-3	4th	Caucasian	SLI	Coll.	Coll.	3	3
3	M	11-5	5th	Caucasian	LD/SLI	12+	12+	2	2
4	F	10-10	5th	Caucasian	LD	Coll.	Coll.	1	3
5	M	10-11	5th	African Am.	SLI	12+	12+	2	2
6	M	11-2	5th	Native Am.	LD/SLI	12+	GED	2	2
7	M	13-9	8th	Caucasian	LD	12+	12	2	2
8	M	13-2	8th	African Am.	LD/SLI	Coll.	12+	3	2
9	M	10-3	5th	Caucasian	LD	Coll.	Coll.	2	3

Note. Diagnostic label = eligibility at school; LD = learning disabilities; POHI = physical or other health impairment (student has Down syndrome but does not qualify as Educable Mentally Impaired); SLI = speech–language impairment involving language. Parental education = highest grade level completed: 12 = high school degree; GED = general education degree; 12+ = some postsecondary education; Coll. = bachelor's degree or higher; NR = not reported. Parental employment = categories based on parental report: 1 = unemployed outside home; 2 = semiprofessional employment (e.g., teacher's aide, water installation mechanic, cosmetologist, police officer); 3 = professional employment (e.g., teacher, research scientist, computer analyst).

TABLE 3.2
Diagnostic Assessment Results for Participants

Student	Grade	Boder	WPT			TOWL-2		
			Devel.	Fluency	Overall	Spon.	Contrived	Overall
1	5th	7th	3 $=^a$ 5		6	25 $=^a$ 25		50
2	4th	5th	6 < 11		8	20 < 33		53
3	5th	3rd	9 > 4		5	24 = 19		43
4	5th	5th	8 = 8		8	50 > 37		87
5	5th	6th	10 > 5		7	44 = 39		83
6	5th	5th	13 > 9		11	31 = 30		61
7	8th	6th	9 = 10		10	28 = 24		52
8	8th	7th	4 < 9		6	29 = 29		58
9	5th	9th	9 = 11		11	29 < 70		99

Note. Boder = Boder Test of Reading-Spelling Patterns grade equivalent scores based on flash reading of isolated words; WPT = Writing Process Test (all standard scores; $M = 10$, $SD = 3$); Devel. = composite score based on six ratings (purpose/focus, audience, vocabulary, style/tone, support/development, organization/coherence); Fluency = composite score based on four ratings (sentence structure/variety, grammar/usage, capitalization/punctuation, spelling); Overall = composite of developmental and fluency scores. TOWL-2 = Test of Written Language-2; Spon. = standard score for spontaneous story ($M = 50$, $SD = 7.5$) based on sum of five standard scores (each with $M = 10$, $SD = 3$) for thematic maturity, contextual vocabulary, syntactic maturity, contextual spelling, and contextual style; Contrived = standard score ($M = 50$, $SD = 7.5$) based on sum of five standard scores (each with $M = 10$, $SD = 3$) for vocabulary, spelling, style, logical sentences, sentence combining; Overall = TOWL-2 standard scores ($M = 100$, $SD = 15$).
[a]Relational signs represent subscores that differ by more than 1 SD for individual subjects; "=" suggests no significant difference between subscores; ">" suggests holistic organizational skills exceeding ability to manage details; "<" suggests ability to manage details exceeding holistic organizational skills.

score) exceeded their ability to manage details (fluency score) by more than 1 *SD*; and as "<" if students' ability to manage details exceeded their organizational abilities by more than 1 *SD*. Using this strategy to characterize individual student profiles, 3 students showed relative *organizational* strengths, 2 showed relative *detail-oriented* strengths, and 4 showed no pattern of relative strength or weakness.

The TOWL-2 is organized differently from the WPT. The two subscores on the TOWL-2 are obtained from (a) a "spontaneous" sample (holistic organizational task) written in response to a picture prompt involving either a space scene or a prehistoric scene, which is rated for thematic maturity, contextual vocabulary, syntactic maturity, contextual spelling, and contextual style, and (b) a set of "contrived" tasks (detail-oriented tasks) designed to measure vocabulary, spelling, style, logical sentences, and sentence combining. Although these two scores represent similar skills measured in different contexts (rather than two sets of diverse skills measured in the same context, as in the WPT), insights into students' individual profiles can be obtained by considering relative strengths in either organizational or detail-oriented areas. Using this strategy to characterize individual student profiles on the TOWL-2, 1 student showed relative organizational strength, 2 showed relative detail-oriented strength, and 6 showed no pattern of relative strength or weakness.

Concurrent Writing Experiences at School.   A questionnaire was sent to the students' referring teachers requesting information about time spent in writing and computer use at school during the time the students were participating in the writing lab. Responses were obtained for 8 of the 9 participants. One question offered choices about how much time was spent each week in handwriting or printing activities. Six respondents reported "more than 5 hours per week," and 2 reported "about 3 to 5 hours per week." Most respondents indicated a range of 0 to 1 hour per week for time spent in writing creative stories. When asked about time spent in using a computer, 5 respondents reported that their students used a computer for "about 0 to 1 hour per week," and 3 reported computer use for "about 1 to 2 hours per week." Thus, results observed in the present study were likely due to work done in the writing lab.

Treatment Procedure

Instructional Approach.   The process approach to writing instruction was implemented consistent with descriptions presented previously in this report. That is, students were encouraged to write about topics of their choice, using the two computer software approaches to scaffold their thinking about possibilities. They participated in author groups with one or two fellow students, who provided peer support and criticism under instructor guidance. They wrote for sustained periods and could decide when a story was done. They also learned about writing as a process. They learned to talk about the three stages of the writing process as (a) planning and organizing, (b) writing your story, and (c) revising and editing. These three stages were a part of the daily routine in the writing lab. Students could name the three stages, which were also prominently listed on an organizing schedule chart displayed in the writing lab rooms.

Instruction in the laboratory was provided by five graduate students in speech–language pathology, each of whom assumed responsibility for an author group of 2 to 3 students. The instructors all had completed bachelor-level requirements for teaching certificates; they had read preparatory materials about the writing process approach prior to beginning the research; they were concurrently enrolled in a course on analysis of language development in context; and they attended twice-weekly practicum meetings in which instructional principles regarding written-language intervention and students' individualized needs were discussed. Two clinically certified supervisors provided daily supervision.

The goal of providing mediator scaffolding as evenly as possible across students and conditions was balanced with the goal of addressing individualized student needs. Mediation was provided in the form of scaffolding dialogues, which were embedded in author group activities, writing time, and review time. The dialogues were designed to convey the presence of a real audience for the students' stories. The mediational instruction was responsive to momentary learning opportunities but also addressed students' individualized objectives at five levels: (a) oral communication and social interaction; (b) story construction and organization; (c) sentence structure; (d) word choice and spelling; and (e) conventions related to the students' sense of sentence, such as punctuation and capitalization.

At the end of each lab session, a review time was held in which students conferred individually with their instructors and filled out a chart indicating which of the three stages of the writing process they had worked on that day. This activity was designed to help students understand the recursive nature of the writing process and to develop their metacognitive control of the process.

Author Groups.   The project directors and supervisor assigned students to author groups with the aim of creating groups that were somewhat heterogeneous, but compatible in age and interests. The two female students were assigned to separate groups. Author-group peers and instructor-mediators were held constant across the two software conditions, although author groups were occasionally combined when student absences would have led to a group of one. Author groups were designed to encourage independence from adult leadership. Value was placed on author conferences in which students spoke directly to each other, rather than directing their comments through the adult who was scaffolding the discussion. As students read their works in progress within the author groups, they were encouraged to ask themselves and their peers, "Is it clear?" and, "Is it interesting?" They also spent one minilesson brainstorming lists of "encouraging" things they could say to themselves and each other, in contrast to a list of "discouraging" things they ought not say.

Writing Software.   The two different software programs the students used were a text-based story grammar prewriting tool and a graphics-based picture-construction prewriting tool. To counterbalance for possible order effects, half of the students wrote with the text-based tool first; the other half wrote with the graphics-based tool first. Both software programs allowed students to generate printed stories. Neither program included options for changing text format, such as font, size, or style; thus, the characters produced with each tool looked similar on paper. The differences lay in the type of planning support available.

The text-based planning tool was customized by the authors using the FrEdWriter (Rogers, 1985) software. FrEdWriter is a public-domain teacher-authoring program that permits teachers to create and place frozen-text prompts in boxes that cannot be affected by students, with space provided below each prompt box, where students can write and edit responses. When students complete a response, they jump the cursor to the next open response space. Students can also return to a space where they worked before and make changes to the text they entered there; but the teacher's prompts stay "frozen."

For this project, the researchers set up a prompted writing file that included 11 questions (see Table 3.3). The first three prompts directed students to think about several story ideas, to pick one, and to think about why they picked it. The remaining eight questions were based on a story grammar model of narrative construction, starting with three questions about setting and characters, followed by five questions about problem, action, goal setting, response, and outcome or ending. For the first few days, students scrolled through the questions and answered them by typing in responses until something was written in each open space, then printed the questions and answers to set beside their work station as they typed in their stories in the final open space. On subsequent

---

TABLE 3.3
Story Grammar Prompts for FrEdWriter

Type your subject number and today's date.

List 2 or 3 ideas for a story.

Choose one of your ideas and type a WORKING TITLE.

Why did you choose this topic?

Who or what is the main character or characters?

Where does the story take place?

When does the story take place?

What happens to the main character or characters?

What does the main character or characters do?

Why does the main character or characters do that?

How does the main character or characters feel?

How will your story end?

---

days, they could go back and review their answers to the questions, make changes or additions, or go directly to work on their stories.

The second software program was the graphics-based planning tool Once Upon a Time (Urban, Rushing, & Star, 1990). Rather than querying students about story grammar elements, this software allowed them to create graphic scenes prior to writing, then generate text to accompany the resulting pictures. The program allowed students to select from among eight backgrounds, then add clip art to the background to create a visual scene. Approximately 100 clip-art objects were organized in categories, which the student could see listed with a click of the mouse on a choice button. Then, as students clicked the mouse on the names of individual objects, the software read the names aloud. To select an object for the picture, students had to type the object name into a space provided. When an object appeared in the scene, students could move it with the mouse, color it one of 16 colors, size it according to three choices, or delete it. There was no limit to the number of items that could be placed in each scene. At the bottom of the screen under the graphic scene were four blank lines for beginning a story. When they were full, the student could continue the story on additional full-text pages or could choose to develop another picture-plus-text page.

Keyboarding Software.   Although keyboarding proficiency is of concern when studying students' abilities to write with computers, it does not constitute a major barrier. After studying students in seven general education classrooms representing a cross section of America's K–12 schools, Dwyer (1994) concluded that

> children, even very young ones, did not find the keyboard a barrier to fluid use of the computer. In fact, with as little as 15 minutes of keyboarding practice daily for six weeks, 2nd and 3rd graders commonly typed 20–30 words per minute with 95 percent accuracy. By comparison, children at that age typically write 9 to 11 words per minute by hand. (p. 5)

Similarly, MacArthur et al. (1991), when discussing students with special education needs, held that "a reasonable goal for typing skill is for students to use correct fingering while looking at the keyboard and to type about as fast as they write by hand (usually about 8 to 10 words per minute)" (p. 233).

In the present study, students practiced the individualized computer-based tutorial typing program Type To Learn (Hermann, 1991) for 15 minutes per session. By the end of the study, one student had completed Lesson 3 of 23; two, Lesson 6; two, Lesson 7; one, Lesson 8; and three, Lesson 9, with at least 90% accuracy and a minimum rate of 10 words per minute.

Treatment Schedule

The study was conducted in the context of a 1-hour, after-school, computer-based writing lab held twice weekly for 11 weeks. The sessions included 2 introductory days, 18 writing days, 1 holiday, and 1 publishing party day. Individual sessions consisted of 15 minutes of keyboarding practice, 10 minutes of author group discussion, 30 minutes of writing, and 5 minutes to print and hold a daily review conference.

The first 2 days of the writing lab were used to introduce the three components of the writing process and the values associated with a process approach to writing instruction. Students met in their author groups for the first time, chose names for their groups, participated in rapport-building activities with their peers, and discussed preliminary ideas for their stories.

Also during the first 2 training days, students received instruction in basic computer operation, including how to turn on the computer, start a program, load and save files, and care for disks. They also practiced accessing and using the Type to Learn keyboarding software.

Writing Days.   After the 2 introductory training days, students began to work on their stories using the text-processing tool to which they had been assigned. They were told that they could write about any topic of their choice, that they would have 9 days to work with each one of the programs, and that they could choose their "best" stories to be published in a class book. The goal was to write one "best" story with each tool. Most of the students worked on a single story for the full 9 days, but a few had to be encouraged to keep working to improve a story they had started rather than repeatedly starting a new one.

The students all gathered in the same room each day for the start of writing lab, but then went directly to their author groups in one of two rooms used for the project. Students assigned to use the FrEdWriter software first worked in an Apple IIgs lab equipped with one computer per student. Students assigned to use the Once Upon a Time software first worked in a Macintosh lab a few doors down the hall. In both conditions, students saved their daily work on disks and kept printouts in their personal writing folders, which they took with them to their author groups the next day.

At the end of the first 9 writing days, all participants turned in one story they considered to be their best work, then they switched labs and worked for another 9 days with the alternate software program. At that point, they again turned in their best stories for publishing.

Publishing Party.   Parents were invited to the final day of the writing lab. Instructors commented on students' special strengths and areas of growth when presenting the plastic-bound books, and parent conferences were held while the students socialized.

Dependent Measures

Several measures were used to evaluate the effects of the two software features on the students' written products and their writing processes. Product-based measures from the students' best stories included linguistic indicators and narrative-maturity scores. Process-based measures from instructors' observations of their students' behavior included daily scaffolding ratings and written anecdotal reports.

Linguistic Indicators. The students' two best stories were analyzed for linguistic length and complexity. To conduct these analyses, the stories were retyped by a research assistant and one of the authors using the software program Systematic Analysis of Language Transcripts (SALT; Miller & Chapman, 1986). For purposes of this analysis, words were divided into free and bound morphemes, and sentences were divided into T-units. T-units are "minimal terminal units," defined by Hunt (1970) as one main clause and any other clause embedded in it or subordinate to it. This unit rewards syntactic maturity without overcrediting run-on sentences, because each coordinate clause is treated as a separate T-unit. The dependent measure, mean length of T-unit (MLT-unit), was used to estimate syntactic maturity in the analyses, and the total number of T-units was used as a measure of discourse construction.

A second coding scheme measured growth in syntactic maturity and yet acknowledged that errors can represent signs of growth (Weaver, 1982). Students who take risks to formulate more complex sentences may at first make more syntactic errors doing so. Thus, the research assistant entered codes to indicate sentences meeting criteria as *simple incorrect, simple correct, complex incorrect,* and *complex correct.* For this analysis, "complex sentences" were defined as including as many as two compound (independent) clauses. To confirm reliability of the transcription and coding process, one of the project directors independently transcribed and coded six of the stories. Reliability for the transcription of words was 99%, and codes were exactly the same for 33 of 35 T-units (94%).

In addition to counting the variables coded directly, the SALT program automatically generated (a) total number of words, (b) total number of different words, and (c) MLT-unit in morphemes. To adjust for different story lengths, the total number of different words was converted to a ratio of different words to total words (type:token ratio), and each sentence type was converted to a ratio of sentence type to total number of sentences in the story.

Narrative Maturity Scores.   Students' best stories were also rated for narrative maturity using the story-grammar–based assessment suggested by Stein and Glenn (1979, 1982) and adapted by several other researchers (Hedberg & Stoel-Gammon, 1986; Hedberg & Westby, 1993; Westby, Van Dongen, & Maggart, 1989). This system requires judges to make a series of decisions about whether a story is merely a set of *isolated descriptions* (score 1); or whether it is (with progressing maturity) an *action sequence,* with a temporally related sequence of events (score 2); a *reactive sequence,* with a causally related sequence of events (score 3); an *abbreviated episode,* with goal-directed behavior implied (score 4); a *complete episode,* with planning to achieve the goal being clear in the story (score 5); a *complex episode,* with an obstacle in the goal path of the story (score 6); *multiple episodes,* with more than one abbreviated or complete episode (score 7); an *embedded episode,* with one complete episode nested within another (score 8); or *interactive episodes,* with story events described deliberately and for effect from the perspective of more than one character (score 9).

To ensure reliability, two of the authors spent approximately 4 hours scoring practice stories, discussing the results, and negotiating decision rules before rating the experimental stories. At that point, they achieved initial agreement on independent ratings for 15 of the 18 experimental stories (83.3%). Ratings on the three discrepant stories varied by only 1 point. The final ratings used in experimental analyses for those three stories were reached by consensus.

Scaffolding Levels.   At the end of each session, instructor-mediators completed individual scaffolding reports for each participant. These reports indicated the level of scaffolding that students required and would accept in each of six areas: software use, reading, spelling, generating text, revising, and conferencing. The scaffolding reports used a 3-point Likert-type scale, where 1 = *required maximum assistance* (defined, e.g., as "instructor told student what and how to revise"); 2 = *required minimal assistance* (defined, e.g., as "student determined what and how to revise with prompts from instructor"); and 3 = *independent* (defined, e.g., as "student initiated revisions without instructor assistance"). NA was recorded for *not applicable* when particular tasks (e.g., revising) were not observed.

Process Observations.   Instructor-mediators also wrote anecdotal comments about the students' use of the software and response to instruction. These comments were written on daily report sheets, in the graduate-student instructors' clinical journals, and in the final reports of progress. Qualitative data from these three sources are reported below to augment the interpretation of quantitative results.

Fidelity of Treatment

All of the students for whom data are reported attended the writing lab on a regular basis, missing no more than two sessions throughout the course of the study. An analysis of the students' story files indicated that they indeed used the relevant features of the software. With the FrEd-Writer software, all of the students entered at least one response to each of the 11 story grammar prompts except 1 student, who did not enter a working title for his story. Some students entered additional responses on subsequent days; others wrote more than one story during the 9 days, and thus had more than one set of responses. An analysis of story files created with the Once Upon a Time software indicated that all of the students used the graphic feature and included at least one scene, consisting of a background and at least one object, in their best stories.

Data Analysis

Due to the small sample size and lack of homogeneity among students in terms of relative writing difficulties, nonparametric statistical procedures were used for all analyses.

The Wilcoxon matched-pairs signed-ranks test, a nonparametric correlate to the related samples t test, was used to compare effects of (a) the two software tools (text-based vs. graphics-based) and (b) time (first 9 writing days vs. last 9 writing days) on each of the eight linguistic indicators and the narrative-maturity scores.

Scaffolding scores were analyzed first by generating six mean scores for each student for each of the two experimental conditions. Wilcoxon matched-pairs signed-ranks tests were used to determine effects of (a) the software tool (text-based vs. graphics-based) and (b) time (first 9 writing days vs. last 9 writing days) on each of the six scaffolding categories. Additionally, the Friedman analysis of variance of ranks with follow-up Wilcoxon matched-pairs signed-ranks tests were used to determine which skills required more scaffolding than others for the entire group.

RESULTS

Linguistic Indicators

Wilcoxon matched-pairs signed-ranks tests comparing each student's two best stories on the eight linguistic indicators revealed no statistically significant differences for total number of words, total number of T-units, percentage of different words, and MLT-unit. In terms of sentence types, however, students produced a higher percentage of complex incorrect sentences with the graphics-based tool than with the text-based tool ($Z = -2.36$, $p < .05$; see Table 3.4). Wilcoxon tests applied to time (first 9 writing days vs. last 9 writing days) revealed no statistically significant differences for any of the eight variables (see Table 3.5).

Narrative-Maturity Scores

Analyses of the narrative-maturity scores revealed that students, as a group, wrote developmentally immature narratives (range = 1 to 5,

TABLE 3.4
Linguistic Indicators for "Best" Stories, by Software Type

Indicator	Text based		Graphics based		
	M	SD	M	SD	Z
Total words	94.22	37.53	68.22	29.85	−1.59
T-units	15.00	5.57	10.56	5.22	−1.36
Different words[a]	.57	.04	.59	.13	−1.12
MLT-unit	7.11	1.74	7.69	3.69	−.05
Simple correct sentences[b]	.48	.23	.48	.32	−.29
Simple incorrect sentences[b]	.13	.15	.05	.07	−1.46
Complex correct sentences[b]	.32	.24	.29	.24	−.41
Complex incorrect sentences[b]	.07	.09	.18	.15	−2.36*

[a]Ratio of different words to total words. [b]Ratio of sentence type to total sentences.
*$p < .05$.

TABLE 3.5
Linguistic Indicators for "Best" Stories, by Time

Indicator	First 9 days		Last 9 days		
	M	SD	M	SD	Z
Total words	90.78	30.93	71.67	38.96	−1.12
T-units	15.00	5.20	10.56	5.59	−1.36
Different words[a]	.58	.04	.59	.13	−.77
MLT-unit	6.75	1.88	8.05	3.51	−1.59
Simple correct sentences[b]	.53	.25	.43	.30	−1.24
Simple incorrect sentences[b]	.09	.11	.08	.13	−.52
Complex correct sentences[b]	.29	.20	.32	.27	−.05
Complex incorrect sentences[b]	.09	.10	.16	.16	−1.01

[a]Ratio of different words to total words. [b]Ratio of sentence type to total sentences.

$M = 2.72$, $SD = 1.41$). The Wilcoxon tests indicated no statistically significant effect for software tool ($Z = -.21$, ns). However, visual inspection of the data showed that 5 of the participants received higher scores on stories produced with the text-based tool, 3 received higher scores on stories produced with the graphics-based tool, and 1 received the same score for both stories. The data also revealed that time did not affect narrative maturity ($Z = -.42$, ns). Table 3.6 depicts narrative maturity scores for each student's best stories.

Scaffolding Levels

Wilcoxon tests revealed that students exhibited similar scaffolding needs with both software programs (text-based vs. graphics-based) for all six skills. However, a comparison between scaffolding scores for the first 9 writing days and scores for the last 9 writing days revealed that significantly more scaffolding was needed for revising during the last 9 days ($Z = -2.36$, $p < .05$). Table 3.7 contains mean scaffolding scores for the two software programs and the two treatment times.

Mean scaffolding scores across conditions indicated that students, as a group, required the least assistance with reading ($M = 2.71$, $SD = .24$) and the most assistance with conferencing ($M = 1.76$, $SD = .39$). The Friedman analysis of variance by ranks revealed significant differences in levels of scaffolding required for the six skills, $\chi^2(5, N = 9) = 27.39$, $p < .0005$. Further analyses with Wilcoxon matched-pairs signed-ranks tests indicated that participants exhibited greater independence with

TABLE 3.6
Narrative-Maturity Scores for "Best" Stories, by Software Type and Time

Student	Text based	Graphics based	First 9 days	Last 9 days
1	3	1	1	3
2	1	1	1	1
3	2	5	5	2
4	4	1	4	1
5	2	5	2	5
6	4	3	3	4
7	2	5	2	5
8	3	2	3	2
9	3	2	3	2
M	2.66	2.77	2.55	2.88
SD	1.00	1.78	1.33	1.53

Note. Scores based on scale of 1 to 9.

reading compared to all five other skills. They were also more independent with spelling than revising or conferencing, and more independent with text generation than software use, revising, or conferencing. Table 3.7 contains results of the paired analyses.

Process Observations

A qualitative analysis of process observations yielded information about students' attitudes toward the two software programs and the writing process. A few students complained to their instructor-mediators that they did not like the FrEdWriter software. While using it, 1 student commented, "This thing asks too many questions." Although all students provided some response to each of the story grammar prompts, some wrote brief responses quickly during the first few days; others spent time developing their responses before writing their stories. All students printed their outlines and had hard copies next to the computer while writing their stories, but at least 1 student could not be persuaded to review the outline while writing.

Students tended to prefer the Once Upon a Time software (it was more "fun"), although they exhibited varied strategies for using it. Seven of the 9 students used the graphics to generate ideas for their stories, but the picture construction activities took time. In one case, an instructor reported that a student "only wanted to make pictures, and it was difficult for the instructor to persuade him to write." Another student expressed that he "had more time to write with FrEdWriter."

Planning Strategies Related to Software Features.   The two students who did not use the graphics feature to plan their stories were Students 2 and 3. Student 2 wrote two isolated description stories, both about "X-Men" (popular superheroes), when using both software tools. The varied planning features seemed to make no difference to him. Student 3 used the graphics tool to create a picture with a bare background and a farmer standing at its center to meet the minimal requirements for using the software feature, but then proceeded to write an unrelated story that he had been planning about an "X-Man" who was kidnapped and later found. That story earned a score of 5 as a complete episode and may have skewed the group results related to software effects on narrative scores.

Students 1 and 4 did use the graphic prompts to develop story ideas, but they adopted the immature strategy of placing objects apparently randomly in their pictures and then writing sentences incorporating the graphic elements. For Student 1, the "what next" picture-construction strategy yielded a "what next" isolated description story:

TABLE 3.7
Scaffolding Scores, by Software Type and Time

Skill	Text based		Graphics based		First 9 days		Last 9 days		Total	
	M	SD	M	SD	M	SD	M	SD	M	SD
Reading[a]	2.66	.29	2.77	.24	2.72	.16	2.70	.35	2.71	.24
Spelling[b]	2.36	.43	2.44	.51	2.53	.27	2.27	.58	2.40	.39
Text generation[c]	2.24	.48	2.22	.40	2.38	.32	2.09	.49	2.23	.37
Software use	1.92	.50	2.02	.37	2.11	.37	1.83	.46	1.97	.37
Revising	1.84	.66	1.88	.46	2.01	.57	1.69	.51	1.83	.52
Conferencing	1.76	.46	1.77	.39	1.82	.35	1.70	.49	1.76	.39

Note. Scores based on scale: 1 = required maximum assistance, 2 = required minimal assistance, 3 = independent.
[a]Reading higher than spelling, text generation, software use, revising, and conferencing (Z = −2.66, p < .05). [b]Spelling higher than revising (Z = −2.07, p < .05) and conferencing (Z = −2.31, p < .05). [c]Text generation higher than software use (Z = −2.13, p < .05), revising (Z = −2.24, p < .05), and conferencing (Z = −2.54, p < .05).

The flying fence went to the moon and skyscraper went to the sun. The bunny rabbit hopped to the lion. Bunny rabbit had a picnic. Lion got hurt. Lion fell down and he went to the hospital and got crutches.

When using the graphics tool, Student 4 also wrote an isolated description story she titled "Crazy Space." Her story might have been developed further if she had allotted more time for writing.

ONCE THERE WAS SPACE. THE NAME WAS CRAZY SPACE. IT GOT THAT NAME BECAUSE ... IT WAS CRAZY. ONE DAY WHEN EVERY-THING WAS GOING GREAT, ALL THE SUDDEN SOMETHING HAP-PENED.

This story contrasts with the abbreviated-episode story the same student wrote with FrEdWriter and the text-based prompting strategy. That story was a fictionalized personal-experience story about children escaping from a big man at a shopping mall and returning safely to their parents.

Student 6 also wrote a well-developed abbreviated episode with FrEdWriter, which he titled "The Rector Set Car." It was about a boy who loved racing and built a car that beat "19 big shots" who "came out and challenged him to a race." This student scored almost as high by using the graphics-based tool in a unique way to create a reactive-sequence time-travel story he titled "The Wildest Space Mission." For this story, the student created a different graphic on each page about a different point in time. For example, the story began with a graphic that mimicked looking through a spaceship window into outer space:

The crew was in space when they headed towards a weird plant. The color was orange. Then they started to spin around and around they went. Suddenly they were in a different time.

The second page included a graphic scene that the student also described in words:

When they got to their new time, it was midieval time. There were 2 jesters, 2 archers, 2 wells, a king and a queen. The archers were aiming at there head. Then they changed times.

The student maintained this strategy for four pages, deteriorating on the last page to an apparently randomly constructed picture and the text, "The crew went to their new time. They seen all types of stuff."

Student 5 responded differently to the two software tools by writing, with the FrEdWriter software, a nonfiction, temporally sequenced personal story about his dog, and, with Once Upon a Time, a fictitious story that went beyond the realm of his direct experience. In his case, the fictitious story was rated as more mature (scoring 5 as a complete episode) because it included a clear statement of goal direction that did not show up in the temporally sequenced personal narrative:

> ONCE UPON A TIME THERE WAS AN ENCOUNTER IN SPACE. THE ALIENS WERE NOT HAPPY. THE ASTRONAUTS WERE TRESPASSING ON THE ALIENS LAND, BUT THE ALIENS WERE FRIENDLY. THE ALIENS LET THE ASTRONAUTS EXPLORE THEIR LAND. THE ASTRONAUTS MADE A DEAL THEY COULD EXPLORE IF THEY KEPT QUIET. THEN THEY ALL GOT ALONG.

Effects on Text-Generation Strategies.   Beyond the effects on planning, the two software programs influenced the process of text generation differentially for some of the students. In particular, the Once Upon a Time feature that required students to consider lists of names for objects and then to type them in themselves seemed to have a positive influence on students' ability to use more mature vocabulary in their stories. Some returned to the menu of object choices several times to check spelling and word choices.

Responsiveness to Stages of the Writing Process.   Responsiveness to the three stages of the writing process also varied. Several students demonstrated a reluctance to revise their stories and required persistent prompting by the instructor-mediators and their peers to stay with a story and improve it. A few students insisted on starting a new story, to avoid the revising phase. Others responded positively to the idea of publishing a book for their peers and engaged in revising and editing in an effort to make their stories as good as possible.

Finally, most of the students were not familiar with the idea of conferencing and had to be instructed about how to listen to others' stories and offer helpful criticism. Several students were quiet in the small author group conferences and required specific prompting to participate. As the semester progressed, most students conformed to the routine and contributed to the conferences. However, a few continued to need maximum scaffolding.

Linking Text-Processing Tools to Student Needs

Attempts to link features of students' diagnostic profiles to features of text-processing tools should be regarded as tentative and speculative at this point. Yet, it is intriguing to note the possible links between response to the varied software features and patterns of relative strength on organizational versus detail-oriented aspects of writing. The 3 students who showed strengths in managing details (relative to weaker holistic organizational skills) in their diagnostic profiles produced stories that scored at the same narrative-maturity level with both software tools (Student 2), or at one level higher with the text-based tool (Students 8 and 9). None of these 3 students wrote a story at a level higher than reactive sequence, however, using either program.

Two of the 3 students (Students 3 and 5) who showed relative holistic organizational strengths wrote stories that scored 3 points higher when using the graphics-based tool than with the text-based tool, although 1 of these was the student who constructed a picture of a farmer but wrote about a missing "X-Man." The third was the student who constructed the time-travel story with the graphics-based tool and the race car narrative with the text-based tool (Student 6).

Two of the 3 students who showed no relative difference between holistic organization and details in the initial assessment (Students 1 and 4) wrote personal narrative stories with the text-based tool that were rated 3 points higher than the fictional stories they produced with the graphics-based tool. Student 7, however, who was the other student showing this profile, was the one who wrote a complete-episode fictional story using the graphics-based software, compared to the temporally sequenced personal narrative he wrote with the text-based software. These results are considered in the discussion that follows.

DISCUSSION

This study was designed to compare the effects of two different software-based planning tools on the story-writing skills of students with language-related learning disabilities. Participants had the opportunity to use both programs in an after-school writing lab that incorporated a process approach to writing instruction. Group results did not clearly favor either tool, although many individual differences were demonstrated.

Although the study sample was relatively small, some preliminary conclusions and implications for practice can be drawn. First, it should be emphasized that writing is a complex process and there is no simple way to analyze the products or students' participation in the process itself. The process involves an interrelated set of skills, beliefs, attitudes, and tools that must be used together to generate a product that can be analyzed using various methods, techniques, and systems. For this study, several well-accepted linguistic indicators and a narrative-maturity rating were used to evaluate the quality of students' writing products. The writing process was examined via daily scaffolding needs for instructor assistance and anecdotal behavioral observations. The findings, then, represent just a fragment of what occurs in a computer-based writing lab that employs process writing instruction.

Analyses of the students' stories revealed no significant differences for software type on seven of the eight linguistic indicators. The single effect for software type was a higher percentage of complex incorrect sentences generated with the graphics-based tool than with the text-based tool, a finding that arguably favors the text-based tool. Results also indicated no significant order effect, suggesting that it did not matter if students used the text-based tool or the graphics-based tool first.

An analysis of the narrative-maturity ratings revealed no significant overall differences; however, it should be noted that 5 of the students received higher ratings on stories they produced with FrEdWriter, the text-based tool, than on their Once Upon a Time stories, whereas 3 students received notably higher story scores when using the graphics-based tool. Several explanations for these varied results seem plausible.

Questions on the FrEdWriter software were designed to prompt students to think about the elements of story grammar. This may have contributed to several students' receiving higher narrative-maturity scores when using the text-based tool. With the text-based tool, students spent all of their writing time either responding to the prompts or generating text. Some students responded to the prompts every day and used those responses in constructing their stories. Others skimmed or skipped some of the prompts each day and went directly to their stories. In either case, students spent all of their writing time either planning their stories or actually writing them. Students who showed relatively weak holistic organizational skills in their diagnostic profiles in particular seemed to benefit from this explicit organizational support.

In contrast, when students used the Once Upon a Time software, they typically spent part of the writing session (and, many times, all of it) creating or modifying their graphic scenes. They appeared to enjoy the graphics tool and returned again and again to use it. Consequently, they spent less time writing and, in some cases, had to hurry their writing near the end of the phase in order to complete a "best" story for publication. The resulting story was sometimes an unfinished, incoherent work that contained a relatively large percentage of incorrect sentences. The exceptions to this pattern were demonstrated by 2 students who showed relative strength in organizational abilities over details prior to writing, and by a third student who showed a profile indicating no relative strength or weakness in the two domains. Thus, although results of the present study agree with prior research by Barenbaum et al. (1987) suggesting that picture-drawing tasks do not facilitate story production for some students, they conflict with the conclusion drawn by those same researchers that a picture-drawing task "interfered with the story production of children who knew how to write stories" (p. 183). In the present study, students who were more proficient at writing stories did benefit from the graphics-based tool.

Another explanation for individual differences in story quality related to software tools may be that the less mature storytellers were also limited in their ability to use the graphics presented in the Once Upon a Time software. When students are provided a word list or a picture to respond to, they may not have the knowledge or background experience to develop a coherent story. If allowed to select their own topic, students have more control over the writing process and can generate text about things they know something about. In the present study, several of the students exhibited this reaction to the software.

These findings suggest that teachers should be cautioned about the relative amount of time students might spend using a graphics component at the expense of their writing time, especially for students who exhibit patterns of organizational weaknesses in spontaneous-writing skills. Teachers may need to develop management strategies to maximize the time students have for planning their stories and generating text, whether or not graphics are available, and text-based computer prompts provide one appropriate means of doing so.

This study also implies that inclusion of a graphics component in text-processing tools may be useful for certain students. For at least 1 student, the graphics tool forced him to think about story ideas that went beyond his range of direct experience. With the text-based tool, he wrote only nonfiction stories relating details of events that had occurred to him; with the graphics-based tool, he created fictitious stories about things that he had not actually experienced, thereby extending his own repertoire of writing topics.

Tentative implications for linking text-processing tools to student needs may be drawn from these findings. If students demonstrate relative difficulty with the holistic organizational aspects of writing, or if they show no relative strengths in their profiles, they may benefit from a software tool that provides more explicit story grammar prompts. Such students may be distracted by a graphics-based tool, and the maturity of their narratives may suffer. On the other hand, if students demonstrate relative strength in the holistic organizational aspects of writing, they may do creative things with a graphics-based tool, or they might not need a planning and organizing tool to scaffold that aspect of story writing at all. For such students, other software features may be more relevant for developing strengths in such detail-oriented areas as sentence construction, punctuation, and spelling.

Despite the fact that several students had difficulty generating stories with the graphics-based tool, they seemed highly motivated to use the software. There has been much discussion in the recent literature about the motivational aspects of computer use and the notion that technology can enhance learning through its motivational value (Gardner & Bates, 1991; Malouf, 1987–88; Roblyer, Castine, & King, 1988; Tolman & Allred, 1991; Yang, 1992). Such technology can provide an initial stimulus to motivate reluctant writers to write. The caution suggested by the present results is that even when students seem motivated to use a program, teachers should pay close attention to what they do with the software and, when using text-processing tools, to what they produce. Teachers cannot assume that because one program is more motivating than another, students will likewise learn more or produce higher quality work with one tool as compared to another.

The results of this study also have implications for process approaches to writing instruction. Analyses of the daily scaffolding scores revealed that the students, as a group, needed much assistance with the tasks of revising and conferencing. Several students resisted revising and editing suggestions from their graduate student leaders or other peers. When they did revise, students tended to add to their stories, often by adding sentences to the end of their story rather than changing text that they had already written. To avoid revising and editing altogether, some students started new stories whenever they ran out of ideas. Thus, revising required much scaffolding throughout the study. In fact, the data showed higher levels of scaffolding for revising during the second half of the study than the first. It is possible that students simply resisted the task more each time they were faced with it and required more scaffolding intervention from the instructor-mediators. Or it may be that the students were more willing to entertain revising and editing suggestions from others later in the study as they allowed their instructor-mediators to spend more time assisting them with the task. In any event, many of the students were not familiar with revising strategies and had to be prompted to make specific changes throughout the course of the project.

A final point is a return to the reminder that the software probably was not the only factor that influenced development of these students' story-writing skills. Text-processing software is but one aspect of a complex writing environment that includes teachers, peers, instructional strategies, computer-based and non–computer-based tools, and ongoing interaction among all components. It is important to consider the contribution of each component to the development of story-writing skills in students with learning disabilities.

AUTHORS' NOTES

1. *This project was supported by Grant No. H180G20005 from the U.S. Department of Education, awarded to the Departments of Special Education and Speech Pathology and Audiology at Western Michigan University, Kalamazoo. The contents of this document do not, however, reflect the policy or views of the Department and no official endorsement should be inferred.*

2. *We gratefully acknowledge the assistance of Kelli Beckman, Chris Bursian, Kristee Guy, Melissa Hoffman, Jolaina Jackson, Laura Johnson, Kara McAlister, and Joani Triezenberg, as well as the students and their families who participated in the writing lab.*

4. Speech-Recognizing Computers: A Written-Communication Tool for Students with Learning Disabilities?

KEITH WETZEL

As particular technologies (e.g., computers, calculators, laser disc players) become more widespread and affordable in the business, professional, and recreation markets, educators have asked whether these innovations might provide meaningful assistance to students with disabilities. Such is the case with computers that recognize commands spoken by a human voice. Voice-input technology is becoming more commonplace as a means of controlling mechanical devices. For example, some videocassette recorders can be operated by a series of voice commands that the user first "teaches" the device to recognize. Recently, radiologists have employed a more sophisticated use of voice-input technology: They dictate observations and diagnoses to a voice-activated computer and see text appear on the screen.

Can these technologies be used to assist students with fluent oral communication skills but disabilities in written communication? Too often we lose the contribution of these students, who may have ideas and knowl-

Reprinted, with changes, from "Speech-recognizing computers: A written-communication tool for students with learning disabilities?" by Keith Wetzel, *Journal of Learning Disabilities,* Vol. 29, 1996, pp. 371–380. Copyright © 1996 by PRO-ED, Inc.

edge worth communicating, but who face frustration and defeat when they attempt to put their ideas in writing. However, a computer with voice-recognition technology could recognize the student's voice, transcribe his or her words into text, and make it available to the student in a word-processing format—which in turn can be edited with keyboard or voice commands. Thus, students could bypass the frustrating and defeating process of writing with pen or pencil and produce compositions that demonstrate their understanding and creativity. The present exploratory study was undertaken to begin to determine whether speech-recognition technology should be pursued as an aid to students with written communication disabilities.

This chapter reviews the related research, describes the available voice-transcription technology, describes the results of using VoiceType (1992) technology, and suggests conclusions and implications from this work.

The problems of students with learning disabilities (LD) in written composition are well documented. Newcomer and Barenbaum's (1991) review of the literature concluded that the problems these students experience with story composition include difficulty with mechanics (punctuation, spelling, and word usage); story schema and cohesion (lack of critical components, inclusion of extraneous ideas, and unclear referents); and modes of production (mechanical aspects of writing). The students' expository writing reveals similar problems and also an apparent inability to develop or maintain a sense of the whole composition.

The teaching of written composition should address three specific areas, as noted by Newcomer and Barenbaum (1991): the mechanics of spelling, grammar, and punctuation; the structure and cohesion of the writing; and the production of words on paper. Some classroom teachers address mechanics and structure problems by instructing their students in the use of strategies such as prewriting, the use of structures to organize the writing, peer editing and feedback, and revision (Wetzel, 1992). Researchers and curriculum developers have made some progress in adapting these strategies and materials for writing instruction for students with LD. For example, Graham and Harris (1988) described a three-step cognitive strategy that students can use to plan and write opinion essays. Englert, Anthony, Fear, and Gregg (1988) described "think sheets" that help students think about and organize each stage of the expository writing process. Graham and Harris (1989) taught students specific strategies (such as the mnemonic device TREE—Topic sentence, Reasons, Examine reasons, and Ending) that emphasize the student's role as an active collaborator with the teacher. Newcomer and Barenbaum (1991) concluded that such training programs show the potential for growth on the part of the student with disabilities, and that in addition to employing these specific strategies, teachers should address the need for (a) practice over time, (b) motivating circumstances for students, and (c) the students' involvement in taking control of the writing process.

To address the problem of production of words on paper, teachers have sometimes used dictation. This strategy has its theoretical background in the Language Experience Approach (Allen & Allen, 1968; Ashton-Warner, 1986; Stauffer, 1970) used in language arts instruction. In that approach, a teacher or other adult writes down the student's words as the student tells a story or report. The written record of the student's speech becomes the medium through which reading and writing are taught. When an adult is not present to transcribe the dictation, a student may dictate into a tape recorder for transcription later. (The low-tech tape-recorder version of dictation differs from student-to-adult dictation in that students who dictate into a tape recorder are not able to see the words as they dictate. Due to limitations on human memory, students quickly lose the context for their writing.)

During the last decade, a few researchers have studied dictation with both normally achieving students and students with learning disabilities to determine the effects of this approach on fluency. MacArthur and Graham (1987) studied the writing of 11 fifth- and sixth-grade students with LD and found that dictation was nine times faster than handwriting and twice as fast as word processing. The authors concluded that the cognitive demands of mechanically producing text (via pen or keyboard) may interfere with the fluency and quality of written expression. Bereiter and Scardamalia (1987) examined the writing processes of 48 fourth- and sixth-grade students. In addition to handwriting and normal dictation, the researchers examined the effects of slow dictation. (In slow dictation, the children dictated to an experimenter, who transcribed according to the rate of each child's previously determined writing rate.) Children produced 86% more words in slow dictation than in writing and 163% more in normal dictation than in writing. These results indicate that the constraints placed on children's fluency by their efforts to write via pen or keyboard can be overcome by the transcription of their dictation. However, although it provides an accurate written record of the student's speech and overcomes the problems of production, transcription is limited by the human resources available to listen to children speak and write down what they say.

VOICE RECOGNITION

The voice-transcription technology currently available allows the user to speak into a microphone and have the spoken word appear on a computer screen in a word processing format. Thus, it could bypass the limitations that students with LD experience in producing text with a pen or keyboard, or in waiting for human transcribers. However, it is not clear whether these students can learn to use the technology, or to what extent the technology will accurately produce text from their speech. If the performance of students and technology on these threshold issues is adequate, will there be improvement in the quantity and quality of students' writing? The present study examines the efforts of fifth- and sixth-grade students to use one form of this technology, VoiceType (a speech-transcription system with a 7,000-word active vocabulary, produced by Dragon Systems, Inc.) and discusses the performance of both the students and technology (see Note for details about VoiceType).

The purpose of this study was to determine whether voice-recognition technology can help intermediate-grade students with written language difficulties communicate more effectively in writing. Three students with LD were instructed in the use of VoiceType for accomplishing assigned writing tasks over a period of 10 weeks.

Three questions guided this study:

1. Can elementary students learn to use VoiceType? To dictate using VoiceType, the student must speak each word clearly, pause between words (for as little as one tenth of a second), and omit nonword sounds (such as saying "ahh" or coughing while dictating into the microphone). In addition, students must learn the procedures for correcting their errors and teaching VoiceType new words.

2. Is the technology powerful enough to support the kind of tasks students try to perform? That is, when the student performs correctly, how accurate is the technology's response?

3. Does the entire process result in students' improved communication? If students can learn to use the technology and the technology performs adequately, thus bypassing students' problems with modes of production, will there be an improvement in the quantity and quality of student writing? This included an examination of the amount of writing produced and the quality of the written product.

At the time of this study, there were no published reports on the use of voice-recognition technology with students with LD. Because this area of study is uncharted, it was deemed of primary importance to expect the unexpected and to gather as much data as possible, so that anything that might prove important would be noted. The remainder of this chapter describes in detail the sixth-grade student's experiences in the study as he worked with the researcher to learn and use VoiceType, and suggests conclusions and implications from this work.

METHOD

Setting and Participants

This study took place at a 600-student urban elementary school in a lower middle class neighborhood of a large southwestern city. The special education resource teacher identified three intermediate-grade students who had normal or above-average intelligence and who, prior to this study, had been identified through standard school procedures as having learning disabilities in the areas of written communication and reading. Because oral skills would be necessary to take advantage of VoiceType, the teacher was asked to select students who were indistinguishable from their classmates on oral participation in social studies or science class; that is, their oral fluency should be average for their class, as judged by teacher observation. The teacher selected two fifth graders, Jeremy and Ashley, and one sixth grader, Steven, to participate in this study. Each of the three students went to the resource room for approximately 2 hours a week for help in reading and writing. The school district's criteria for identifying students as learning disabled were (a) teacher referral in the areas of mathematics, reading, or language; (b) normal or above-normal intelligence; and (c) discrepancy of two or more grade levels between expected and actual academic performance in the above areas.

Ashley.   Ashley was referred for testing when she was in fourth grade. Her scores on the Wechsler Intelligence Scale for Children–Revised (WISC-R; Wechsler, 1974) were Verbal, 92; Performance, 121; and Full Scale, 105. She was given achievement tests the following year, and her cluster scores on the Woodcock-Johnson Tests of Achievement (Woodcock, 1989) when her grade level was 5.5 were reading, 4.9; math, 4.7; and language, 5.0. Subtests revealed lower scores in Proofing (4.3), Word Attack (4.4), and Quantitative Concepts (3.7).

Jeremy.   Jeremy was referred for testing when he was in fifth grade. His scores on the WISC-R were Verbal, 113; Performance, 120; and Full Scale, 117. He was given achievement tests the same year, and his cluster scores on the Woodcock-Johnson Tests of Achievement when his grade level was 5.3 were reading, 4.0; math, 5.7; and language, 4.2. Subtests revealed lower scores in Punctuation (2.9), Spelling (3.9), and Word Attack (2.4).

Steven.   Steven, a sixth grader, was referred for testing when he was in fifth grade. His WISC-R scores were as follows: Verbal, 106; Performance, 115; and Full Scale, 111. He was given achievement tests that year, and his cluster scores on the Woodcock-Johnson Tests of Achievement when his grade level was 5.7 were: reading 4.0; math, 5.8; and language 4.2. Subtests revealed lower scores in Proofing (3.7), Spelling (3.9), and Word Attack (3.0). This chapter focuses on Steven because he was able to participate in the most sessions in which actual dictation took place and because he fit the profile of a student with fluent oral communication.

The Technology

VoiceType was selected for this study because it was the most affordable among large vocabulary systems available at the time. This system recognizes discrete speech, which means that the user must pause briefly between each word while dictating. The system works most efficiently if the user "pretrains" it by repeating several hundred preselected words three times each. The system compares each utterance with its expectation for the specified word and adjusts an internal template to conform to that user's distinctive speech patterns. After one has pretrained the system, one can begin to dictate, and VoiceType places the dictated words on the computer screen in a word-processing format. As soon as the machine "hears" the word, it places its best guess on the screen with a box appearing below giving the selected word and alternatives. If the selected word is correct, the user continues by dictating the next word. If the selected word is an error, the user can select from a menu of other suggestions or, if the word does not appear on the menu, type it in (see Appendix A for examples of the correction procedures). These corrections are added to the voice template that began with the repetition of the training words. Each user's personal voice template is saved to the hard drive and updated whenever new words are taught, thus increasing the probability that VoiceType will produce the correct match in the future.

Procedure

The researcher was scheduled to meet with each student twice a week for 10 weeks in sessions lasting 20 to 40 minutes each. However, the number of sessions and the total time was somewhat less than that, due to schedule changes, school programs, and prior student commitments. At the end of 10 weeks, the researcher had met with Steven for fourteen 30-minute sessions.

It was expected that students would produce pieces of personal-narrative writing, using VoiceType to input the story orally and editing with the keyboard and voice commands. To reach this goal, students needed to be able to keep a coherent story in mind, and they needed the specific skills to operate VoiceType (e.g., learning the commands, speaking into the microphone with short pauses between words). The intervention consisted of teaching skills in both areas.

Oral composition is difficult because one must hold all of the complex thought processes required for writing in memory simultaneously. This difficulty was exacerbated for students in this study because they were also trying to remember the VoiceType commands they had to utter (e.g., "Capitalize next word"). In order to help them overcome this memory limitation and speak fluently and coherently, the researcher taught students to use two prewriting skills developed by participants in the National Writing Project (California State Department of Education, 1986): oral rehearsal and a keyword bank. *Oral rehearsal* is a process by which students think aloud about the personal narrative they will tell. The researcher engaged in a dialogue with the students by asking questions that prompted clarification and extended descriptions. Then students were encouraged to tell the story again, writing down *keywords* as they spoke. The list of keywords served as a planning guide for recalling both the content and the order of the ideas as students dictated to the computer. The keywords had the additional advantage of allowing the student and researcher to discuss specific words that might be difficult for VoiceType to recognize, and to plan a strategy to avoid those recognition problems. For example, "birthday" can be said with a natural pause but should be said quickly so VoiceType recognizes it as one word rather than two. Although these strategies were an integral part of the intervention, the focus of the study was on the students' attempts to use VoiceType.

The VoiceType portion of the intervention was based on the sequence of skills and procedures explained in the VoiceType manual. The researcher modeled the procedures in a manner similar to that on the publisher's videotape that accompanied the program. While pretraining the system, the user practices maintaining the required tenth-of-a-second pause between utterances. Following directions in the manual, students began training the system to recognize their own voice patterns by repeating each of several hundred preselected words three times. These words include general vocabulary (e.g., number and color words) and command phrases (e.g., "Begin paragraph," "Capitalize next word"). The ability to correct recognition errors is a critical component of using VoiceType and this was a key learning task for the students. VoiceType commands and procedures were taught in each session. In later lessons, previously introduced procedures were reviewed and reinforced within the context of the personal narratives.

A description of the first four sessions provides a context for understanding the nature and results of the intervention.

Session 1.   Upon meeting the researcher, Steven was initially somewhat reserved but responded readily to conversational overtures. He reported that his parents had a computer and that he was interested in computer technology. He had used the word processor and had played a few games on his home computer. He was very willing to use the computer and try VoiceType. The researcher explained that voice recognition was another way to communicate and that he would be trying it to see if it was an effective way to write. During this first session, Steven received preliminary instruction in both pretraining the system and the correction procedure. Steven started with the words that are used to begin and close the program (e.g., "Voice console," "Wake up," "Go to sleep"). Training for each group of words required 2 to 10 minutes. The correction procedure was explained. At the close of the session, Steven put on the headset microphone and repeated this short sentence several times: "Hello, how are you?" and then said "I am having fun" twice. Here is what appeared on the screen.

yemnt roome hello how are you aid been.
lo how are you in room room
hello how are? Been
i am further further in further
i am having fun. ago in
hi vicotry every

Although most of the words that he spoke were recognized by VoiceType, extra nonsensical words were added. This occurred when Steven made extraneous sounds, for example, when he breathed deeply or coughed while the microphone was on.

Session 2.   This session emphasized the importance of pausing for one tenth of a second between words. As he practiced, Steven noticed that coughing and saying "aah" or "eh" into the microphone caused words unrelated to the writing task to be displayed on the screen. He practiced the procedures for eliminating unwanted words.

Session 3.   In this session Steven was introduced to the "hot key" (normally, the "+" key), which turned the microphone off when he needed to cough or to talk to the researcher. He pretrained the number-word and punctuation-word groups; he learned the command "Begin document," for starting a new piece of writing and for capitalizing the first word of the opening sentence. He reviewed the need to pause one tenth of a second between words and reviewed how to respond to VoiceType's word choice.

Session 4.   The researcher demonstrated the fluent use of VoiceType. Steven observed that VoiceType could display dictated words quickly and accurately; and, as a result of the demonstration, he spoke into the microphone more clearly and with more confidence.

In summary, each session with Steven started with a review of VoiceType commands and procedures, the teaching of new procedures, and a writing segment. During the writing segment, Steven would engage one or more aspects of the writing process: prewriting with oral rehearsal and listing keywords, dictation, and correction procedures. A debriefing followed in which procedures that worked and did not work were discussed, as was as the focus of the next meeting. Using these strategies, Steven dictated seven short personal narratives over the course of the study.

Data Collection

Steven dictated using VoiceType for 14 sessions. The researcher took notes during each session. The notes included (a) a videotape of the screen during dictation, (b) a verbatim transcription of the interaction between Steven and VoiceType, (c) Steven's oral rehearsal before dictation, (d) his keyword lists, and (e) each draft that Steven dictated. Examination of these data sources provides information about the student's mastery of the system, the adequacy of the system's response for this purpose, and the potential for improvement of student writing.

RESULTS

Question 1

Can elementary students learn to use VoiceType? To use VoiceType effectively, a student must master the skills of pausing between words, pronouncing words correctly, using the correction procedure, and controlling extraneous sounds. Steven quickly mastered the ability to pause briefly between words, and he spoke each word clearly. In the final session there were no errors due to a failure to pause between words or pronunciation of words (see transcription of the dictation in Appendix B).

The researcher's observation and a transcription of the videotapes revealed no instance in which the researcher found the student's speech to be unrecognizable. That is, the researcher would have correctly transcribed the words as uttered. This may be considered an indication that the student's speech was sufficiently clear for a human transcriber. The ability of VoiceType to recognize Steven's speech was less proficient, though it improved as the system was trained and responded to Steven's corrections. In the first two sessions, VoiceType recognized 40% and 23%, respectively, of Steven's utterances with a correct guess on the menu. In the last two sessions, the recognition levels were 71% and 74%, respectively.

Mastery of Correction Procedure.   Another indication of mastery was whether the student had learned the procedure for correcting errors. There were two error types: (a) the correct match of the user's utterance was not the first choice on the menu but was listed in the menu, or (b) the correct match was not listed on the menu. An examination of actual instances when the student needed to correct VoiceType errors revealed that the student learned to correctly select from the menu the word that matched the utterance. The transcript of the dictation sessions showed that as Steven practiced he learned to make the selection on his own and that his rate of dictation improved. However, when the match for the utterance was not on the menu and Steven was required to spell the word, the data showed that he had trouble correcting words if he had difficulty spelling them. For example, VoiceType supplied "said" for "should." Steven tried to sound out the word by saying "sh." VoiceType supplied "see" for "sh."

A summary of errors Steven attempted to correct in the 13th session (see Appendix B for transcript) included 9 instances out of 58 words dictated in which the desired word did not appear on the menu and he had to spell it entirely, or it appeared after he begin typing it in, and 10 instances whereby he merely had to select it from the menu.

Monitoring Extraneous Sounds.   In the first sessions, Steven made utterances that produced many unwanted words on the screen. By the final session he had only 5 utterances during the dictation of 58 words that resulted in extraneous words on the screen (one sniffle, two voiced deep breaths, one instance of two words whispered, and the beginning sound of a word). Steven produced no extraneous sounds as he was dictating as long as VoiceType recognized his words or placed the correct word in the menu. However, in one instance it failed to recognize a second consecutive word, and Steven took a deep breath prior to beginning the correction procedure. VoiceType "heard" his deep breath and suggested yet another unwanted word, resulting in two erroneous words that had to be deleted. He pressed *F10* (reject) to delete the most recent unwanted word he wanted, and he began to sound out the word, saying the beginning "sh," and immediately VoiceType suggested "see" for "sh."

Although Steven knew what to do, it took an effort to simultaneously engage in the correction procedure and restrain unwanted sounds.

Question 2

Is the technology powerful enough to support the kinds of tasks students are assigned? The power of this technology to support communication tasks can be evaluated by focusing on the speed and accuracy of transcription. Although this depends on the student's ability to speak clearly, it also is dependent on the system's ability to recognize the user's speech. This is evident in the dictation instances in which Steven did everything correctly, yet VoiceType failed to transcribe accurately. For 74% of the words Steven dictated, either VoiceType transcribed them correctly (ranked them first on the menu) or were lower ranked, but on the menu. Twenty-six percent of the words were not on the menu, although Steven stated them clearly and paused before saying the next word. In these instances, great concentration was required to monitor the correction procedure, spell words and remove the unwanted words and start again.

Steven's dictation rate provides data that illustrates the rate of this procedure. In early sessions the dictation rate was 2.5 words per minute; in the final sessions it was 5.5 words per minute. As with the accuracy, this measure was a reflection of both Steven's proficiency and the characteristics of VoiceType.

Question 3

Does the entire process result in students' improved communication? If students could learn to use the technology, and if the performance of voice-recognition technology were adequate, one might expect students' written communication to improve. Steven was able to dictate six short narrative pieces of writing over the period of 10 weeks. The teacher indicated that this was an improvement for Steven, who typically produced no written work of his own. However, because of VoiceType's limitations and Steven's only partial mastery of the correction and self-monitoring procedure, it is not possible to draw conclusions about his written work.

DISCUSSION

An analysis of the transcriptions of early and late dictation showed that Steven improved his speed of dictation, and VoiceType more accurately transcribed his utterances, but he continued to be troubled with VoiceType's failure to recognize words. Over the 10-week period, Steven learned to speak clearly and pause slightly between words. By the 13th session, VoiceType's top-ranked suggestion or a suggestion on the menu matched Steven's utterance 74% of the time. Although there are no benchmarks for determining whether a student has mastered the procedures, VoiceType promotional literature indicates that adults develop rates of accuracy over 90%.

Steven's problems occurred when VoiceType did not recognize an utterance and the word match had to be input through the keyboard. This was the case in 26% of the words dictated in the last sessions. During the correction procedure, Steven had trouble spelling some of the words VoiceType did not recognize. His problems were compounded when, in his attempt to spell a word, he would begin sounding out words while the microphone was on, which resulted in unwanted words appearing on the screen. As Steven's frustration grew, other inappropriate behaviors became evident; for example, he breathed deeply or coughed, adding unwanted words to the screen. Each unwanted word had to be considered and deleted. Although he did not give up or ask to stop, it was evident that he became frustrated, as these problems slowed the correction procedure and interfered with the dictation.

In addition to Steven, 2 other students were trained to use the system. Ashley, a fifth-grade girl, was more fluent than Steven and thus required less time in oral rehearsal. However, the report that she dictated used numerous scientific and geographical terms that were not recognized by VoiceType, such as *radium, polonium, Sorbonne,* and *Warsaw.* Using the correction procedure to teach VoiceType these new words was difficult, and she preferred to use the keyboard for entering subject-specific vocabulary. The third student, Jeremy, was the least verbally fluent of the 3 students and wrote very short samples. The oral rehearsal strategies produced little oral narrative; he responded to questions with answers of only a few words and did not elaborate. The researcher concluded that he did not fit the profile of a student who was orally fluent but deficit in written composition skills, and thus was a poor subject for the study. In summary, all 3 students successfully learned to use the dictation system and experienced similar difficulties with the correction procedure. In addition, individual differences in each student's verbal fluency and task selection influenced the usefulness of this technology for their written communication.

CONCLUSIONS

For VoiceType to take advantage of Steven's natural verbal fluency, the program needed to have recognized more than 74% of his utterances. Employing correction procedures 26% of the time would likely be unacceptable to adults who were fluent readers and writers; for students who have difficulty with decoding the alternatives suggested by VoiceType and correctly spelling their choices, this level of recognition is even less acceptable.

One might take some measures to enhance the level of recognition. More frequent training sessions over a longer period of time might (a) allow for more time to develop the template for Steven's voice, (b) increase recognition, and (c) enable Steven to self-monitor his dictation. Additional training could help students use the correction process with more ease. At a minimum, they might learn to self-monitor to the degree that they would remember to turn off the microphone and program when sounding out words and making extraneous noises.

Alternatively, one might anticipate through oral rehearsal the new words that would be used for a particular narrative and teach them to VoiceType prior to dictation. This would require the student to say the word and engage in the correction procedure until VoiceType learned the word. The student's fluency would be interrupted less often. This is a time-consuming process that requires an aide. However, for specific students who have consistent access to trained assistants, this approach may be worthwhile and workable. For example, a school psychologist (Jacobson, 1994) reported using VoiceType successfully with a high school student who took VoiceType to college and continued to use it independently for his written work. The psychologist explained that the training period supervised by a trained aide required a half hour daily for 6 months. During this time, new words relating to daily writing assignments were anticipated and were added to the student's voice template. For the remainder of the day, he used the system to do his writing.

Another strategy would be to ignore the recognition errors and dictate as much as possible with fluency. If VoiceType's recognition rate improved to 90%, this would be a strategy to consider, but at the present time it seems impractical because too much meaning is lost when one of every four words is substantially incorrect. If the errors are to be corrected later, too much is left to revise. Also, during Steven's dictation lessons, the researcher thought that each misrecognized word should be corrected immediately because this improved the odds that VoiceType would recognize that word the next time it was uttered. However, some improvements in VoiceType's accuracy of recognition are needed before this strategy is worth investigating further.

Attributes of a Voice-Recognizing Computer

What are the minimal requirements of a speech-recognizing computer that would be workable for students? Students need a system they can master in a reasonable period of time, and one that can produce a high percentage of accurate word matches. A combination of factors might serve to ensure this. First, the accuracy of the system must be high enough that students do not get bogged down with the correction procedure: generally 90% or better. The accuracy rate should be a level that allows a transcription rate that exceeds writing by pencil. Second, the ease of correction or the ease of adding new words to one's template should be such that the correction procedure would not cause students to lose their concentration or train of thought. Third, the system should screen out close-range nonword sounds, such as a deep breath. VoiceType was lacking in these areas.

On the other hand, two VoiceType functions were adequate. First, VoiceType required that users pause between dictated words, and these students were able to use discrete speech dictation. The tenth-of-a-second pause between words did not cause them a problem. They were able to monitor their speaking by pausing slightly before saying the next word, and the pauses did not require so much thought that fluency was affected. This indicates that a computer that would recognize natural (continuous) speech does not appear to be a prerequisite for student use. Second, the system was adequate at screening middle- and far-distance noises, so that voices 20 feet away or a door closing in the hallway did not degrade the system's performance.

Schools

This exploratory study begins to build a research base to determine the usefulness of current voice-to-speech technology. Although the use of this technology may intrigue parents and educators, it should be regarded as experimental at this time; schools should exercise care regarding the purchase of this technology for students who in theory may benefit from it. The potential benefits are intuitively obvious; for example, when VoiceType recognized a string of Steven's words without error, his face would light up. However, this potential is constrained at present by the cost and physical limitations of the technology, and the amount of training required. In this study, it was evident that fourteen 30-minute sessions were insufficient for teaching the student to use it competently. Given these limitations, it may be advisable to wait for improvements in the technology before seriously considering it for use by students with LD.

Suggestions for Further Research

Because the use of this technology with students is so new, there are unlimited directions for research. It appears that four areas should receive priority: First, voice-recognition systems other than VoiceType are on the market and they should be investigated to determine whether any may prove more usable for students with LD, especially with regard to rate of recognition and correction procedures. Second, because speech-to-text technology is more efficient when oral dictation is fluent, strategies that boost students' speech fluency should be investigated. The model used in this study to assist fluency was borrowed from the strategies promoted by the National Writing Project, but there may be differences among effective prewriting and pre-dictating strategies. Third, one might explore differences in the final product between writing by pen and writing through dictation. And, finally, some students with LD may benefit more from this technology than others. How do we select students who would likely benefit from speech-to-text transcription?

NOTE

VoiceType was developed by Dragon Systems, Inc., and is distributed by IBM. VoiceType requires an IBM-compatible computer equivalent to a PS/2 or greater (Intel 80386SX processor or greater), six Mb of RAM memory, a 30 Mb hard disk drive or larger, one floppy drive, an IBM M-Audio Capture and Playback Adapter card and VoiceType software. VoiceType was selected because it has a 7,000-word active vocabulary, integrates with many off-the-shelf MS-DOS PC-based applications, and is moderately priced, compared to larger vocabulary systems. The 1993 cost of the audio capture card was approximately $300 and VoiceType software approximately $3,000. (In 1995, the cost of a similar software, Dragon Dictate Starter Edition, was $395.) The student-appropriate word processing program IBM's Primary Editor Plus ($95) was used with VoiceType. (It is important to note that, in 1996, IBM distributed a new product called VoiceType; however, it is not based on the Dragon Systems technology. The results of this study are based on the earlier version. The new product, although titled the same, should be considered as a separate system.)

APPENDIX A: CORRECTION PROCEDURE

To illustrate the procedure, consider dictation of the sentence, "Everyone likes computers." The user says, "Everyone." If VoiceType recognizes the word, this screen would appear:

Everyone_
F1	everyone
F2	every
F3	many
F10	[reject]

Because the first choice is correct, the user continues by speaking the next word, *likes*. However, VoiceType may not correctly recognize the word *everyone* and instead presents the following screen:

Everything_
F1	everything
F2	federal
F4	many
F5	every
F6	everyone
F10	[reject]

To correct, the user presses the *F6* key and *everyone* replaces *everything* on the screen. A final possibility is that VoiceType may fail to recognize the word and, furthermore, may not include the correct word on the menu of choices, as shown below:

Something_
F1	something
F2	Mary
F3	many
F4	cherry
F5	fairy
F10	[reject]

In this case, the user must spell the desired word. As each letter is keyed, the menu of choices changes to words that conform to the keyed-in letters, and the correct choice often appears on the menu by the third letter. It then may be selected by pressing the appropriate function key. The user may also spell the word by saying each letter using the International Communication Alphabet—in this case by saying, "Echo," "Victor," "Echo," "Romeo," and so forth. VoiceType updates the user's speech template, so the next time the user says "everyone," the probability rises that VoiceType will produce the correct word on the screen.

APPENDIX B: DICTATION SESSION NO. 13

The section below describes Session 13 using the transcript from the videotape. The transcript documents Steven's dictation word for word, VoiceType's response to each word uttered, and Steven's use of the correction procedure. In addition, the time required to complete the dictation was noted in the transcript, to allow an examination of the fluency of the dictation. A detailed examination of this next-to-last session provides some information about both Steven's experiences and the responses of the technology.

Steven rehearsed and dictated the following story about his favorite basketball team during the session:

> When the Suns come on TV we always rush to the TV. I think that the Suns will win the series, but if they want to win they must get the ball inside and play better defense. Barkley should block more. Kevin should pass more and drive more.

What actually took place when the words were dictated? Steven began by saying, "When," and VoiceType placed the word *When* on the screen. As soon as Steven saw that "When" was the correct word, he continued speaking the next word in the sentence, "the," and VoiceType placed "the" on the screen.

Steven said, "Suns." This was a word that VoiceType did not recognize, and "stretch" appeared on the screen, as shown below. Under this phrase, a box appeared on the screen with words preceded by corresponding F keys. These words were VoiceType's next-best guesses for Steven's spoken word: "Suns":

> When the *stretch*
>   F1 stretch
>   F2 string
>   F3 sunk
>   F4 ton
>   F5 top
>   F6 [reject]

Because none of the words were correct, Steven began spelling the word by typing the first letter, "S." The words on the menu changed as he typed each subsequent letter, but VoiceType did not guess the word, so Steven typed each letter of "Suns." The menu now showed only two choices:

> F1 Suns
> F2 [reject]

F1 was correct so Steven continued by speaking the next word in his sentence: "come." As soon as he spoke this word, VoiceType automatically accepted "Suns" and added it to Steven's voice template. It also placed "come" on the screen:

> When the Suns *come*

Steven continued by dictating "on," and that word appeared correctly on the screen. He said "TV" and "he" appeared as VoiceType's first choice. "TV" was not on the menu so Steven typed "T.V." without hesitation. He said "we" to begin the next sentence paused briefly, saw that it was correct, and said "always." Once again, he followed with a pause, then said "rush." VoiceType suggested "rest" for "rush," as shown in the sentence below.

When the Suns come on T.V. we always *rest*

The flow of speech was interrupted as Steven stopped speaking to determine the next step. "Rush" was not on the menu, so he typed "r-u-s." As he typed the "r," "rush" appeared as the third choice on the menu (F3) because VoiceType continues to update its suggestions as the program receives more information. Steven pressed F3, noticed at a glance that the screen was correct, and continued dictating "to" (pause) "the" (pause) "T.V." VoiceType once again selected "he" for "T.V." as shown below:

When the Suns come on T.V. we always rush to the *he*

"T.V." was not a menu selection. Steven typed "T," and immediately "T.V." appeared on the menu as the first choice. This was an example of the process by which VoiceType learned a new word that was missed initially, spelled by Steven, and saved in his voice template. Each time his oral pronunciation of "T.V." was associated with the word he spelled, the association with the word was strengthened. After several repetitions, VoiceType presented the word as the first choice. He finished the sentence by saying "period" and the punctuation mark appeared at the end of the sentence. He continued by dictating the new sentence: "I" (pause) "think" (pause) "that." VoiceType suggested "at" for "that," as shown below:

When the Suns come on T.V. we always rush to the T.V. I think *at*
    F1 at
    F2 that
    F3 mat
    F4 sat
    F5 chat
    F6 [reject]

Here, Steven did not spell the word because he noticed that "that" was the second choice on the menu, and he pressed F2. Once again the program associated his utterance "that" with the graphical form "that," and the chances were improved that VoiceType would select "that" as the first choice next time it was uttered. Steven continued with "Barkley," and VoiceType suggested "breakfast." He spelled "Barkley" without any problem and continued by saying "should." VoiceType suggested "said" for "should." Notice that VoiceType misrecognized two consecutive words. Steven took a deep breath prior to proceeding. VoiceType "heard" his deep breath and suggested the word "room" for the breath. The sentence now read:

When the Suns come on T.V. we always rush to the T.V. I think that Barkley *said room.*

Steven pressed F10 [reject] to delete the unwanted "room" and attempted to spell "should" to replace "said." He began to sound out the word, saying "sh" and immediately VoiceType suggested "see" for "sh."

When the Suns come on T.V. we always rush to the T.V. I think that Barkley *said see.*

Frustration was beginning to show on Steven's face. However, he continued by pressing F10 to remove "see" and then he typed "s-h-o" and pressed F1 because "should" now appeared as the first choice on the menu. He continued dictating "block" (pause) "more" (pause) "period." VoiceType suggested "for" for "more," but "more" was the second menu choice. Steven quickly pressed F2 and said "period." This type of interruption (merely pressing an F key to select the correct word from the menu) was fairly minor and did not derail the continuity of his dictation.

He continued with the last sentence by saying "Kevin," and VoiceType responded by suggesting "in" for "Kevin." Steven took a deep breath to tackle this correction and VoiceType suggested "1993K" in response to the voiced breath. He correctly selected F10 [reject] and said "Kevin" again. This time VoiceType suggested "said" and Steven started to type "K-e." As he typed, VoiceType updated the choices on the menu and F3 "Kevin" (F3) appeared. He pressed F3 and continued speaking: "should - pass - more - drive - more." Once again VoiceType suggested another word for "more." However, because the correct word appeared as F7 on the menu, he pressed that key and continued. "Tried" was suggested for "drive," but again Steven pressed F7 ("drive") and completed the sentence without losing momentum. When VoiceType's first suggestion was incorrect, but the correct word appeared on the menu, Steven was able to continue without losing his line of thought. In the last sentence, he did omit saying "and" and he failed to notice it was missing.

5. The Effects of Computer-Assisted Versus Teacher-Directed Instruction on the Multiplication Performance of Elementary Students with Learning Disabilities

RICH WILSON, DAVID MAJSTEREK, AND DEBORAH SIMMONS

Access to computers in public schools has increased dramatically for students in the past decade (Becker, 1991). Based on meta-analyses of the effects of technological support, the increased investment in technology has been positively related to performance for many learners without identified disabilities (C. Kulik & J. Kulik, 1991; J. Kulik & C. Kulik, 1987). Support for computer-assisted instruction (CAI), also known as *computer-based instruction,* has also been reported for students with identified disabilities (Schmidt, Weinstein, Niemic, & Walberg, 1985–86), though empirical investigations with these students have been fewer.

Applications and investigations of CAI in special education have been largely limited to drill and practice programs (Cosden & Abernathy, 1990). A probable cause for this limitation is that most published software, especially early CAI applications, was designed to teach or reinforce specific skills. It is important to note that although most empirical inves-

Reprinted, with changes, from "The effects of computer-assisted versus teacher-directed instruction on the multiplication performance of elementary students with learning disabilities," by Rich Wilson, David Majsterek, and Deborah Simmons, *Journal of Learning Disabilities,* Vol. 29, 1996, pp. 382–390. Copyright © 1996 by PRO-ED, Inc.

tigations involve drill-and-practice software, recent CAI products (e.g., CD programs, QuickTime movies, PlainTalk, and other interactive and multimedia applications) incorporate sophisticated developments that may be appropriately used in learning disabilities (LD) settings. Basic skill-building CAI, however, addresses an empirically validated need of students with learning disabilities. For example, in their analysis of multiplication errors made by students with LD, Miller and Milam (1987) found that most errors were due to basic-fact deficits. Because the higher order mathematical processes involved in solving story problems are contingent on basic-fact mastery (Pellegrino & Goldman, 1987), it is no wonder that teachers opt for skill-building software applications to address Individualized Education Program (IEP) arithmetic objectives. Thus, the combination of teachers' willingness to employ easy-to-use CAI and empirical support of the need for skill building in arithmetic makes drill-and-practice computer applications a logical instructional component for students with arithmetic learning disabilities.

Reviewers of CAI (e.g., Majsterek & Wilson, 1989, 1993) found that the instructional features of software are associated with effective computer applications. For example, researchers have found that effective software includes sufficient opportunities to respond (Salisbury, 1990), provides contingent and frequent feedback (Collins, Carnine, & Gersten, 1987), and is linked to teacher-directed instruction (Woodward et al., 1986).

Research comparing teacher delivery and computer delivery to students with LD, however, has been difficult to interpret due to a lack of adequate intervention description. For example, one early study suggested that using CAI in an augmentative capacity produced greater achievement gains than the same instruction without the CAI component (Watkins & Webb, 1981), an advantage the treatment group maintained over time. Unfortunately, classroom application of these findings would be difficult because the interventions were inadequately described. Other researchers (Trifiletti, Frith, & Armstrong, 1984) found that a data-based CAI system produced greater gains in math skills and problem-solving fluency than workbook-based "traditional" instruction in the resource room. But, again, details of the instructional delivery systems were incomplete, making implementation problematic. Finally, Chiang (1986) found benefits for CAI programs that included a skill-building component. Although his was not a comparison study, Chiang's results demonstrated that speed of fact recall for the students with LD increased over time and transferred from the computer-based activities to paper-and-pencil tasks.

In general, special education teachers report that they are familiar with the principles of effective teaching but characterize their competence in technology as introductory (Cosden, 1988). This suggests that teachers may be less comfortable applying instructional design principles to computer applications in the classroom. This perception, coupled with the limitations of previous findings, suggests a need for in-school research that includes detailed descriptions of the interventions so that comparisons of computer-directed and teacher-directed instruction (TDI) can be made both for student achievement and on selected instructional variables. Although a wide range of skill-building software is currently in use in special education programs, there exists a need to translate research on effective teaching into information about how CAI can best be used for students with LD. The present research was designed to compare student performance in a specific CAI program to performance under similarly structured teacher-directed instruction. Thus, the purposes of this investigation were to (a) compare the relative effect of two instructional delivery formats (computer and teacher) on the mastery of multiplication facts by elementary students with LD, and (b) compare the two teaching formats on two critical instructional variables: opportunities to respond and success rate.

METHOD

Participants

Four elementary students with LD, ranging in age from 9 years 2 months to 10 years 10 months, participated in this study. All students attended school in a local education agency (LEA) of 3,200 students located in a city of 25,000 in northwest Ohio. All students received at least 1 hour per day of instruction in the resource room but received half or more of their academic instruction in their general education classrooms. Each student was previously identified as LD by a multidisciplinary team, was currently attending third or fourth grade, received math instruction from the resource teacher, had at least one annual IEP goal in math, and had returned signed parental and student permission. The study was approved by the Human Subjects Review Board at Bowling Green State University. Ohio criteria for LD eligibility require that students demonstrate a severe discrepancy between actual and predicted achievement—a discrepancy statistically evidenced by a difference of 2 or more standard deviations between scores on intelligence and achievement tests. In addition, students had missed at least 24 multiplication facts on the pretest. This last criterion ensured that each student had missed enough facts to guarantee that there would be at least 12 facts in each of the two learning sets. Additional student characteristics are provided in Table 5.1.

TABLE 5.1
Student Characteristics

Student	Gender	Age	Ethnicity	Estimated SES	Full-Scale IQ (WISC-R)	Overall academic achievement[a] (K-TEA)	Math achievement[a] (K-TEA)	Grade level	Hours/day in SLD resource room
Samuel	M	10-6	C	MC	106	66	49	4	1
Sebastian	M	10-10	C	UMC	92	24	15	4	2½
Sally	F	9-2	C	MC	88	21	13	3	2½
John	M	10-4	C	LMC	105	63	21	3	2

Note. C = Caucasian; K-TEA = Kaufman Test of Educational Achievement (Kaufman & Kaufman, 1985); WISC-R = Wechsler Intelligence Scale for Children–Revised (Wechsler, 1974); MC = middle class; UMC = upper middle class; LMC = lower middle class.
[a]In percentile ranks.

Dependent Measures

The dependent measure of primary interest was the number of multiplication facts mastered by each student. A fact was defined as mastered when a student wrote the answer correctly within 3 seconds on two consecutive probes. Dependent measures of secondary interest were opportunities to respond (defined as verbal, written, or typed student responses following a teacher's or CAI program's question) and success rate (defined as the percentage of correct verbal, written, or typed responses by a student during the lessons).

Fact Selection. Careful attention was paid to the selection of facts to be learned by each student and to the assignment of facts to instructional format, to ensure that (a) only facts the student did not know were taught in the lessons and (b) the difficulty level of facts was controlled and balanced for each teaching method. First, students were pretested on multiplication facts from 0 through 9, and only facts that were not answered correctly were taught. Next, difficulty level was determined for each multiplication fact by (a) administering written tests to intact classes of general education third-grade students in the same LEA, (b) scoring correct and incorrect responses, and (c) assigning a difficulty index to each fact that corresponded to the proportion of third-grade students who responded correctly (Wilson, Majsterek, & Simmons, 1994). The same procedure was followed to determine difficulty indices for facts for fourth-grade students.

Assignment of Facts to Teaching Format. Pretest results identified facts that were known by the student, facts that were unknown, and facts that were "nearly known" (i.e., facts that were answered correctly in more than 3 seconds and facts that were self-corrected). Unknown and nearly known facts were then randomly assigned to two instructional sets of equal difficulty for each student. Each set contained a minimum of 12 facts and the same number of unknown and nearly known facts. For example, 40 of the facts that John missed on the pretest (6 nearly known facts and 34 unknown facts) were taught in two 20-fact sets, each with 3 nearly known facts and 17 unknown facts (see Table 5.2). An added stipulation: A fact and its reciprocal (e.g., 6×8 and 8×6) were assigned to the same treatment, and the same number of fact and reciprocal fact pairs were assigned to both treatments. In addition, if 2 students missed the same fact, and the fact had been assigned to the computer-assisted set for the first student, the fact was assigned to the teacher-directed set for the second student. These procedures ensured that the two sets of facts for each student contained the same number of equally difficult facts.

TABLE 5.2
John's Facts

Order	CAI set		TDI set	
	Fact	Difficulty index	Fact	Difficulty index
1.	2 × 2[a]	.98	1 × 1[a]	.98
2.	6 × 2[a]	.95	2 × 3[a]	.95
3.	2 × 4[a]	.93	5 × 2[a]	.93
4.	2 × 9	.90	7 × 2	.88
5.	3 × 3	.90	5 × 5	.83
6.	3 × 5	.88	2 × 8	.88
7.	4 × 5	.85	4 × 3	.78
8.	8 × 5	.68	6 × 5	.71
9.	5 × 7	.68	3 × 6	.68
10.	9 × 5	.54	9 × 3	.54
11.	7 × 3	.51	8 × 3	.41
12.	2 × 6	.93	3 × 2	.93
13.	4 × 2	.93	2 × 5	.90
14.	9 × 2	.83	2 × 7	.88
15.	5 × 3	.85	8 × 2	.88
16.	5 × 4	.71	3 × 4	.71
17.	5 × 8	.44	5 × 6	.71
18.	7 × 5	.59	6 × 3	.61
19.	5 × 9	.51	3 × 9	.29
20.	3 × 7	.41	3 × 8	.41
	Average	.75	Average	.74

Note. CAI = computer-assisted instruction; TDI = teacher-directed instruction.
[a]Nearly known fact.

Presentation of Facts During Lessons.   After instructional sets were created, facts were sequenced in the order they would be taught. Nearly known facts were taught first, followed by easier and then harder unknown facts. Thus, the facts in Table 5.2 were taught in the order listed. CAI facts and TDI facts were always taught in separate lessons.

Facts to be taught during CAI and TDI lessons were selected in the same way for both treatments. The first five facts in a given ordered set were designated for instruction and constituted the instructional objectives for the first lesson. These five facts were taught until probes administered prior to each lesson indicated that one or more facts had been mastered (i.e., answered correctly on two consecutive probes). If mastered, a fact was replaced in the five-fact teaching group with a new, unknown fact, and the new five-fact set became the lesson's instructional objectives. Fact mastery and replacement of mastered facts by new, unknown facts continued until all facts in the ordered instructional set of CAI or TDI facts were mastered.

Monitoring Student Performance.   A series of pretests, probes, and posttests were administered to monitor fact acquisition. Through pretests, the researchers identified the facts to be taught. Written probes containing only facts missed on the pretest were administered prior to each lesson. Four probe forms, which contained the same facts in varied order, were developed to guard against potential order and memorization effects. Written posttests identical to the written pretests were administered 1 and 3 weeks after the lessons ended. Administering and scoring written tests and probes followed the same format. Students were provided test pages of multiplication facts and instructed to work as quickly and accurately as possible. Students were instructed to examine each problem carefully, write the answer to problems they knew, and cross out problems whose answers they did not know. As students responded, observers watched and recorded on observer test pages problems that students (a) answered correctly within 3 seconds, (b) crossed out, (c) answered correctly in more than 3 seconds, and (d) answered incorrectly. Ultimately, a problem was deemed correct only if the answer was accurate and the student responded within 3 seconds. A fact was defined as mastered when a student wrote the correct answer on two consecutive lesson probes.

Research Design

A single-subject, alternating treatments design (ATD; Sindelar, Rosenberg, & Wilson, 1989) was used for data display and analysis. The ATD permits visual comparison of the effects of two (or more) interventions through observation of the difference in acquisition of the dependent variable. Two important considerations must be met when the ATD is used to assess academic learning. First, the sets of items to be learned must be of equal difficulty to control for effect due to task complexity. Second, the order of intervention presentation must be counterbalanced (e.g., the same intervention cannot always occur first or in the morning) to control for effect due to time of day and order of presentation. For the purposes of this study, extended baseline data were not gathered; rather, initial data points for all students were zero, because only unknown facts were introduced during the study.

Independent Measures

The primary purpose of the study was to compare student learning under computer-assisted instruction versus teacher-directed instruction. Both teaching formats were designed to result in fact automaticity (Hasselbring, Goin, & Bransford, 1988) by incorporating sound assessment and instructional methods in the lessons. Fact automaticity is attained when students respond immediately and correctly and do not require time for silent computation or involved processing.

Both interventions incorporated three basic components in all lessons: demonstration, controlled practice, and "game-style" practice. The lesson components are described below.

CAI Treatment.   The basis for the CAI lessons was the popular computer math software program Math Blaster (MB; Eckert & Davidson, 1987). One of the desirable features of this software is that teachers can select specific math facts (or sets of facts) to be studied. The demonstration component of MB was called "Look & Learn." In this activity, facts and answers were presented vertically on the screen:

$$\frac{\begin{array}{r} 5 \\ \times 7 \end{array}}{35}$$

When the fact and answer appeared, students were instructed to vocalize the entire problem softly. Each of the five facts taught during an individual CAI lesson was presented during "Look & Learn." This entire sequence was then repeated.

During "Build Your Skill," the controlled-practice component of MB, facts were presented without answers and students were given 3 to 10 seconds to respond. Longer response times occurred during initial fact instruction, shorter times as students approached automaticity. If a student responded correctly within the designated time, MB delivered a brief praise statement. If the student erred, MB indicated that the answer was wrong and requested a second attempt to answer. If the second attempt was incorrect, MB provided the correct answer, and students were instructed to verbalize the fact and answer. At the conclusion of "Build Your Skill," MB provided a scoreboard containing the percentage of correct responses. Missed facts were recycled until 100% correct responding was attained.

The final component of MB was an arcade-style game involving practice on facts previously mastered and facts studied during the current lesson. During the game, students had a teacher-determined number of seconds (from 2 to 6) to respond to a fact presentation. Responding correctly within the allotted time landed the "Blasternaut" on the space station and scored points. Correct answers were provided when responses were incorrect.

TDI Treatment.   The foundation of the TDI lessons was a flashcard program also designed to result in fact automaticity. The demonstration component always occurred first, wherein students were shown one of the five facts (with answer) and the teacher verbalized the problem and answer (e.g., "My turn. Two times nine equals eighteen"). Next, the student and teacher said the fact and answer together (e.g., "Say it with me. Two times nine equals eighteen"). Finally, students read the problem and answer alone. This procedure was completed twice for each fact. Errors were corrected immediately by repeating the three-step instructional sequence (teacher alone, student and teacher together, student alone). Correct responses were followed by teacher praise, self-corrections and slow-but-accurate responses by encouraging verbal feedback.

The controlled practice component was designed to develop fact automaticity by generating fast and accurate responding. First, students responded verbally to problems on flashcards without printed answers. The flip side of the flashcard contained the problem with the answer, and wrong answers were corrected by the teacher showing the problem and answer and the student restating both. A "no response" resulted in the teacher supplying the correct answer after 5 seconds. Next, students gave written responses to the same problems. Positive feedback and correct answers, as appropriate, were provided at the end of each row of five problems. The last part of the controlled practice component consisted of 1-minute fluency drills, during which students wrote answers to as many problems as possible while being timed by the teacher.

The final component of the TDI lesson was a timed game, during which a student tried to beat her or his own best time for responding correctly. Problems taught during the current lesson, as well as all previously mastered problems, were presented during game practice. A stopwatch was used for timing, results were recorded by the teacher and student, and the student was encouraged to attain faster times for correct responding.

Typical Daily Lesson Sequence. The three-part lesson sequence (probe, CAI or TDI lesson, TDI or CAI lesson) lasted approximately 30 minutes. The probe (a written test containing all missed facts) was always administered first and took less than 5 minutes. Next, a 10-minute CAI (or TDI) lesson was delivered, followed by a 10-minute TDI (or CAI) lesson. The order of the CAI and TDI lessons was alternated for every second lesson sequence.

RESULTS

Reliability

Reliability data were gathered on two variables: student performance on lesson probes and length of the lesson. Approximately one third of the probes were checked for scoring reliability by two independent observers. Reliability ranged from 88% to 100% and averaged over 98% agreement between observers. In addition, the same lessons were timed, to ensure that CAI and TDI lessons were of equal duration. All timed lessons lasted 10 minutes, with one exception—1 student lingered for 1 extra minute on the Math Blaster game during one CAI lesson.

Fact Mastery

Results are presented graphically in Figures 5.1 through 5.4. Note that the pattern of fact acquisition is the same for all students: First, all students mastered multiplication facts under both experimental condi-

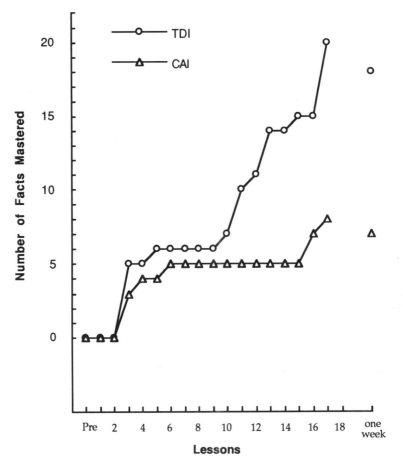

Figure 5.1. John's performance.

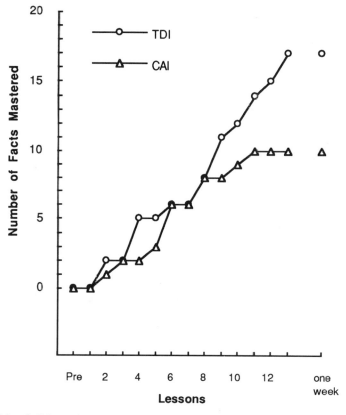

Figure 5.2. Sally's performance.

tions. Second, there was a period of time at the beginning of the study, ranging from 8 to 21 lessons, during which fact acquisition was approximately equal for all students under both teaching formats. Finally, and most important, all students mastered more facts under teacher-directed instruction, and that difference is clearly discernible through visual inspection.

Opportunities to Respond

Data on opportunities to respond are presented in Table 5.3. Analysis indicates a pattern of difference between the two teaching formats favoring the TDI condition for all students. The magnitude of difference varies across students, ranging from two to four times as many opportunities to respond in the TDI condition.

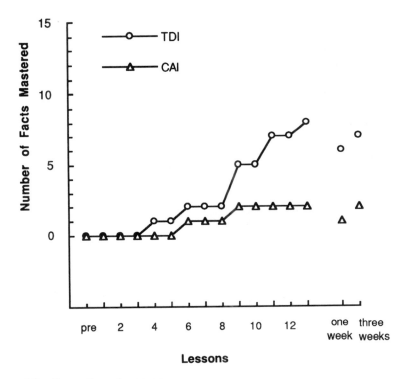

Figure 5.3. Samuel's performance.

Success Rate

Success rate data are presented in Table 5.4. Analysis reveals a pattern of difference between the two teaching formats favoring the TDI condition for all students. The magnitude of difference varies across students, ranging from 4% to 34% higher success rates in the TDI condition.

DISCUSSION

In this study, components of instructional design were made comparable to examine the relative effects of teacher-directed versus computer-assisted instruction on the multiplication performance of students with identified learning disabilities. The results suggest that both instructional formats can promote mastery and enhance automaticity of multiplication facts. However, the findings indicate consistent trends favoring the teacher-directed condition on fact mastery, and an average success rate as

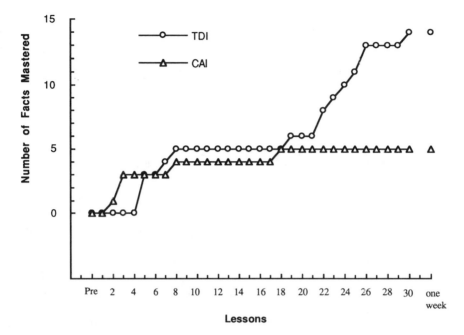

Figure 5.4. Sebastian's performance.

TABLE 5.3
Opportunities to Respond Per Lesson

Student	CAI lesson	TDI lesson
Samuel	55	100
Sebastian	33	86
Sally	32	135
John	37	154

Note. CAI = computer-assisted instruction; TDI = teacher-directed instruction.

evidenced in the performance of all four students. Across acquisition and success-rate data, the findings are robust but nevertheless cannot be explained by mere comparison of instructional components.

The apparent efficacy achieved through teacher-directed instruction must be considered in light of several instructional and ecological variables. First, care was taken to ensure that instructional "design" was not the differentiating factor between treatments. Drawing upon the teacher effects literature (e.g., Rosenshine, 1983), lesson components were designed to teach multiplication facts according to empirically validated

TABLE 5.4
Average Success Rate

Student	CAI lesson (%)	TDI lesson (%)
Samuel	90	94
Sebastian	53	87
Sally	83	99
John	72	100

Note. CAI = computer-assisted instruction; TDI = teacher-directed instruction.

procedures. A model, guided-practice, and independent practice instructional format was used in both conditions. As Rosenshine noted, this teaching structure was designed to teach information akin to basic facts.

Despite our attempts to keep the instructional features comparable between the two interventions, an unanticipated but perhaps illuminative difference arose. Specifically, opportunities to respond were substantively greater in the teacher-directed than in the computer-assisted condition. Empirical research clearly documents the advantage of opportunities to respond and the corollary benefits of feedback associated with these learning opportunities (e.g., Wilson & Wesson, 1986). In the teacher-directed condition, students received two to four times more opportunities to see facts and answers, respond to problems, and receive feedback. These markedly consistent opportunities should be considered not merely *opportunities to respond,* but, more accurately, *opportunities for instruction.*

The flexible and responsive nature of the teacher-directed condition allowed teachers to move at a quicker pace, remediate errors more immediately and differentially, and build fluency through greater opportunities for practice. Our objective was to compare treatment efficacy based on equal allocated time; we did not anticipate substantive differences in the number of presentations during a single lesson. Therefore, the unexpected benefit of increased opportunities to receive, practice, and respond to problems could largely explain the achievement differences between the two conditions.

An interesting observation was the latent effectiveness of TDI. We think it would be a mistake to interpret this finding solely as a quantity-of-opportunities issue. Rather, the unintended benefits of quality of instruction must be recognized when interpreting findings (Carroll, 1963). Prior to the study, the novelty of CAI and its accompanying special effects (i.e., color, sound, and graphic feedback) were perceived as potential benefits over TDI. As the learning profiles of the 4 students indicated, actual advantages of TDI were not evidenced until after eight or more lessons. This finding may indicate that certain elements of CAI were effective initially but waned over time.

At least two limitations must be noted. First, although the MB software is popular, well designed, and generally representative of quality CAI drill-and-practice programs, the results of this study should be generalized to other CAI software with caution. Given the differences across software and the rapidly increasing sophistication of CAI programs, such generalizations must be limited. Second, although student performance under the TDI condition was consistently superior to performance under the CAI condition, the one-on-one teaching format of TDI is an atypical classroom practice for many teachers. The 183% increase in the special education population since 1976–1977, when P.L. 94-142 was first instated (U.S. Department of Education, 1992), suggests that opportunities for individualized, teacher-led instruction are decreasing over time.

Conclusion

These findings parallel those of previous studies of basic fact–type information corroborating that "relatively simple procedures . . . may be more powerful when a task is less complex or when a student's needs are straightforward" (Harris, Graham, Reid, McElroy, & Hamby, 1994, p. 137). The issue at hand, however, is not whether simple instructional procedures are effective for basic-fact acquisition. Rather, as special educators and general educators face increasing numbers of students with special needs (Fuchs & Fuchs, 1994), they must be able to match the instructional needs of students with the ecological conditions of classrooms to design methods that optimize learning. Our findings suggest that for these students, teacher-directed procedures were the more efficient and effective method of achieving basic-fact automaticity. Nevertheless, this advantage must be countered by the limited time teachers have for individualized instruction. Effectiveness of CAI for automaticity development is clearly substantiated by these findings and provides teachers a feasible means of extending limited instructional resources.

Thus, although the present findings support the superiority of TDI over CAI in one-to-one instructional situations, results of observational studies in special and general education indicate that students spend a majority of their time working independently, not in individualized teaching conditions (Haynes & Jenkins, 1986). Given the increasingly diverse and complex conditions encountered in general and special education classrooms, instructional research must move beyond providing an either/or analysis of interventions and instructional practices, to specifying the conditions and effects of particular interventions. Such information can be gained from the types of questions examined and findings provided by this study of multiplication-fact acquisition. Armed with this information, practitioners can make informed decisions regarding how best to structure instructional time.

Additional research exploring the effects of teacher-directed and computer-assisted instruction in small groups and authentic instructional situations appears warranted. Small-group instruction more closely reflects current practice by LD teachers, and the results of such research would increase our understanding of instructional efficacy. Increasing the number of CAI programs investigated would also extend the findings of the present study.

6. Using Hypermedia to Improve the Mathematics Problem-Solving Skills of Students with Learning Disabilities

BEATRICE C. BABBITT AND SUSAN PETERSON MILLER

Several national initiatives related to mathematics instruction have emerged in recent years. The nation's America 2000 plan (U.S. Department of Education, 1991) for restructuring American education stressed the importance of teaching mathematical problem-solving skills. Similarly, a report prepared by the U.S. Department of Labor (1991) emphasized the importance of thinking, reasoning, and problem-solving skills. Moreover, the National Council of Teachers of Mathematics (NCTM) has become involved in identifying appropriate mathematics curricula and recently published the Curriculum and Evaluation Standards for School Mathematics (NCTM, 1980, 1989). These standards advocate teaching mathematics through a problem-solving perspective and emphasize finding mathematical applications in everyday situations. In fact, the council stated that problem-solving skills should be a top priority in math instruction and that problem-solving approaches should be used to teach mathematical content.

Reprinted, with changes, from "Using hypermedia to improve the mathematics problem-solving skills of students with learning disabilities," by Beatrice C. Babbitt and Susan Peterson Miller, *Journal of Learning Disabilities,* Vol. 29, 1996, pp. 391–401, 412. Copyright © 1996 by PRO-ED, Inc.

Understanding what is meant by mathematical problem solving has been challenging for educators. There appear to be a variety of definitions for problem solving. Mercer (1992) inspected 10 books and numerous articles about problem solving and students with learning problems and identified 37 different descriptors of mathematics problem solving. However, most authorities interpret problem solving within the context of word problems (e.g., Cawley, Miller, & School, 1987; Fleischner, Nuzum, & Marzola, 1987; Kameenui & Simmons, 1990). Therefore, the scope of this chapter will emphasize elementary and complex problem solving as it relates to mathematics word problems.

Historically, word problems in mathematics have been difficult for many students, but students with learning disabilities (LD) tend to find these problems particularly challenging (Lee & Hudson, 1981). The components of word problems that are especially difficult for students with learning disabilities include determining the correct operational process for solving the problem (Lee & Hudson, 1981), identifying and ignoring extraneous information (Blankenship & Lovitt, 1976; Englert, Culatta, & Horn, 1987; Fafard, 1976), reading the problems accurately (Dunlap & Strope, 1982; Montague & Bos, 1986), completing all the steps or carrying out the procedures necessary for solving the problem (Montague & Bos, 1992), and computing basic facts (Zentall, 1990). Havertape and Kass (1978) found that adolescents with learning disabilities had more trouble than their normally achieving peers in identifying critical information, understanding the word problem, and organizing an efficient strategy for solving it.

The language difficulties common to many students with learning disabilities also contribute to problem-solving deficits. Language disorders may cause confusion with mathematics vocabulary, such as "take away," "minus," "add," "plus," "carrying," and "borrowing" (Lerner, 1993). When students lack the prerequisite skills of language proficiency, vocabulary usage, and sequencing, solving word problems becomes extremely difficult (Bley & Thornton, 1989). Students need to understand the underlying language structures of math word problems in order to plan and perform the tasks required to find the answer (Bley & Thornton, 1989; Cawley et al., 1987). In some cases, students have no difficulty with the language they encounter in their daily lives but are confused when math problems do not use language exactly like their own. This confusion results in an inability to decipher the clues and solve the problems (Polloway & Patton, 1993).

The deficits discussed in the preceding paragraphs have resulted in poor problem-solving performance among many students with learning disabilities. Cawley and Miller (1989) found that the problem-solving skills of 17-year-old students with learning disabilities peaked at the fifth-grade level, whereas Greenstein and Strains (1977) reported that adolescents with learning disabilities plateaued at fourth-grade performance. Moreover, Smith (1985) found that students with learning disabilities were unable to solve word problems at a level equivalent to their computation skills.

In response to the increased emphasis on mathematics problem solving and the poor performance of students with learning disabilities, researchers have begun to explore appropriate methods for teaching these skills with greater effectiveness and efficiency. Fortunately, a body of research is emerging that will greatly enhance teachers' abilities to teach mathematics word problems (e.g., Case, Harris, & Graham, 1992; Miller & Mercer, 1993a; Nuzum, 1987; Watanabe, 1991). Concurrent to these investigations, other researchers (e.g., Gleason, Carnine, & Boriero, 1990; Robinson, DePascale, & Roberts, 1989; Trifiletti, Frith, & Armstrong, 1984) are examining the use of technology to enhance instruction provided to students with learning disabilities. It seems that combining the knowledge obtained from both groups of researchers could result in a highly effective approach for teaching problem solving using state-of-the-art technology.

The next three sections of this chapter discuss current knowledge about teaching problem solving to students with learning disabilities, using computers for teaching math to students with learning disabilities, and using computers to teach problem solving to students with learning problems. The remainder of the chapter provides ideas and suggestions for merging these knowledge bases to develop instructional technology that will increase the likelihood that students with learning disabilities can succeed in their mathematics problem-solving endeavors.

TEACHING PROBLEM SOLVING TO STUDENTS WITH LD

Research indicates that students with learning disabilities lack specific strategies for approaching problem-solving tasks (Mellard & Alley, 1981; Montague & Bos, 1986). For this reason, many researchers (e.g., Case et al., 1992; Hutchinson, 1993; Montague & Applegate, 1993; Montague, Applegate, & Marquard, 1993) advocate the teaching of cognitive and metacognitive strategies to remediate poor problem-solving performance. These strategies typically involve four to eight steps that cue students to perform the specific cognitive and physical processes that are needed to solve the problem. Direct instruction is frequently used to help students memorize and understand the steps in the strategies. Table 6.1 lists a variety of strategies that have been successfully used to teach problem solving. It is interesting to note the similarities across the strategies. The most critical components among these strategies seem to be reading

TABLE 6.1
Problem-Solving Strategies

Researchers	Strategy steps
Babbitt (1993)	Read the problem. Understand the problem. Choose solution strategy and solve. Check, "Is the question answered?" Check, "Does the answer make sense?" Consider applications and extensions.

Bennett (1982)
  Preorganizer
 	
  Postorganizer
	Read the problem.
	Underline numbers.
	Reread the problem.
	Decide on the operation.
	Write the mathematical sentence.
	Read.
	Check operation.
	Check math statement.
	Check calculations.
	Write labels.

Case et al. (1992)	Read the problem out loud. Look for important words and circle them. Draw pictures to help tell what is happening. Write down the math sentence. Write down the answer.
Fleischner et al. (1987)	Read. Reread. Think. Solve. Check.
Kramer (1970)	Read the problem. Reread the problem. Use objects to show the problem. Write the problem. Work the problem. Check your answer. Show your answer.

Miller & Mercer (1993b)
 	
  Then to compute
  answer . . .
	Find what you're solving for.
	Ask what are the parts of the problem.
	Set up the numbers.
	Tie down the sign.
	Discover the sign.
	Read the problem.
	Answer, or draw and check.
	Write the answer.

(table continues)

TABLE 6.1. Continued.

Researchers	Strategy steps
Montague et al. (1993)	Read. Paraphrase. Visualize. Hypothesize. Estimate. Compute. Check.
Polya (1957)	Understand the problem. Devise a plan. Carry out the plan. Look back to verify that the answer is reasonable.
Snyder (1988)	**R**ead the problem. **I** *know* statement. **D**raw a picture. **Go**al statement. **E**quation development. **S**olve the equation.
Watanabe (1991)	**S**urvey question. **I**dentify key words and labels. **G**raphically draw problem. **N**ote type of operation(s) needed. **S**olve and check problem.

the problems carefully; thinking about the problem via self-questioning or drawing, visualizing, underlining, or circling relevant information; determining the correct operation or solution strategy; writing the equation(s); and computing and checking the answer.

Another approach for teaching problem solving to students with learning disabilities is to introduce a graduated word-problem sequence (Miller & Mercer, 1993a). Using this approach, teachers introduce word problems concurrently with elementary computation instruction. Initially, the word problems contain one or two words. If the computation instruction involves the use of a manipulative device, such as cubes for addition, the word problems would look something like this:

$$
\begin{array}{r}
5 \quad \underline{\text{cubes}} \\
+3 \quad \underline{\text{cubes}} \\
\hline
\underline{\text{cubes}}
\end{array}
$$

Likewise, if the computation lesson involves teaching students to draw tallies to figure out the answer, the word problems would look something like this:

$$
\begin{array}{r}
4 \quad \underline{\text{tallies}} \\
\underline{+2} \quad \underline{\text{tallies}} \\
\underline{\text{tallies}}
\end{array}
$$

If, however, the student is learning to solve computation problems at the abstract level without using manipulative devices, drawings, or tallies, then the word problems would include one or two words from the student's environment. For example:

$$
\begin{array}{r}
5 \quad \underline{\text{dolls}} \\
\underline{+2} \quad \underline{\text{dolls}} \\
\underline{\text{dolls}}
\end{array}
\qquad
\begin{array}{r}
3 \quad \underline{\text{big balls}} \\
\underline{+2} \quad \underline{\text{big balls}} \\
\underline{\text{big balls}}
\end{array}
$$

The graduated word-problem sequence progresses from words to phrases to sentences, with the numbers still aligned.

Next, the traditional word-problem paragraph format is presented to the student. The first word problems presented in the traditional paragraph format are single-step problems that do not contain any extraneous information. Once mastery is reached on these word problems, problems with extraneous information are introduced. Finally, the student learns to make up his or her own word problems (see Table 6.2). The entire graduated sequence can be taught to students with learning disabilities in 21 lessons.

Another popular teaching approach for solving word problems has been the keyword method: Students are taught to look for certain cue words (e.g., *how many more, altogether, less*) in their word problems. They are taught that these keywords frequently indicate the operation they should use to solve the problem. Several authorities (e.g., Mahlios, 1988; Sowder, 1989) have criticized this approach, however, because the keywords do not always cue the appropriate operation; thus, student errors are likely to occur.

Current research on problem-solving approaches for mathematics indicates that students need to learn to attack word problems in a systematic and strategic manner (Mastropieri, Scruggs, & Shiah, 1991; Watanabe, 1991). Moreover, students need to begin solving word problems in the elementary grades and be provided frequent opportunities to practice their skills (Willoughby, 1990).

USING COMPUTERS TO TEACH MATHEMATICS TO STUDENTS WITH LD

The use of microcomputers for teaching mathematics to students with learning disabilities has increased significantly over the past decade.

TABLE 6.2
Graduated Word-Problem Sequence

Level of instruction	Lesson no.	Sample problem
Concrete	1	9 (name of manipulative device used in lesson) − 2 (name of manipulative device used in lesson) (name of manipulative device used in lesson)
Concrete	2	8 (name of manipulative device used in lesson) − 4 (name of manipulative device used in lesson) (name of manipulative device used in lesson)
Concrete	3	3 (name of manipulative device used in lesson) − 2 (name of manipulative device used in lesson) (name of manipulative device used in lesson)
Semiconcrete	1	6 (name of drawings used in lesson) − 4 (name of drawings used in lesson) (name of drawings used in lesson)
Semiconcrete	2	8 (name of drawings used in lesson) − 5 (name of drawings used in lesson) (name of drawings used in lesson)
Semiconcrete	3	6 *tallies* (assuming tallies were used in lesson) − 3 *tallies* (assuming tallies were used in lesson) *tallies*
Abstract	1	5 dolls (single words) − 2 dolls dolls
Abstract	2	6 pieces of pie (phrases) − 1 pieces of pie pieces of pie
Abstract (numbers aligned)	3	Stevie had 4 pens. (sentences) He lost 2 of them. He has pens left.
Abstract (no extraneous)	4	Bev has 4 homework assignments. She has finished 1. How many more does she have to do?
Abstract (extraneous)	5	José had 5 notebooks. Larry had 6 birds. José gave his 5 notebooks to Ray. How many notebooks does José have left?
Abstract	6	Students are taught to make up their own word problems that will use the operation being taught (e.g., subtraction).

Note. Additional abstract lessons would present a variety of the last three formats in the sequence to promote effective discrimination skills.

Much has been written about the benefits of computer-assisted instruction in special education, but relatively few studies have produced conclusive findings related to math instruction for students with learning disabilities. Much of the math and computer research has involved investigating software programs designed to provide practice with computation skills. For example, extended practice using computers has been shown to support increased automaticity in basic mathematics tasks for students with learning disabilities (Goldman & Pellegrino, 1987). Several other researchers have been interested in comparing simple drill-and-practice software programs to more lively game formats for building acquisition and fluency skills. Some studies (e.g., Bahr & Rieth, 1989; Okolo, 1992) have revealed that both practice formats are effective, whereas others have suggested that drill-and-practice programs are better than game programs (e.g., Christensen & Gerber, 1990).

Researchers also have been interested in comparing the use of computers to more traditional instruction. Again, the findings are mixed. Trifiletti et al. (1984) compared the SPARK-80 Computerized Mathematics System to traditional resource room instruction using Steck-Vaughn math workbooks. They found that the computerized program was more effective. Berthold and Sachs (1974) reported that the use of microcomputers with students with learning disabilities produced inferior gains when compared to traditional, teacher-delivered instruction. Other studies have shown that the combination of directed teacher intervention and computer-assisted instruction is more effective than computer-assisted instruction alone (Bahr & Rieth, 1989; Howell, Sidorenko, & Jurica, 1987).

Several explanations are offered for the mixed findings related to computers and math instruction. First, many of the comparison studies have not reflected adequate experimental control; thus, consistent results are not likely. Second, the instructional design variables have not been held constant in most of the comparison studies. Researchers now realize that the computer is simply a vehicle for delivering instruction; *software design* is the critical variable related to its effectiveness (Kolich, 1985; Wager, 1992). Therefore, it is important to keep the curricular and instructional design variables consistent when comparing computer- and teacher-delivered instruction for students with learning disabilities. Gleason et al. (1990) conducted such a study, whereby multiplication and division word problems were taught to middle school students with mild disabilities. No significant differences were found between the students who received instruction via the computer and the students who received teacher-directed instruction. In fact, both groups showed a significant improvement from pretest to posttest scores. These findings suggest that effective curricular design variables are equally important for computer- and teacher-delivered instruction.

Research has demonstrated that several curricular design variables enhance student acquisition of new concepts. For example, Darch, Carnine, and Gersten (1984) found that step-by-step strategies are effective for teaching concepts and solving various problem types in mathematics. They also found that systematic practice in discriminating among similar problem types is important to prevent algorithm confusion. In another study, Carnine (1980a) found that it was important to separate confusing elements and terminology when teaching new concepts. Moreover, he found that a wide range of examples should be used when teaching new concepts, otherwise students form misconceptions and emit mathematical errors (Carnine, 1980b). Although these curricular-design studies did not involve computer-assisted instruction, it makes sense that integrating these variables into computer programs would enhance student achievement.

Using Computers to Teach Problem Solving to Students with LD

Although little research has been done related to the use of computers for teaching problem solving to students with disabilities, several researchers (e.g., Bransford, Sherwood, Hasselbring, Kinzer, & Williams, 1990; Cognition and Technology Group at Vanderbilt University, 1991, 1992) have begun to explore the use of anchored instruction. According to these researchers, anchored instruction involves bringing real-life problem-solving contexts into the classroom via computer videodiscs. Students learn to solve multistep, complex problems by first identifying pertinent information and then formulating their own strategies for finding appropriate solutions.

Bottge and Hasselbring (1993) compared the ability of two groups of adolescents with learning difficulties to generate solutions to a contextualized problem after being taught problem-solving skills under two conditions, one involving standard word problems, the other involving anchored instruction on videodisc. The problems for both conditions required the addition and subtraction of fractions in relation to money and linear measurement. The anchored instruction was integrated with effective teacher guidance. Teachers and students discussed the challenge posed by the video and referred back to the video to better define the problem. Supplemental worksheets were used to review the video's content, and subproblems were solved with teacher guidance. Video presentation allowed problems to be set in rich contexts, and computer control allowed students to reaccess information as it was needed. Although both groups showed improved word problem–solving performance, students in the contextualized problem group who used anchored instruction did significantly better on the posttest and on transfer tasks.

Because research on the development of effective problem-solving technology for students with learning disabilities is limited, it seems that a viable approach to increasing contributions in this area would be to apply what we know about effective problem-solving instruction to the development of relevant computer software and hypermedia. Such an approach would provide a foundation for further study and refinement of current knowledge. The remainder of this article will describe the application of hypermedia to the delivery of effective instruction in mathematical problem solving for students with learning disabilities.

APPLYING HYPERMEDIA TO PROBLEM-SOLVING INSTRUCTION

Early approaches to computer-assisted instruction in mathematics were limited by the memory capacity of computers and inadequate attention to instructional design. Progress in the development of mega-memory computers and disc drives has opened the door of opportunity in technology-assisted instruction. Currently, hypermedia programs that incorporate text, graphics, sound, animation, and video hold promise for the development of sophisticated problem-solving software. *Hypermedia* is multimedia information linked and accessed by a computer (Lynch, 1991). Hypermedia environments go beyond text and traditional computer-assisted instruction to incorporate sound, animation, photographic images, and video clips in sophisticated ways. The new multimedia encyclopedias on CD-ROM are examples of the merging of computer and media technologies.

For mathematics instruction, hypermedia graphics can range from simple diagrams of mathematical shapes to digitized photographic images of natural phenomena illustrating mathematical principles. Digitized music can be incorporated to set the mood for a mathematical problem, show the passage of time, or cue important information. Video clips and computer animation can show dynamic problem sequences. Computer control allows instant access to any sequence and easy review of previously viewed sequences. If appropriate digital cameras and microphones are available, students can create and input their own photographic depictions of problem situations with accompanying voice-overs.

Mathematics instruction can be enhanced in several ways by hypermedia use. First, hypermedia has dramatically expanded the media available for computer-assisted instruction and made it instantly accessible. Multiple representations of information in a variety of formats, which is an important feature of hypermedia, have been found to result in better retention and retrieval (Paivio, 1971). Second, movement through many hypermedia programs is accomplished in a nonsequential manner, which gives the user instant access to multiple resources (e.g., synthesized speech, definitions of terms, mathematical diagrams) on a need-to-know basis. Babbitt and Usnick (1993) suggested that although easy access to resources is useful for all students, it offers special support for students with learning difficulties, who might not easily access traditional supplementary resources. Finally, the many choices available to students and multiple representations of ideas support an interactive presentation of mathematical ideas that is ideal for low-achieving students (Bos & Anders, 1990). The interactive feature is especially supportive of a strategic approach to problem solving.

Anchored instruction already incorporates some hypermedia principles through the use of videotaped real-life problem situations (Cognition and Technology Group at Vanderbilt University, 1992), but other problem-solving approaches may also profit from hypermedia use. Hence, we will discuss possibilities for enhancing cognitive strategy instruction and the graduated problem sequence using hypermedia.

Application of Hypermedia to Cognitive Strategy Instruction

The teaching of cognitive and metacognitive strategies has been advocated to remediate poor problem-solving performance among students with learning disabilities (Montague et al., 1993). Hypermedia is an effective tool for supporting the use of specific cognitive and metacognitive problem-solving strategies. For example, in Babbitt's (1993) six-step problem-solving model, the student is taught to (a) read the problem, (b) understand the problem situation, (c) choose a solution strategy and solve the problem, (d) check to make sure that the question is answered, (e) check the reasonableness of the answer, and (f) consider applications and extensions of the problem. Hypermedia can be used to prompt and cue cognitive processes that will help students successfully perform each of these six steps. Adapted from an original hypercard program (Babbitt & Kubala, 1991), Figures 6.1 through 6.3 illustrate sample screens that are designed to guide students through the first three steps of this model. Although these steps are being illustrated with static text and graphics, it should be remembered that with hypermedia, dynamic graphics, video clips, and sound can be used to enhance the instructional process.

The use of cognitive and metacognitive strategies involves recalling the appropriate strategy and then using the strategy effectively. Each screen of the problem-solving program prompts the student to use the

Speech Button

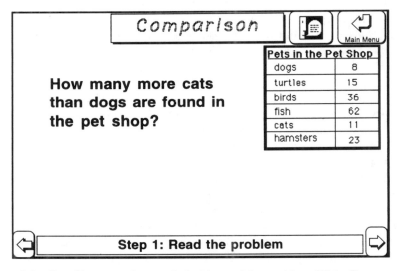

Figure 6.1. Cognitive prompt cues student to read the problem. (*Note.* From Mathematics Assistant Program (MAP) [Hypercard software]. Copyright 1991 by B. Babbitt and D. Kubala, Las Vegas, NV. Adapted with permission.)

appropriate cognitive strategy. For example, in Step 1, students are reminded to use the first cognitive strategy, "read the problem," by a prompt that lists the strategy on the screen and subsequently highlights the problem text (see Figure 6.1). This prompting could also be done through digitized speech. Hypermedia can also make synthesized speech available for those students who need help reading the problem. Students can highlight individual words, phrases, or sentences, or the entire problem; click on the speech button (see Figure 6.1); and have the selected text read to them. Thus, students can continue to develop mathematical problem-solving skills in spite of poor reading abilities.

Understanding the problem situation is frequently a multistep process involving identification of the question being asked and the relevant information needed to solve the problem. These steps are divided into three parts (see Figure 6.2): "What do you want to know?" (Step 2a); "What do you know already?" (Step 2b); and "What else do you know?" (Step 2c). Students are guided through the steps with graphics, animation, and sound. The cognitive prompt is highlighted and then the relevant problem text is identified through highlighting or changing the typeface. The student can click on the Pictures button to have the "object" pictured or on the Letters/Numbers button to have the words and numerals

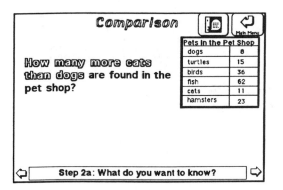

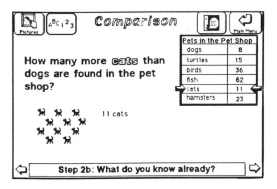

Figure 6.2.   Cognitive prompt cues student to think about what he or she wants to know and what he or she already knows. (*Note*. From Mathematics Assistant Program (MAP) [Hypercard software]. Copyright 1991 by B. Babbitt and D. Kubala, Las Vegas, NV. Adapted with permission.)

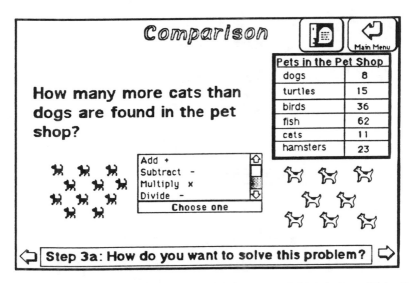

Figure 6.3. Cognitive prompt cues student to choose a solution strategy. (*Note.* From Mathematics Assistant Program (MAP) [Hypercard software]. Copyright 1991 by B. Babbitt and D. Kubala, Las Vegas, NV. Adapted with permission.)

placed on the screen. Both options are shown in Figure 6.2. An animation or video clip of the problem situation could precede the cognitive prompts.

Step 3—"How do you want to solve this problem?"—typically requires the selection of a computation operation (see Figure 6.3). The computation solution can be linked to the problem representation developed in Step 2 (see Figure 6.2, Steps 2b and 2c). Management options within the program can be set to allow access to a calculator for complex computations, thus expanding the realm of solvable problems for students with calculation difficulties.

The final three steps of this problem-solving strategy can continue in similar fashion to guide the student through the checking process and extension activities. Although traditionally "checking" has meant comparing an answer with the correct answer, redoing the problem, or doing it in another way, hypermedia can also present feedback through video clips. For example, a video might depict the problem situation with its accompanying solution, to which student work can be compared.

As Figures 6.1 through 6.3 illustrate, hypermedia is very adept at prompting cognitive and metacognitive processes using interactive, integrated media. Each of the recommended problem-solving approaches described in Table 6.1 can be translated to a hypermedia environment. Appropriate student tools can be made available depending on the particular emphasis of the strategy. Moreover, cognitive strategy prompts can be faded over time as students become more proficient in their use.

Application of Hypermedia to Graduated Word-Problem Sequence

The second problem-solving approach, using a graduated word-problem sequence, can also be taught in a hypermedia environment. This word-problem sequence is typically taught in conjunction with computation using the concrete-to-representational-to-abstract teaching sequence. As was discussed earlier, at the concrete level of instruction, word problems involve the names of the manipulative devices used to teach the computational problems in the lessons. Because these initial word problems involve hands-on manipulation of objects, they would be solved without the use of hypermedia. At the representational level of learning, however, students are taught to solve computational and word problems using pictures or tallies. At this point in the instructional sequence, hypermedia can be used to enhance students' conceptual understanding of word problems. Moreover, the use of hypermedia can greatly assist students with learning disabilities who have difficulty drawing objects or tallies in an organized manner. Hypermedia programming can also assist students who have difficulty counting accurately as they solve problems using manipulative devices or tallies.

Sample frames that are designed to guide students through a very basic multiplication word problem when representational-level teaching is taking place are shown in Figure 6.4. Frame 1 sets up the original problem. In Frame 2, students use the grab tool to move six successive circles (representing the groups) to the work area. In Frame 3, students use the grab tool to move seven cubes into each circle. The screen is self-checking, so that if students select the incorrect set of cubes, they are prompted to try again. Students next fill in the name of the objects they are counting—in this case, "cubes." In Frame 4, students are prompted to begin to count the cubes in the groups. Students click and count each cube. The cubes fill with color as they are counted. A click, beep, or other sound can accompany each count. In Frame 5, students are prompted to type their answer. If they have completed the problem correctly, they receive positive feedback and they go on to a new problem. If they have made an error, the program loops back to Frame 4 for a recount. More advanced students might count by the number of objects in the group. This can be done with paper and pencil rather than on screen.

Similar hypermedia lessons can be designed to provide the student with effective practice throughout the remainder of the graduated problem-solving sequence (i.e., word problems involving phrases, sentences, and

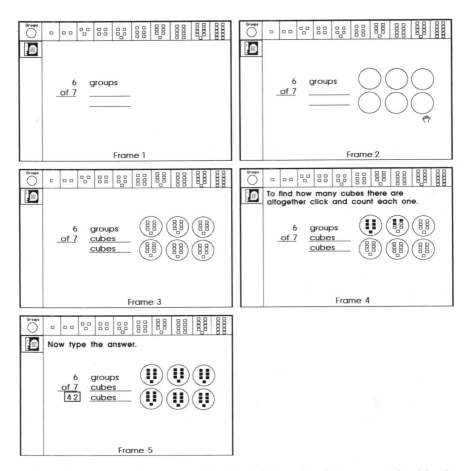

Figure 6.4.   Initial multiplication word problem displayed at the representational level.

paragraphs with and without extraneous information). The last component of the graduated sequence is having the student create his or her own word problems. This can be done using a basic word-processing program, with paper and pencil, or through the use of tape recorders. Whichever approach is used, the teacher needs to evaluate the student's word problems after they are created and then provide feedback to ensure adequate understanding.

As the illustrated examples show, previously identified effective design principles can be incorporated into hypermedia instruction. Cognitive strategies can be clearly defined, modeled, prompted, and practiced in creative ways using hypermedia. Direct instruction procedures can be incorporated into hypermedia instruction as well. Lessons can be presented in a systematic fashion. Students can be prompted to respond to maintain an active learning environment. Feedback can be designed to be frequent and specific. In fact, there is evidence that direct math instruction combined with media presentations is effective in teaching standard word problems (Hasselbring et al., 1987–1988; Moore & Carnine, 1989). Finally, a wide range of problem-solving examples can be explored and terminology illustrated by fully using the multimedia available in the hypermedia environment.

Several cautions are in order as we embark on the development of hypermedia problem-solving software. We can predict that some students will have difficulty with the complexity of options available in hypermedia environments, just as they have had problems with fast-moving game formats, visually confusing math software, or decision making during traditional problem solving. Effective curricular design variables are critical to student success within hypermedia environments. In addition, help features must be carefully designed to support students when they have difficulty remembering what to do next.

It is likely that the combination of teacher intervention and technology-assisted instruction will become an effective intervention approach in the area of mathematical problem solving (Goldman & Pellegrino, 1987). In some problem-solving tasks (e.g., graduated word-problem sequence), teacher instruction must precede *and follow* technology-assisted instruction to ensure student understanding and achievement. In other problem-solving tasks (e.g., cognitive and metacognitive strategies), the teacher needs to provide instruction on how and when to use a particular strategy. Similarly, anchored instruction is dependent on engaging problem situations and effective teacher guidance.

There is much work to be done on developing effective hypermedia instructional designs and testing their effectiveness. Hypermedia can model and prompt cognitive and metacognitive strategies and depict problem situations in realistic ways. It can systematically lead a student through a graduated problem sequence or provide multiple routes to a problem's solution. It can readily provide a full range of assistive tools to match the problem-solving requirements of a wide range of students.

Of interest to teachers and researchers, hypermedia authoring programs—for example, Hypercard (Apple Computer, Inc., 1995), Linkway (IBM Corp., 1992), Hyperstudio (Roger Wagner Publishing, Inc., 1993)—have some advantages over other programming languages for novice programmers. Unlike BASIC or Fortran, chunks of hypermedia code can be easily moved from one program to another. A beginner can easily develop new programs by borrowing good ideas from existing programs. In addition, program parts can be connected without using complicated subroutines. Although it is expected that some teachers will develop their own programs, most will wait for the development of commercial software using hypermedia principles.

It is important to note that although we have described hypermedia applications that are consistent with what we know about mathematical problem-solving instruction and computer-assisted instruction, the evidence supporting their use is only beginning to become available. Most of these applications require additional evaluation across instructional environments with a variety of students.

7. Hypertext Support for Remedial Students and Students with Learning Disabilities

KYLE HIGGINS, RANDALL BOONE, AND THOMAS C. LOVITT

Educational hypermedia and multimedia have made a successful arrival into the home and school marketplace. Multimedia and hypermedia versions of popular children's books such as Mercer Mayer's (1992) *Just Grandma and Me* and Beatrix Potter's (1990) *The Tale of Peter Rabbit* are available. Many include teacher guides for facilitating their integration into a classroom setting. Some textbook publishers now offer a hypermedia CD-ROM supplemental version of basal reader stories as well as other content area texts (Cohen, 1993; Macmillan/McGraw-Hill, 1994); and many teachers are creating their own hypermedia and multimedia educational materials for use in their classrooms (Boone, Higgins, Falba, & Langley, 1993; Prickett, Higgins, & Boone, 1994); with authoring systems such as HyperCard (Apple Computer, 1989) and HyperStudio (Wagner, 1990).

During the past 7 or 8 years (since hypermedia and multimedia capabilities became readily available for microcomputers), there has been

Reprinted, with changes, from "Hypertext support for remedial students and students with learning disabilities," by Kyle Higgins, Randall Boone, and Thomas C. Lovitt, *Journal of Learning Disabilities*, Vol. 29, 1996, pp. 402–412. Copyright © 1996 by PRO-ED, Inc.

a seemingly endless parade of new capabilities for the medium. Hypertext systems quickly gave way to hypermedia as new media, such as sound, graphics, and digital video, technologies provided alternate modes of text support and enhancement. Hardly a month goes by without a computer industry announcement of some new hardware or software release that has implications for enriching the media milieu that educational software developers and researchers have available. Digital video is an interesting example. First available only on computers with specific additional hardware, digital video capability next was provided for most machines with a software upgrade to the operating system. This gave users a tiny video window displaying a grainy, jerky video clip. The latest upgrade to that same software now offers large screen size and broadcast-quality video and audio.

Obviously, in light of this rapid expansion of technological tools, educational applications of hypermedia and multimedia need to keep up with the cutting edge of the technology. Improved sound and music, color graphics and photo-realistic pictures, and high-quality digital video are appealing enhancements to text in educational hypermedia and multimedia. However, the one medium of hypermedia and multimedia that has not undergone great technological advances may still provide reasonable clues for assessing the educational efficacy of the technology as a whole. That medium is text.

Textbooks represent the primary means of presenting new information to students in secondary content area classrooms (Anderson & Armbruster, 1984; Lovitt & Horton, 1994). Much of what is taught in these classrooms involves factual learning, including new vocabulary, relationships of vocabulary to concepts, and testing. Although many educators are beginning to realize the need to teach students to analyze, synthesize, and evaluate information, in most classrooms facts are what are taught and tested (Mastropieri & Scruggs, 1994).

The structure of the text in content area textbooks has received considerable attention in the research literature. The organization of the text (Anderson & Armbruster, 1984; Meyer, 1979; Shimmerlik, 1978), sufficient repetition of vocabulary (Nagy, 1988), and the use of structural signals to highlight important information (Lorch & Lorch, 1986; Meyer, 1979) have all been identified as effective curricular features when incorporated into content area instructional materials.

Armbruster and Anderson (1988) termed texts that incorporate such features "considerate text." The goal of these considerate texts is to enable the reader to gather salient information with minimal effort. Incorporating these types of features directly into educational materials provides an effective instructional design for content area instruction (Carnine, Kameenui, & Dixon, 1993; Tyree, Fiore, & Cook, 1994).

The paradigm of hypermedia and multimedia as "cooperative text systems" (Boone et al., 1993, p. 29) that provide readers with additional related information in a nonlinear environment encompasses many of the same instructional features as considerate text (Armbruster & Anderson, 1988). It has also served as the basis for several hypermedia research studies including such topics as (a) subject matter knowledge and interest (Alexander, Kulikowich, & Jetton, 1994), (b) semantic relationships between words and information that are linked within a hypermedia document (Harris & Grandgenett, 1993), (c) instructional cuing (Lee & Lehman, 1993), (d) color coding (Chapman, 1993), and (e) learner control (Becker & Dwyer, 1994), all using hypermedia or multimedia in a design for supporting or extending text.

The purpose of the present study was to determine the effect of hypermedia text presentation on the comprehension of content area reading material of students with learning disabilities and remedial students. The hypermedia study guides used in this study were designed for use within a mainstreamed high school social studies classroom.

Student use of pop-up text windows that supported or extended information found in a high school social studies text provided a detailed look into the instructional effectiveness of a set of hypermedia study guides for students with learning disabilities and remedial students. Content enhancements limited to the familiar medium of text provided an opportunity for answering the following critical questions surrounding student use of educational materials in a hypermedia or multimedia format.

1. Does text-only information support provide adequate reinforcement to motivate students into continued, unprompted use?

2. Do students read a text passage from a text-only information support window with short-term comprehension?

3. Do students retain information found in a text-only information support window (nonlinear information format) as well as information found in the main body of text (linear information format)?

4. Does the nonlinear access of information through a hypermedia system such as the notes function interrupt or compromise the comprehension process?

Answering these questions regarding text-only hypermedia support will help to provide a framework for assessing the utility of less conventional media support, such as sound, photo-realistic graphics, and digital video.

METHOD

Setting and Students

The study took place in a mainstreamed social studies classroom and in a computer lab, containing 25 Macintosh computers, located next to the classroom. The class included students with learning disabilities and students identified as remedial according to school district guidelines.

Twenty-five ninth-grade students enrolled in Washington State History participated in this study (see Table 7.1). There were 13 students with learning disabilities and 12 remedial students. The 25 students were taught by the same teacher who had been teaching Washington State History for 15 years and mainstreamed social studies classes for 2 years.

Remedial students were defined by the school district as students without disabilities scoring below the 35th percentile on both quantitative and verbal subtests of the Metropolitan Achievement Test (Prescott, Balow, Hogan, & Farr, 1984). In Washington, students with learning disabilities in Grade 7 and above are defined as students whose intellectual functioning is above mental retardation and who exhibit a severe discrepancy between intellectual ability and academic achievement in one or

TABLE 7.1
Student Characteristics by Educational Method

Characteristic	Lecture	Lecture/hypermedia study guide	Hypermedia study guide
Numbers			
Male	6	4	9
Female	3	2	1
Total	9	6	10
Age			
Mean	14.6	14.6	14.6
Ethnicity			
White	8	6	9
Hispanic	1	0	0
Black	0	0	0
Asian	0	0	1
SES	UN	UN	UN
IQ	UN	UN	UN
Overall achievement	UN	UN	UN
Specific achievement	UN	UN	UN
Educational group			
LD	6	2	5
Remedial	3	4	5

Note. UN indicates unavailable information.

more of the following areas: oral expression, listening comprehension, written expression, basic reading skill, reading comprehension, mathematics calculations, and mathematics reasoning. A severe discrepancy is defined as a functioning level of two-thirds or below expected performance and a functioning level below chronological age/grade in one or more of the seven areas described in the definition of a student with learning disabilities. Socioeconomic status, overall and specific achievement scores, and IQ information were not available.

Although specific reading levels for the students were unavailable, informal observation during a pilot test of the software and reading materials gave no indication that students had difficulty in reading the materials used in the study.

Materials

Textbook.   This study used *The Washington Story: A History of Our State* (Pelz, 1979) as the textbook. The first two chapters were adapted to a hypermedia format and broken down into 10 reading sections, which varied in length from 500 to 700 words. Readability of the text used in the lessons was determined to be at the junior high school level (Flesch Index of 68).

Hypermedia Authoring System.   We used the *Guide* (Owl International, 1987) hypermedia authoring system in this study to create the hypermedia study guides. Three hypermedia functions were used in designing the study guides:

1. "Notes," indicated in the text by an underlined word or phrase, were used by students to access short explanatory text passages of related information.

2. "Replacements" provided direct replacement of a word or phrase in the main body of text. A typical replacement might be a synonym. Replacement functions were indicated in the text by boldface type.

3. "Inquiry" was used to control student movement through the multiple choice questions. Students could not move on to the next text screen until they had answered a multiple choice question correctly. An incorrect answer rerouted the student back to the appropriate text and the multiple choice question. A correct answer was reinforced with text and graphics directly related to the question. Students were then allowed to continue to the next page of the study guide.

Hypermedia Computer-Assisted Study Guides.   The hypermedia study guides incorporated the components of good screen design as identified by Grimm (1983) and Heines (1983). These include the avoidance of screen scrolling, the use of titled pages when appropriate, functional organization of information, and uncrowded screens. The cooperating teacher's suggestions on vocabulary, concepts, charts, maps, or graphics were used in creating the hypermedia enhancements.

The hypermedia study guides were from 9 to 13 screens of text, depending on the length of the reading passage and the number of words, graphics, concepts, maps, or charts included in the lesson. Each study guide contained eight multiple choice questions that were presented on the same screen as the text to which they related. A lesson was designed so that a student could complete it during a 15-minute period.

A screen in the hypermedia study guide was made up of text (with word or graphic enhancements), text plus a multiple choice question (with word or graphic enhancements), or a graphic (with word enhancements). Enhancements could be a definition, graphic, or further clarification of a word or phrase. Students accessed the enhancements by placing the cursor on the word or graphic and clicking the mouse. The enhancement appeared on the screen for the student to view. The student returned to the original text by clicking the mouse again.

For the purposes of this study, information in the hypermedia instructional materials was coded as *factual information* (information that was explicitly stated in the reading passage), *inferential information* (information that was implicitly presented in the identified reading passage from which the student would have to draw a conclusion or inference), or *note information* (information that a student would have access to only if he or she had read the pop-up text windows associated with the note function). Types of information for creating factual, inferential, and note questions from the study guides are show in Figure 7.1. An example Note is depicted in the information box in the bottom-right corner of the screen. This pop-up window appears when the phrase "the Dalles" is selected. A Factual multiple choice question is shown at the bottom-left of the screen. The answer to the question is explicitly stated in the first sentence on the screen. An Inferential question might ask about the similarity of the fishing technologies of the Plateau and Coastal tribes in order to have students pull together information from two or more places in the story. For example, one sentence states that both groups were "fishers." The final sentence indicates that yearly trips took place between tribes. A hidden Note on the phrase "they ate salmon" indicates that salmon were caught "up the rivers" each year, giving the different tribes an opportunity to fish together and learn each other's techniques.

Teacher-Presented Instructional Materials.   Teacher-presented instructional materials included the same information as the hypermedia computer-assisted study guides. These materials were (a) teacher lecture, (b) the identified reading passage, and (c) a student worksheet containing the eight multiple choice questions included in the hypermedia study guides.

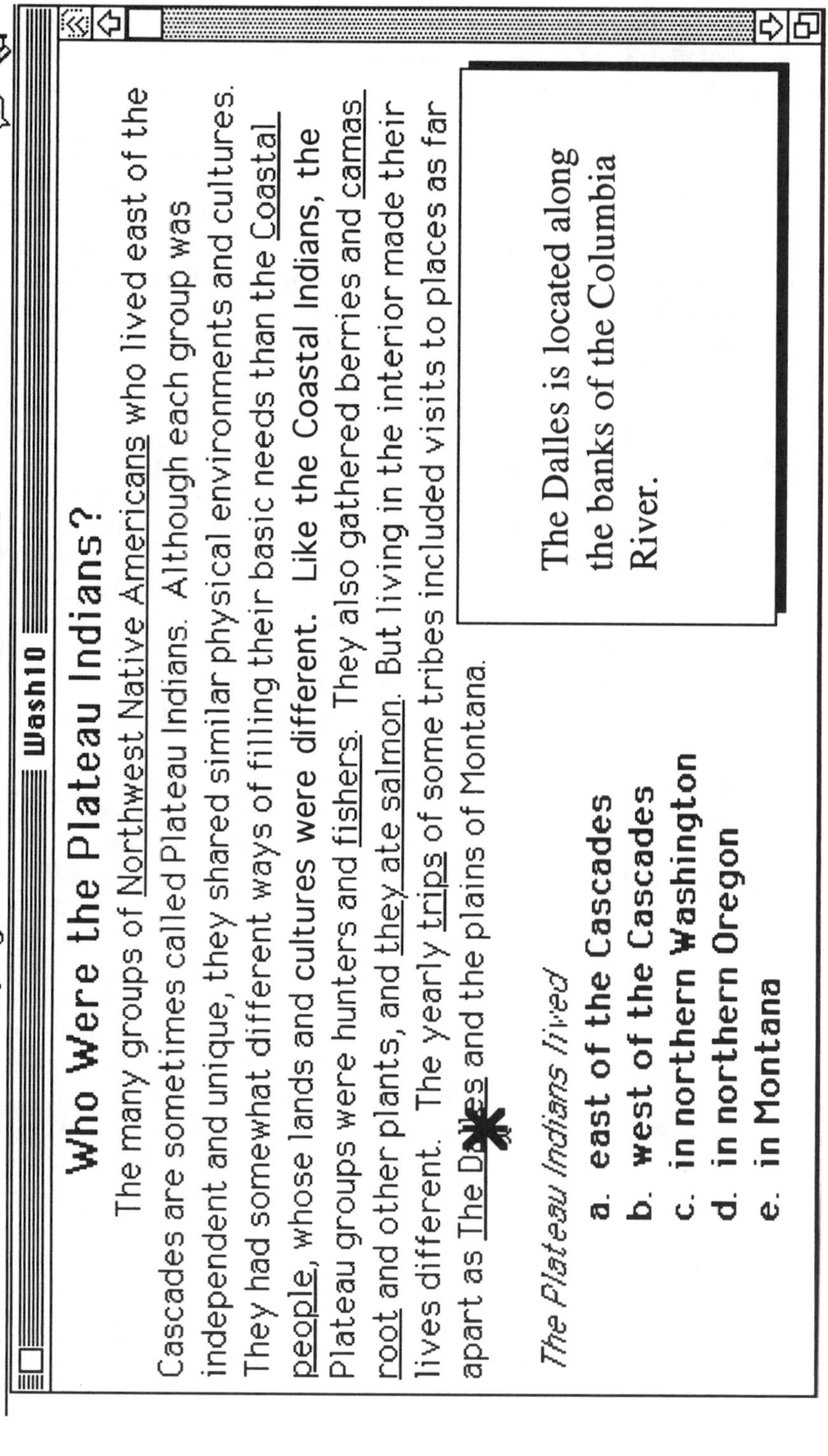

🍎 **File Edit Search Display Format Font Size Make**

⬜️ ▭▭▭ 〓〓〓 **Wash10** 〓〓〓

Who Were the Plateau Indians?

The many groups of Northwest Native Americans who lived east of the Cascades are sometimes called Plateau Indians. Although each group was independent and unique, they shared similar physical environments and cultures. They had somewhat different ways of filling their basic needs than the Coastal people, whose lands and cultures were different. Like the Coastal Indians, the Plateau groups were hunters and fishers. They also gathered berries and camas root and other plants, and they ate salmon. But living in the interior made their lives different. The yearly trips of some tribes included visits to places as far apart as The Dalles and the plains of Montana.

The Plateau Indians lived

   a. east of the Cascades

   b. west of the Cascades

   c. in northern Washington

   d. in northern Oregon

   e. in Montana

The Dalles is located along the banks of the Columbia River.

Figure 7.1. Types of information for creating factual, inferential, and note questions from the study guides are shown in this page about the Plateau Indians.

A protocol containing directions for the teacher was developed for each lecture. Daily reading passages in the lecture condition were the same as those adapted for the hypermedia study guides. The students were assigned the 500- to 700-word reading passage in the textbook following the teacher's lecture.

Information in the teacher-presented instructional materials for the purpose of this study was coded as factual information (information that was explicitly stated in the reading passage), inferential information (information that was implicitly presented in the identified reading passage from which the student would have to draw a conclusion or inference), or note information (information that a student would have access to only if he or she had read the assigned reading passage or listened during the teacher's lecture).

Tests.   All tests were prepared following the guidelines for multiple choice tests suggested by Sarnacki (1979). A 50-item multiple choice test, drawn from the daily quizzes, was administered as a pretest prior to the study, as a posttest the day after the completion of the 10-day Washington State History unit, and as a retention test administered to the students 2 weeks after the unit test. Thirty-five of the questions were based on information coded as factual and 15 were based on information coded as inferential. Of the 35 factual questions, 21 were additionally coded as note information questions. None of the 15 inferential questions were coded as note information. Each question had five possible answers from which to choose.

The daily multiple choice quizzes were based on each reading passage. Each quiz contained 25 questions. Twenty were coded as factual questions and 5 as inferential questions. The same eight questions contained in the hypermedia study guides and the student worksheets appeared on the daily quizzes.

For the purposes of this study, a factual question was defined as a question for which the answer was explicitly stated in the reading passage and an inferential question was defined as a question for which the answer was not explicitly stated in the reading passage, from either the textbook or the computer screen (Gillet & Temple, 1994). A question based on a note was defined as a factual question for which the answer was found in a hypermedia pop-up text window enhancement in the hypermedia study guides and concurrently presented by the teacher through lecture, classroom worksheets, or textbook reading assignments.

Design and Procedure

Prior to the study, the students attended two 1-hour computer training sessions. In these sessions the students learned how to operate the

Macintosh computer and how to navigate through the hypermedia study guides.

This Washington State History instructional unit was conducted over 10 consecutive school days with students randomly assigned to one of three educational methods: (a) lecture, (b) lecture/hypermedia study guide, and (c) hypermedia study guide. Each educational method involved a 30-minute instructional period followed by a 10-minute multiple choice quiz.

Students assigned to the lecture method listened to and took notes from a lecture given by the teacher for 15 minutes. The students were then assigned a reading passage from the textbook and given a worksheet containing eight multiple choice questions to complete in the last 15 minutes of the instructional period. They were allowed to use their notes or the book to complete the worksheet. Prior to taking the quiz, students turned in their notes and worksheets.

Students assigned to the lecture/hypermedia study guide method listened to and took notes from the lecture given by the teacher for 15 minutes. They then turned in their notes and moved to the computer lab, where they went through the hypermedia study guide as many times as possible for the remaining 15 minutes of the instructional period. Progression through the hypermedia study guide involved reading the text on the screen, selecting enhanced words, reading the notes behind the enhancements, and moving on to the next screen of text. Students were able to pace their movement through the lesson. Responses to the multiple choice questions generated feedback and routed students back to the question or to the next screen of text as appropriate.

Students in the hypermedia study guide method worked with the hypermedia study guide for the entire 30 minutes of the instructional period. These students were also able to go through the study guide as many times as possible in the allotted time.

The day after the conclusion of the 10-day instructional unit, the 50-item multiple choice test that had been administered as a pretest was given again. Two weeks after the conclusion of the instructional unit, the 50-item multiple choice test was readministered as a retention measure.

Scoring and Reliability

Data included scores of the 10 daily quizzes and the retention test. All quizzes and tests were machine scored.

Reliability data on the daily teacher lecture were taken in order to measure the extent to which the lecture protocol was followed. This ensured that students in all three educational methods received the information necessary to complete the tests and quizzes (e.g., all students received the same information but through different media).

RESULTS

Test Scores

The data analyzed in this study were the scores from the 10 daily quizzes and the scores from the retention test. Data were also analyzed according to the two educational groups (students with learning disabilities and remedial students); three educational methods (lecture, lecture/ hypermedia study guide, and hypermedia study guide); and question type (factual, inferential, and questions based on a hypermedia note enhancement). A three-way ANOVA with repeated measures on the third factor (question type) was the design used. There were no missing values among the retention test scores, and missing values among the daily quiz scores were omitted as they were not systematically missing in any way.

Retention Test Scores

Main effect means and standard deviations of the retention test scores, broken down by educational group, educational method, and question type, are found in Table 7.2. Means and standard deviations are also presented, broken down by educational group, educational method, and question type (see Table 7.3); educational method and question type (see Table 7.4); and educational group, educational method, and question type (see Table 7.5).

The results from the three-way ANOVA indicated a significant educational method ($p = .08$). Because there were unequal numbers of students in the three educational methods, the Tukey-Kramer procedure was used to detect significant differences between means corresponding to the different educational methods. Alpha was set at .05. No significant differences were found. This can be attributed to the lack of power in the procedure due to the small sample size.

Question-type effect was also found to be significant ($p = .006$). The Newman-Keuls procedure was used to detect significant differences between pairs of means. Alpha was set at .05. Factual questions whose answers were displayed through a hypermedia note window were answered correctly significantly more often than inferential questions. Additionally, factual questions whose answers were displayed in the body of the text were answered correctly significantly more often than inferen-

TABLE 7.2
Main Effect Means for the Retention Test

Educational group		Educational method			Question type		
Students with LD	Remedial students	Lecture	Hypermedia study guide	Lecture/hypermedia study guide	Factual	Inferential	From a note
59	65	54	65	73	65	57	66
(.18)	(.18)	(.18)	(.15)	(.19)	(.19)	(.18)	(.15)

Note. Scores expressed as mean percentage correct on 50-item test. Standard deviations in parentheses.

TABLE 7.3
Educational Group, Educational Method, and Question Type Means for the Retention Test

Group	Educational method			Question type		
	Lecture	Hypermedia study guide	Lecture/hypermedia study guide	Factual	Inferential	From a note
Students with LD	49 (.17)	61 (.16)	81 (.09)	61 (.14)	53 (.21)	62 (.18)
Remedial students	57 (.17)	71 (.12)	71 (.21)	68 (.22)	59 (.17)	68 (.13)

Note. Scores expressed as mean percentage correct on 50-item test. Standard deviations in parentheses. LD = learning disabilities.

TABLE 7.4
Comparison of Educational Method and Question Type Means
for the Retention Test

Educational method	Question type		
	Factual	Inferential	From a note
Lecture	57	47	58
	(.21)	(.16)	(.14)
Hypermedia study guide	66	61	70
	(.15)	(.18)	(.11)
Lecture/hypermedia study guide	79	64	75
	(.20)	(.20)	(.19)

Note. Scores expressed as mean percentage correct on 50-item test. Standard deviations in parentheses.

tial questions. There were no significant differences between factual questions whose answers were displayed through a hypermedia note window and factual questions whose answers were found in the body of the text. These questions were answered an equal proportion of the time.

The three-way interaction effect was found to be significant ($p = .05$); however, there is not much interpretative value, as the educational-group effect and the two-way interaction effects were not found to be significant.

Daily Quiz Scores

Main effect means and standard deviations of the daily quiz scores, broken down by educational group, educational method, and question type, are shown in Table 7.6. Means and standard deviations, broken down by educational group, educational method, and question type (see Table 7.7); educational method and question type (see Table 7.8); and educational group, educational method, and question type (see Table 7.9), are also presented.

The results from the three-way ANOVA indicated a significant educational method ($p = .04$). The Tukey-Kramer procedure was used to detect significant differences among means corresponding to the different educational methods. Alpha was set at .05. No significant pair differences were found. Again, this can be attributed to the lack of power in the procedure due to the small sample size.

The question-type effect was also found to be significant ($p = .00$). The Newman-Keuls procedure was used to detect significant differences between pairs of means. Alpha was set at .05. Once again, factual ques-

TABLE 7.5
Comparison of Educational Group, Educational Method, and Question Type Means for the Retention Test

Group	Lecture			Hypermedia study guide			Lecture/hypermedia study guide		
	Factual	Inferential	From a note	Factual	Inferential	From a note	Factual	Inferential	From a note
Students with LD	57 (.19)	47 (.24)	43 (.10)	61 (.13)	53 (.21)	67 (.11)	79 (—)	73 (—)	90 (—)
Remedial students	57 (.23)	48 (.13)	65 (.09)	73 (.17)	71 (.09)	69 (.12)	79 (.23)	62 (.22)	71 (.20)

Note. Scores expressed as mean percentage correct on 50-item test. Standard deviations in parentheses. LD = learning disabilities.

TABLE 7.6
Main Effect Means for the Average Daily Quiz

Educational group		Educational method			Question type		
Students with LD	Remedial students	Lecture	Hypermedia study guide	Lecture/hypermedia study guide	Factual	Inferential	From a note
69	70	62	75	73	69	65	75
(.12)	(.14)	(.13)	(.11)	(.12)	(.13)	(.12)	(.12)

Note. Scores expressed as mean percentage correct on 25-item test. Standard deviations in parentheses. LD = learning disabilities.

TABLE 7.7
Educational Group, Educational Method, and Question Type Means for the Average Daily Quiz

Group	Educational method			Question type		
	Lecture	Hypermedia study guide	Lecture/hypermedia study guide	Factual	Inferential	From a note
Students with LD	63 (.14)	71 (.11)	72 (.06)	68 (.11)	73 (.12)	75 (.11)
Remedial students	61 (.12)	79 (.09)	73 (.13)	70 (.14)	66 (.13)	75 (.14)

Note. Scores expressed as mean percentage correct on 25-item test. Standard deviations in parentheses. LD = learning disabilities.

TABLE 7.8
Comparison of Educational Method and Question Type Means
for the Average Daily Quiz

Educational method	Question type		
	Factual	Inferential	From a note
Lecture	61	56	67
	(.14)	(.10)	(.13)
Hypermedia study guide	74	70	80
	(.09)	(.11)	(.10)
Lecture/hypermedia study guide	72	69	78
	(.14)	(.11)	(.10)

Note. Scores expressed as mean percentage correct on 25-item test. Standard deviations in parentheses.

tions whose answers were displayed through a hypermedia note window were correctly answered significantly more often than inferential questions. No significant differences were found between factual questions whose answers were displayed in the body of the text and inferential questions, or between factual questions whose answers were displayed through a hypermedia note window and factual questions whose answers were found in the body of the text. No interaction effects were significant.

Reliability of Teacher Lecture Presentation

Reliability observations of the teacher's 10 lectures were conducted in order to ensure that all students received the same information. A checklist of topics contained in each lecture was used. Lecture reliability was calculated by summing the number of topics covered in a lecture and dividing by the total number of possible topics in a lecture. The average for the 10-day period was .91.

DISCUSSION

Educational Method

Retention Test.   Scores indicate that there was a significant effect for the educational method used in the study. Unfortunately, due to the small sample size, it is unclear where this difference lies. Mean retention test

TABLE 7.9
Comparison of Educational Group, Educational Method, and Question Type Means for the Average Daily Quiz

Group	Lecture			Hypermedia study guide			Lecture/hypermedia study guide		
	Factual	Inferential	From a note	Factual	Inferential	From a note	Factual	Inferential	From a note
Students with LD	61 (.13)	55 (.13)	72 (.14)	71 (.10)	67 (.12)	76 (.11)	73 (—)	66 (—)	77 (—)
Remedial students	62 (.15)	57 (.10)	65 (.12)	78 (.07)	74 (.10)	86 (.06)	72 (.16)	69 (.13)	78 (.12)

Note. Scores expressed as mean percentage correct on 25-item test. Standard deviations in parentheses. LD = learning disabilities.

scores for students with learning disabilities indicate that information was retained best over time by students who participated in the lecture/ hypermedia study guide method. Students with learning disabilities who participated in the hypermedia study guide method had the next high-est mean retention test scores. Students with learning disabilities who participated in the lecture educational method had the lowest retention test score mean.

Remedial students who participated in the hypermedia study guide method or the lecture/hypermedia study guide educational method had equivocal retention test score means, indicating no clear preference for either method. For this group of students, the lecture educational method produced the lowest retention scores.

Average Daily Quiz.   Scores of students with learning disabilities were higher when they worked with the lecture/hypermedia study guide method. However, these daily quiz averages were closely followed by those of the students who participated in the hypermedia study guide method. These two educational methods produced similar results on a daily basis. Students who participated in the lecture educational method had the lowest daily quiz score averages.

Remedial students who worked with the hypermedia study guide method had the highest daily quiz score averages, followed by the reme-dial students who worked in the lecture/hypermedia study guide method. Remedial students who participated in the lecture educational method had the lowest daily quiz scores.

Question Type

The most interesting results of this study deal with the findings con-cerning the question type (factual, inferential, note) answered correctly by the students in relation to the educational method.

Retention Test.   Scores indicated that there was a significant effect for the question types used in the study. Factual questions whose answers were displayed through a hypermedia note window were correctly answered significantly more often than inferential questions. Factual questions whose answers were displayed in the body of the text were correctly answered significantly more often than inferential questions. Factual questions whose answers were displayed through a hypermedia note window and factual questions whose answers were found in the body of the text were answered an equal proportion of the time.

When viewed by educational group, the students with learning dis-abilities had higher retention test scores on information they had read from a hypermedia note in both the hypermedia study guide and the lecture/hypermedia study guide methods than from inferential information or factual information contained in the body of the reading passage (see Table 7.5). Retention of factual information from the main body of text was higher than that of inferential. These findings, although not statistically significant, are particularly interesting.

Although mean test scores for inferential information were lower than those for factual information in both the hypermedia and the lecture/hypermedia study guide methods, retention of inferential information was much higher for both of those groups than for students who participated in the lecture method. This difference was particularly marked for students in the lecture/hypermedia study guide method.

The retention test score means for factual, inferential, and note information for remedial students in the hypermedia study guide and lecture/hypermedia study guide methods were very similar. For these students, both the hypermedia study guide method and the lecture/hypermedia study guide method produced higher retention in all three types of questions than the lecture method.

Daily Quiz Scores. Results indicated that daily retention of information for students with learning disabilities was increased when the information was included in a hypermedia note as opposed to including the information in the body of the text for both the hypermedia study guide method and the lecture/hypermedia study guide method (see Table 7.9). Although factual information was retained at a higher rate than inferential information on a daily basis, it is interesting to note that students who worked with the hypermedia study guide for at least some portion of their instructional time had higher inferential comprehension scores than the students who participated in the lecture educational method. These findings are also mirrored in the daily quiz score means of the remedial students for factual, inferential, and note comprehension. Again, these data do not reflect statistical significance, but they do provide interesting comparisons.

These data suggest that for students with learning disabilities and remedial students, retention of factual and inferential information is increased by access to a teacher lecture that is followed by a hypermedia study guide. An interesting finding for these students was the increase in retention over time when the information was contained in a hypermedia enhancement note as compared to when it was contained in the main body of text. This suggests that, at the very least, students accessed the note windows and read the information. Moreover, the increase in retention for a note may have indicated a "hidden" message to the student that information included in the note was important, by its very existence.

Another interesting finding of the study involved the retention of inferential information for remedial students and students with learning disabilities in the hypermedia study guide and the lecture/hypermedia study guide methods. These students had higher retention and daily quiz means for inferential information than students in the lecture method. This may suggest that the interaction of the hypermedia study guides indirectly provided some help in inferential comprehension.

CONCLUSIONS

Several conclusions can be drawn from this study:

1. Text-only information support provides adequate reinforcement to move students with learning disabilities and remedial students toward continued, unprompted use of a hypermedia study guide. Student retention of information based on analyses of question types indicated that, at the very least, students were utilizing and reading a substantial number of the unprompted note window enhancements.

2. Short-term and long-term retention of information by students with learning disabilities and remedial students can be expected from text-only information support in a hypermedia study guide. The results of this study suggest that retention of factual and inferential information is increased by access to a teacher lecture that is followed by a hypermedia study guide. An interesting finding for these students was the increase in retention over time when the information was contained in a hypermedia enhancement note as compared to when it was contained in the main body of text.

3. The nonlinear access of information through a hypermedia study guide does not seem to interrupt or compromise the comprehension process of students with learning disabilities or remedial students. In every situation investigated in this study, students who had access to the hypermedia study guides exhibited better information retention than students who did not use the hypermedia study guides. Using the note functions did not seem to be a detriment with regard to reading from the main body of text.

The following limitations of this study should be considered: (a) the short duration of the study (10 days), (b) the small number of students who participated in the study (25), and (c) the emphasis placed on student retention of factual information as an indicator of comprehension.

With an increasing variety of hypermedia reading materials coming into the marketplace, it is imperative that educators and researchers attend to the educational components that will benefit students with learning disabilities and students who are struggling to learn. Too often in educational technology, educational software is developed without adequate knowledge of instructional methods that have been found to benefit particular groups of learners. The results and conclusions of this study indicate that for students with learning disabilities and remedial students, a hypermedia study guide is a viable educational tool that leads to retention of factual information. The results also indicate that the design of the hypermedia study guide can affect these students' comprehension. Students with learning disabilities and remedial students will access and read text notes in hypermedia study guides, and it appears that as they interact more with the text, both factual and inferential comprehension is improved.

Research concerning the use of hypermedia for instructional purposes is being undertaken at an ever-increasing rate. With still so little known about the effects of this instructional medium on student learning, it is important for researchers to attend to (a) the components of instructional design that benefit certain groups of learners; (b) the integration of the hypermedia software into the instructional process; (c) student interaction with the hypermedia enhancements (e.g., whether students are more likely to access one type of enhancement over another); and (d) specific educational outcomes correlated to hypermedia enhancement types.

AUTHORS' NOTES

1. Research reported in this chapter was supported by U.S. Department of Education Grant No. 84158G to Thomas C. Lovitt. The contents of this document do not, however, reflect the policy or view of the Department and no official endorsement should be inferred.

2. We gratefully acknowledge the assistance of Mary McClutchy, Kathleen Opie, and Rob Nelson in implementing this research.

8. Authenticity in Learning: Multimedia Design Projects in Social Studies for Students with Disabilities

RALPH P. FERRETTI AND CYNTHIA M. OKOLO

The discipline of education is currently enjoying the unprecedented attention of parents, policymakers, and public officials. A seemingly endless stream of reports from prestigious state, regional, and national commissions (e.g., National Commission on Excellence in Education, 1983; National Commission on Social Studies in the Schools, 1989) lament the failure of educational institutions to prepare our children for the challenges of life. Most advocates of educational reform would probably agree that schools should prepare students to contribute to constructive, personally satisfying, and socially valued activities in a representative democracy. There is much less agreement, however, about the specific strategies and educational processes that are proposed to achieve this goal. For some, the focus is the acquisition of basic skills, for others, it is a national curriculum or standardized assessments, and for yet others, the student's capacity to think critically and analyze information is emphasized (Cherryholmes, 1990; Engle, 1990; Epstein & Evans, 1990; Nelson, 1990).

Reprinted, with changes, from "Authenticity in learning: Multimedia design projects in social studies for students with disabilities," by Ralph P. Ferretti and Cynthia M. Okolo, *Journal of Learning Disabilities*, Vol. 29, 1996, pp. 450–460. Copyright © 1996 by PRO-ED, Inc.

In this chapter, we discuss our beliefs about the goals of social studies education and the conditions that are conducive to promoting those goals. Our work is predicated upon the premise that education should encourage students' disposition toward thoughtfulness and reflection (Dewey, 1916; 1933; Wiggins, 1993), and that it is possible to design learning environments that encourage students' construction of knowledge and active problem solving. Further, we argue that the social studies curriculum is a fertile and as yet largely untapped domain in which to foster thinking and problem solving. Finally, we believe that multimedia technologies can serve as tools to advance these educational goals. In this chapter, we discuss some of the reasons for the current revival of interest in thinking and problem solving, explain our reasons for focusing on the social studies, discuss the use of multimedia technology in supporting projects in the social studies, discuss some considerations in implementing multimedia design projects, give an example from our research of multimedia design, and, finally, discuss some challenges to the implementation of multimedia design projects in the classroom.

WHY THINKING AND PROBLEM SOLVING?

Bransford, Goldman, and Vye (1991) offered a compelling account of the issues that have shaped views about thinking and problem solving over the last decade. First, many students score poorly on tests of problem solving, essay writing, reasoning, experiment design, and the like (e.g., Gentile, 1992; National Assessment of Educational Progress, 1981; National Commission on Excellence in Education, 1983). Second, business leaders have serious concerns about workers' reading, writing, speaking, learning new skills and adapting old ones for use in the workplace; using quantitative skills to manage and produce job-related information; and assessing and generating arguments and explanations (Resnick, 1987). Third, there is a growing awareness that rapid technological change and our nation's economic competiveness will compel workers to adapt existing skills and learn new ones to optimize performance. Finally, our very system of government depends upon an informed and literate electorate to protect against abuses of tyranny (Bransford et al., 1991).

As noted, interest in thinking and problem solving has been renewed, but traditional approaches to teaching these skills have met with very mixed results (Nickerson, Perkins, & Smith, 1986). It now appears that the efficacy of these efforts was determined by at least three interrelated factors: First, instructional designers often failed to appreciate the importance of domain-specific knowledge in effective thinking and problem solving (Chi, Glaser, & Farr, 1988). Programs that emphasize the use of generic reasoning and problem-solving heuristics may be theoretically generalizable across situations, but they usually lack power in any specific situation (Anderson, 1987). Therefore, students must adapt these heuristics to the requirements of particular tasks. The research evidence shows that this is a daunting challenge that may not be met by many students with learning handicaps (Ferretti & Cavalier, 1991; Torgesen, Kistner, & Morgan, 1987).

Second, thinking strategies have not often been illustrated in the context of authentic problems. Authenticity involves the application of skills and knowledge to genuine problems that people must tackle in adapting to the requirements of life. According to Wiggins (1993), authentic problems are nonalgorithmic, complex, and amenable to multiple solutions; involve judgment; require the use of multiple criteria; are uncertain; involve self-regulation and the imposition of meaning; and are effortful. In contrast, many teachers rely very heavily on the use of textbook problems to illustrate thinking strategies (Brophy, 1988; Simon 1980). As a consequence, students assume that these skills are to be used for simple, school-like exercises instead of as tools for managing real-life problems. Students may be able to recall information when prompted to do so, but they are unable to spontaneously use knowledge and skills even when they are pertinent to the problem at hand. Said differently, students' knowledge and skills become inert (Cognition and Technology Group at Vanderbilt, 1990; Sherwood, Kinzer, Hasselbring, & Bransford, 1987).

Finally, there is a growing recognition that thinking and problem solving are shaped by social context and interaction (Adams, 1990; Feuerstein, Rand, Hoffman, Hoffman, & Miller, 1987; Vygotsky, 1978). Traditional perspectives on thinking and learning emphasize the individual's performance in the absence of social supports (Resnick, 1987). In contrast, the social constructivist perspective (Carver, Lehrer, Connell, & Erickson, 1992; Harris & Graham, 1994) emphasizes the learner's active organization of meaning in a socially mediated environment. In this view, students engage in a cognitive apprenticeship (Brown, Collins, & Duguid, 1989; Collins, Brown, & Newman, 1989) with teachers who support the acquisition of strategies and skills by explicit instruction and modeling.

WHY SOCIAL STUDIES?

We believe that the domain of social studies affords a nearly inexhaustible set of opportunities to promote the child's critical construction of knowledge (Ferretti & Okolo, 1993). First, there is a general consensus that the principal goal of social studies education is the preparation of an informed and critical citizenry (Cornbleth, 1985; Dewey, 1916; Oliver & Shaver, 1966; Parker, 1991). Second, the social studies curriculum affords students opportunities to construct elaborate, deep, and tightly interconnected knowledge bases about problems whose solutions inform challenges to contemporary society. This should increase the likelihood that students will develop real expertise (Voss, Greene, Post, & Penner, 1983; Voss, Tyler, & Yengo, 1983).

Third, social studies problems are representative of the kinds of ill-defined problems (Bransford & Stein, 1984; Simon, 1980) that people confront in life. Like everyday problems, social studies problems often have ambiguous or vague resolutions that are highly idiosyncratic (Voss, 1991; Voss, Greene, et al., 1983; Voss & Post, 1988; Voss, Tyler, & Yengo, 1983). For example, a social studies problem may involve reducing racial inequalities, or balancing the costs of increasing the federal debt against the advantages of expanding the nation's money supply. Problems such of these do not usually have an explicit and generally accepted end state against which all possible outcomes can be evaluated. Further, there may be many different and apparently contradictory strategies for accomplishing any goal in social studies education. Ill-defined problems challenge students to define goals, identify and analyze evidence that can be used to evaluate plausible strategies, develop persuasive arguments in support of proposed solutions, and critically evaluate the arguments and proposed solutions of others (Kuhn, 1991; in press; Newmann, 1990; 1991; Toulmin, 1958).

Social Studies for Students with Disabilities

Social studies and special educators agree that a primary goal of social studies education is citizenship preparation (Curtis, 1991). All citizens, including persons with disabilities, are expected to participate in the processes of democratic decision making. In fact, the guarantee of a free, appropriate public education for students with disabilities is largely due to the application of these democratic and political processes in practice. However, surveys of social studies programs in more and less restrictive placements show that social studies instruction often is not provided for students with disabilities. For example, Patton, Polloway, and Cronin (1987) studied the availability of social studies instruction for students with disabilities in seven states. Over 90% of the students served by respondents had mild disabilities; over 70% of the students in resource rooms and 61% of those in half-day instructional programs received no social studies instruction. Perhaps more surprising, 25% of elementary teachers and 50% of secondary teachers of students with disabilities in full-time instructional programs did not provide social studies instruction.

These data are mirrored by the paucity of empirical investigations about social studies instruction for students with disabilities. In a comprehensive review of this literature, Curtis (1991) identified 39 studies, only 22 of which appeared in professional journals and periodicals. In fact, that count overestimates the size of the literature, because many of those studies were actually conducted with at-risk students for whom compelling diagnostic data were not reported. These studies survey a very wide range of traditional intervention strategies, topics, content, and materials. The plurality of these studies and the majority of the published reports focus on the relative effects of cooperative learning, as compared to competitive or individualistic approaches, on the attitudes, interactions, and academic achievement of students with and without disabilities. These studies show that students who learn about social studies in cooperative rather than competitive or individualistic learning environments evidence greater self-esteem (Smith, Johnson, & Johnson, 1982), greater interpersonal attraction between students with and without disabilities (Johnson & Johnson, 1981; 1982; 1984; Smith et al., 1982), and more and better interpersonal relationships between students with and without disabilities (Cooper, Johnson, Johnson, & Wilderson, 1980; Johnson & Johnson, 1983; 1985). The effects of learning environments on social studies achievement have been studied less frequently (Curtis, 1991), but the evidence suggests that cooperative learning is associated with better recall of declarative information about social studies content than alternative approaches (Johnson & Johnson, 1984; Smith et al., 1982; Yager, Johnson, Johnson, & Snider, 1985). To our knowledge, none of these studies report information about the effects of cooperative learning on the generative performance of students with disabilities, including project design, thinking, and problem solving.

Project-Based Learning

Project-based learning is particularly well suited to achieving the citizenship and instructional goals we previously discussed. Contemporary approaches to project-based learning originated with Dewey's (1933) contention that scientific and technical knowledge arises from the need to meet practical exigencies of life. Dewey believed that projects could be designed so that practical activities would "inevitably result not only in students' amassing information of practical and scientific importance . . . but also (what is more significant) in their becoming versed in methods of experimental inquiry and proof" (p. 217). Project-based investigation affords opportunities for students to develop the habits of mind that characterize independent learners (Dewey, 1933).

Five essential features characterize project-based instruction (Krajcik, Blumenfeld, Marx, & Soloway, 1994). First, an authentic question or problem provides a framework for organizing concepts and principles. Second, students engage in investigations that enable them to formulate and refine specific questions, locate data sources or collect original data, analyze and interpret information, and draw conclusions (Blumenfeld et al., 1991). Third, these investigations lead to the development of artifacts that represent students' proposed solutions to problems, reflect their emerging understanding about the domain, and are presented for the critical consideration of their colleagues. Fourth, teachers, students, and other members of the community of learners (Brown, 1994) collaborate to complete their projects, share expertise, make decisions about the division of labor, and construct a socially mediated understanding of their topic. Finally, cognitive tools, such as multimedia technology (Cognition and Technology Group at Vanderbilt, 1990; Salomon, Perkins, & Globerson, 1991), are used to extend and amplify students' representational and analytic capacities.

Social studies instruction has been criticized for its focus on isolated facts, reliance on textbooks, and oversimplification of complex issues (Beck & McKeown, 1991; Brophy, 1990; Kinder & Bursuck, 1991). Project-based learning offers an intrinsically interesting and pedagogically promising alternative to an exclusive reliance on textbooks. When students have the opportunity to engage in meaningful investigation of interesting problems for the purpose of communicating their findings to others, their interest in learning is enhanced (Blumenfeld et al., 1991). Increased interest can yield significant cognitive benefits, including improved attention, activation and utilization of background knowledge, use of learning strategies, and greater effort and persistence (Hidi, 1990; Hidi, Renninger, & Krapp, 1992; Pintrich, 1989; Pintrich & Garcia, 1991; Tobias, 1994). Moreover, during project-based learning activities, students have the opportunity to cooperate and collaborate with peers. According to Curtis (1991), cooperative learning can been viewed as citizenship training because it provides a context for the dispositions and skills that are needed to function in a democratic society.

MULTIMEDIA DESIGN PROJECTS

Educational multimedia, in which text, graphics, animation, sound, voice, music, still pictures, and motion video are incorporated into a single system, afford unique advantages for project-based learning. Students can explore multimedia environments and exercise control over their own learning in ways not possible with traditional instructional materials. They can focus on information of the most importance to them, set personal learning goals, and acquire information in highly individualized ways that may facilitate connections with prior knowledge (Schmalhofer & Kähn, 1988). The video component of multimedia can bring events to life in a way that text cannot, enabling learners to construct richer mental models of events or situations (McNamara, Miller, & Bransford, 1991). This capability is especially important for low achievers with little background knowledge about a topic (Bransford, Kinzer, Risko, Rowe, & Vye, 1989). In addition, video can circumvent the text barrier encountered by many students with reading difficulties. As a component of project-based learning, multimedia instructional programs and databases can provide access to rich sources of information. We believe that multimedia's most profitable use, however, is in conjunction with authoring tools that enable students to develop presentations that integrate text, sound, and visuals to illustrate the results of their investigations. These presentations publicly display the students' definition of project goals, their positions about controversial topics, evidence offered in support of their position, and conclusions drawn from their research and the research of others.

Armed with multimedia authoring tools, students become designers, rather than mere consumers of information (Perkins, 1986). As designers, students can be involved in creating instructional environments for their peers; for younger students; for the local media; or for libraries, museums, and other community sites (Carver et al., 1992). We call this type of project-based learning, in which students use multimedia technology to illustrate the results of their investigations of a topic, *multimedia design projects*. The design of a multimedia project requires students to engage in a complex set of tasks, including decomposing a topic into subtopics, sequencing subtopics appropriately, integrating diverse sets of information, translating ideas into a presentation format, and considering design elements based on audience needs and characteristics (Carver et al., 1992). The potential for representing ideas through text, pictures, and sound increases the likelihood that students will acquire an understanding of complex information. Students can communicate the interconnectedness of concepts by creating links that connect different units of information or different and sometimes conflicting representations of the same information. Furthermore, when working collaboratively to construct multimedia projects, and presenting work to their peers and other audiences, students have opportunities to discuss and defend their ideas, revise their positions, correct misconceptions, deepen their understanding, and learn to work with others in productive and mutually satisfying ways.

Outcomes Associated with Multimedia Design Projects

A growing literature describes the forms that multimedia design projects can take, ranging from autobiographies and studies of one's own culture (e.g., Apple Computer & LIST Services, 1991; McMillan, 1990;

Smith, 1992) to investigations of social studies and science topics, such as history, astronomy, and ecology (e.g., Carver, in press; Lehrer, Erickson, & Connell, 1993; McMillan, 1990; Perlbachs, 1992; Prickett, 1992; Turner & Dipinto, 1992). The majority of the extant reports provide anecdotal evidence that participation in multimedia design projects helps students develop interconnected knowledge and problem-solving skills (Apple Computer & LIST Services, 1991; Prickett, 1992). Teachers report that students are highly motivated by these learning opportunities, take pride in displaying their work to others, and enjoy collaborating (McMillan, 1990; Muir, 1992; Perlbachs, 1992; Prickett, 1992; Smith, 1992). One research team found that students' views of writing and the number of their spontaneous revisions were affected by the opportunity to create a product that could be used by others (Turner & Dipinto, 1992). Most authors note that students are able to acquire the technical skills necessary to use multimedia authoring tools if instruction is structured and sequential (e.g., Muir, 1992).

We are aware of three research teams that have collected systematic data about the impact of multimedia design projects on students' learning and motivation. Carver (in press) and her colleagues have implemented five different project-based learning activities over 3 years in urban middle-school classrooms. Most of these activities have included a multimedia design project component. Investigations were organized around themes relevant to students' interests and community, such as teenage life 20 years ago and students' roles in preserving the environment. In all cases, students were taught a set of explicit research and communication skills, and used computers to develop HyperCard stacks or create written reports. Students gave oral presentations or created work that was viewed by peers and other audiences. In one activity, students' projects were showcased in a local museum. Across the five projects, Carver observed a general shift from didactic instructional practices to collaborative activity, high rates of student engagement, and increased student initiative. She also reported decreases in classroom disruption and improved student ability to work in groups while remaining on task. However, she found that teachers experienced difficulties in providing explicit instruction and modeling research and communication skills for students. Furthermore, managing student behavior and assessing progress posed challenges to the efficacy of project-based learning activities.

Lehrer and his colleagues (Lehrer et al., 1993; Lehrer, Erickson, & Connell, in press), have worked with middle-school students who developed projects to help peers learn about history and social studies topics. These investigators documented increases in the percentage of time devoted to design and collaboration and decreases in off-task behavior and teacher guidance, suggesting a gradual progression from teacher involvement to autonomous functioning. Student self-report data, taken before and after the completion of projects, provided evidence of high levels of student involvement, mental effort, interest, planning, and collaboration. Students readily mastered the technical aspects of project construction and the authoring software, and thus were able to concentrate on higher level design tasks. However, students with less knowledge about a topic tended to focus on surface features of the design process. Analyses of students' multimedia documents showed they made extensive use of multiple representations of ideas. Although student teams were able to revise their projects based on feedback from peers who used them as learning tools, they were not inclined to solicit feedback during project development. In another study, Lehrer (1993) found little difference between the cognitive structures and declarative knowledge of students who participated in traditional instruction versus those who designed multimedia projects about the Civil War. However, a follow-up study with both groups 1 year later found that design students were more likely than those given traditional instruction to view history as interpretation, rather than as a compilation of facts. Design students were able to articulate effects of the Civil War on modern life, recalled more about their instructional experience, and were less apt to have confused recall of facts and events.

We have investigated the impact of multimedia design projects on students' knowledge and attitudes in two studies. In the first (Okolo & Ferretti, 1994), adolescents with learning disabilities investigated either the British or the Colonial perspective about events leading up to the American Revolution. They designed their projects over ten 60-minute sessions and then presented their work to peers. We found that participation had no impact on students' attitudes toward social studies or the Revolutionary War; however, significant differences emerged in students' knowledge of Revolutionary War events, their causes, and their consequences. In our second study (Okolo & Ferretti, in press), fourth-grade students with and without learning disabilities investigated either the advantages or disadvantages of industrialization. Pre- and posttesting demonstrated that students' attitudes toward social studies and toward collaborating improved significantly over the course of the study. Moreover, students' knowledge of industrialization significantly improved. The most encouraging result of this study was that outcomes were similar for students with and without learning disabilities, and the students with learning disabilities learned as much as their nondisabled peers.

In summary, three teams of researchers have shown that multimedia design projects can be successfully implemented in social studies classrooms. Students experience high levels of involvement, effort, and motivation. There is some evidence to suggest that students develop autonomous research and communication skills that are both necessary for completing their projects and important for lifelong learning. Students take pride in their work, are motivated to make revisions and improvements based on peer feedback, and learn content information. Preliminary information suggests that students both with and without learning disabilities benefit from these experiences.

Implementation Considerations

In our work, we have found it important to take into account a number of factors in implementing multimedia design projects with students. First, we select a topic in close consultation with students' teachers. The topic should be one that is sufficiently rich to engage students for an extended period of time (Blumenfeld et al., 1991). Fortunately, students find many social studies topics to be of interest because social studies is essentially the study of people and their communities (VanSledright & Brophy, 1992).

Second, we carefully consider the availability of materials in selecting a topic for investigation. In a study described previously (Okolo & Ferretti, 1994), we asked groups of middle school students to investigate the American and British perspectives on events leading up to the American Revolution. Although students were interested in the topic, we found very few materials that represented the British point of view. Those materials we located were often journals, personal accounts, or letters— usually written in Old English and the script of the period. These materials would be daunting to students *without* reading problems. Unfortunately, our students could not bypass inaccessible text by interviewing persons who had participated in the Revolutionary War, or by viewing films or photographs taken during this period in history. Consequently, we have concluded that contemporary topics, for which there are archives of audio, photographic, and film material, are better suited for multimedia design projects.

Third, teachers must sacrifice breadth of curricular coverage for detailed investigation of a specific topic, because projects take extensive amounts of time. Teachers often express concerns about how students will obtain exposure to the material listed on the curriculum guide or covered on standardized tests (Blumenfeld, Krajcik, Marx, & Soloway, 1994; Carver, in press; Lundberg, Coballes-Vega, Standiford, Langer, & Dibble, 1992). This issue has led us to select topics that encompass content found in the standard social studies curriculum, such as industrialization and colonization.

Fourth, we deliberately choose topics that are controversial, or about which students can take different positions. Controversy forces students to attend to multiple perspectives on an issue, stimulates dialogue, and increases motivation to learn (Johnson & Johnson, 1979). Confronted with controversy, students may engage in an active search for information and a cognitive restructuring of their initial position (Johnson, 1979). In future work, students in our projects will be asked to take and defend a specific position. For example, students could be asked to investigate either the advantages or the disadvantages of industrialization; after taking and defending a position, they will present their work to peers who investigated the opposing viewpoint.

Fifth, students complete their projects in cooperative learning groups. We have relied on the extensive cooperative learning literature to guide the selection of groups and inform group activities (e.g., Johnson & Johnson, 1982; Sharan & Sharan, 1992; Slavin, 1990). Students are assigned to heterogenous groups of four or five; groups are of mixed race and gender and include students with and without disabilities. We attempt to distribute expertise within each group, with at least one good reader and one student who has some prior knowledge of the topic to be studied assigned to each group. Initial sessions focus on establishing guidelines for cooperation through discussion, role-playing, group-building activities, and self-evaluation. The topics encompass a broad range of ideas and materials, so we do not expect individuals to become experts on all facets of an issue (Brown, 1994). Rather, we distribute responsibility by asking subgroups of students to become expert about specific subtopics. For example, subtopics for the Revolutionary War might include the French and Indian War, taxation, the Boston Tea Party, the Boston Massacre, and the Declaration of Independence. We have found that investigating subtopics helps to focus students' reading and note taking and enables them to better organize their projects. Each subgroup then contributes what they have learned toward the construction of a final project that represents the group's work.

Sixth, we provide students with guidance and assistance in specific components of project construction, even though each group is responsible for the selection of information in its project. We rely on a combination of teacher-directed instruction and explicit modeling, dialogue with individuals and groups, and scaffolding through worksheets and the authoring software itself. Thus, we have developed modules to teach students how to read source materials with a partner, how to take notes, how to select pictures that represent desired content, and how to segment information onto cards and link those cards within the authoring software. We provide students with planning sheets that scaffold many of the activities they must utilize, such as taking notes or organizing information on a card. We are mindful of the caution that too much teacher direction can constrain and routinize interaction within a group, impeding interaction and creative problem solving (Cohen, 1994; Salomon, Perkins, & Globerson, 1989). However, we are convinced that teachers must actively support and provide structure to students' learning. We always embed instruction about skills and procedures in project design activities (cf. Harris & Graham, 1994).

Seventh, we have learned that it is useful to design introductory activities that enable students to understand the gist of a project, and acquaint them with the hardware and software they will use in its design (cf. Brown et al., 1989). Students are guided through the creation of a miniproject, which contains features that we ask students to include in their final project. These include computer screens that (a) state the purpose of the project, (b) state the position each group is assigned to take, (c) provide reasons for each position, and (d) summarize positions. The miniproject also introduces students to the multimedia elements they can include in their projects, including text, scanned and digitized pictures, and digitized movies and sound. By participating in these activities, students develop an understanding of the goals that guide their work and the purposes for which they are acquiring skills.

Finally, we collaborate extensively with teachers in the design and implementation of projects. Project-based learning is labor-intensive for both teachers and students. Projects do not lend themselves well to the typical school schedule, which is segmented into 30- to 60-minute periods of discrete subjects. Rather, projects cross disciplinary boundaries and require extensive blocks of time for students to engage in research, analysis, and collaboration. Teachers in our studies have worked with us to provide the time blocks necessary for project activities, assisted in the selection of topics, helped delineate the skills that students need to learn, developed ways to teach those skills, informally assessed the success of projects as they unfolded in the classroom, and advised us about ways to adjust procedures so that students benefit more fully from project design experiences.

An Example of a Multimedia Design Project

To give the reader a more explicit picture of the way in which we have implemented multimedia design projects, we describe a study (Okolo & Ferretti, in press) that we conducted with two integrated fourth-grade classrooms. Each classroom was staffed by a special educator and a general educator. One classroom was assigned to study the advantages of industrialization, for which we selected the subtopics of transportation and com-munication. The other classroom investigated the disadvantages, which included pollution and depletion of natural resources. Our intention was for students from one classroom to share their presentation with students from the other. Thus, we nested topics within classrooms. Students were assigned to heterogenous groups of four or five, taking into consideration the student characteristics we described above. Each group was then divided in half, with a pair or trio of students assigned to work together to investigate one of the four subtopics.

We equipped each classroom with a multimedia-ready computer, a color scanner, and a printer. To create their presentations, students used a multimedia authoring system called HyperAuthor (Learning with Hyper-Media Group, 1989–1991). This program allows students to create multimedia documents that include text and scanned and digitized pictures. Students worked on their projects for approximately 25 sessions, about three times a week, for 60 to 90 minutes per session. One research assistant (RA) worked in each classroom, providing instruction and guidance to students in the cognitive and technical skills necessary for project design. Classroom teachers assisted groups and individuals as they learned specific skills and developed their projects. In the first four sessions, we discussed the project and its general objectives with each class. Then, we familiarized each group with the computer and software, as described above. Finally, we introduced students to guidelines for working in cooperative groups and engaged them in discussion, role-playing, group-building activities, and self-evaluation designed to reinforce cooperation.

In the fifth through seventh sessions, we acquainted students with the presentation topics by showing two videotapes, discussing major terms and concepts covered, and assigning group activities to review that content. Each group then decided upon a division of labor for their project, with each pair or trio assigned one subtopic. We then introduced students to issues of project design by guiding them through the development of the first two cards in their HyperAuthor stack. Students were given planning sheets, on which they designed their cards prior to entering them into the computer.

In the 8th through 15th sessions, we taught students a series of procedures to assist them in creating the substance of their presentation. First, students learned a modified version of reciprocal teaching (Palincsar, 1986; Palincsar & Brown, 1984) to assist them in reading source materials. Next, we instructed students in a procedure for taking notes from source material and provided them with planning sheets to facilitate note taking. Then, we discussed with students ways to organize cards within a presentation. Finally, students learned a process for selecting pictures to accompany their text. We taught the procedures described above through a sequence of discussion, demonstration, guided practice with the whole class, and supervised independent practice within groups. (Modules for teaching each procedure are available from the authors upon request.)

For the 16th through the 20th sessions, students worked independently in groups, reading, taking notes, and creating cards on their planning sheets. Teachers intervened when students began to experience difficulties with the note-taking task, and met with groups of students to assist them in reading source materials and identifying main ideas. As students began to translate information from their notes into HyperAuthor cards, we discussed with them an organizational structure for their stack that included cards containing a title, a statement of the purpose, introductions to each subtopic, specific information about each subtopic, and a summary. The remaining sessions were devoted to constructing the presentations. Students worked in pairs or trios to design their cards on planning sheets, assisted by their teachers. The RA then assisted groups of students in placing their cards on the computer.

The process of entering cards into the computer took much longer than we had planned, primarily because we did not anticipate how students' lack of keyboarding skills would affect the process. Students were still creating their cards on the computer during the last week of school, and thus we had to forgo the final phase of the study. We had hoped that students who investigated the advantages of industrialization would present their work to students who investigated the disadvantages, and vice versa; students would then receive feedback about their presentations and would have revised their presentations in light of that feedback (Carver et al., 1992). Also, we were unable to provide students with the opportunity to showcase their work (Carver, in press). We scheduled an open house, during which students could show their work to their parents, and students rehearsed for this event. Unfortunately, a spring flood closed the school on that day, and the open house was canceled.

Peer feedback and showcase events are important components of multimedia design projects. Students are asked to create their projects for specific audiences; authentic forums for displaying their work can help motivate them to consider their audience, to revise, to learn presentation skills, and to take pride in their performance. We will include both peer feedback and showcases in our future studies and examine their impact on students' project construction and revision.

CHALLENGES

We have described many potential advantages of multimedia design projects, but we would be remiss if we did not acknowledge some of the challenges inherent in implementing projects in general, and multimedia design projects in particular. Like other constructivist approaches, project-based learning necessitates new roles for teacher and student. Project-based learning is "messy" in the sense that the outcomes are not easily defined, there is no set of right answers, and there are many ways to complete an activity. To date, most of our understanding of classroom management is predicated on instruction in well-structured domains. We know little about how to effectively manage the multiple goals and needs of groups of students who are simultaneously pursuing individual learning activities. In our own work we have found that project-based learning quickly degenerates into chaos unless teachers have well-established routines for gaining and maintaining student attention.

Based on a preliminary analysis of videotaped interactions from our most recent study (Okolo & Ferretti, in press), we are convinced that getting students involved in productive, positive collaborations that are critical to the success of project-based learning can be extremely difficult. Our videotapes suggest that some groups work effectively in collaboration. In other groups, a few students do the majority of the work, or students work without sharing information or consulting one another about decisions. The latter pattern may be especially problematic for heterogeneous groups, because students with less skill or motivation may be prone to depending on more able students. Further, high achievers may purposefully exclude students with less skill for fear that the latter's contributions will diminish the quality of the final product.

Undoubtedly, students with and without disabilities need explicit instruction and guided practice in the social skills necessary for positive group interaction (e.g., Barnes & Todd, 1977; Cosden, Goldman, & Hine, 1990; Nastasi & Clements, 1991). Furthermore, students also need instruction and guidance if they are to engage in group problem solving, decision making, and other higher level cognitive skills (Cohen, 1994). Our preliminary analyses also suggest that the teacher can have a significant impact on group functioning. In one classroom, teachers facilitated interaction by questioning groups about how they planned to complete a task, asking how responsibilities were divided, and suggesting alternatives when groups reached an impasse. In the second classroom, teachers focused much more extensively on behavior management, and typically admonished students for misbehavior. Students in the first classroom appeared more engaged, and groups seemed to function more effectively. We are encouraged by the year-long investigation of project-based learning conducted by Marx et al. (1994), who found that with experience, students' collaborations became more productive, with greater participation in discussion and decision making occurring from students of all ability levels.

A final challenge that will receive more attention in our future work is that of assessment. To date, no clear standards exist for assessing the impact of project-based learning or multimedia design projects. As Lehrer's (1993) study suggests, measures of declarative knowledge may be insufficient for documenting the depth and interconnectedness of knowledge that students acquire. In addition, traditional measures of student products, such as those employed in assessing written reports, do not fully analyze all the features of multimedia projects, which include multiple and overlapping representations of information. Along with other researchers and educators, we are attempting to develop alternative ways to assess students' knowledge and products.

Moreover, we contend that assessment should not only focus on knowledge acquired and products produced, but also address the processes that we hope to cultivate in students. We believe that performance-based assessments (Wiggins, 1993) can be extremely useful in documenting students' proficiency at meeting the challenges of authentic learning situations. To this end, we are developing instruments to assess students' abilities to engage in research, to give an oral presentation, and to defend a point of view. The performance-based assessments we envision must be conducted with individuals and thus are labor-intensive and time-consuming. Our approach as researchers will be to conduct these assessments with representative samples of students. Sampling may not be appropriate for classroom teachers, however, who need to collect performance data about all students in a class. Carver (1992) and Chomyn (1992) recommended mini-assessments of project components, such as computer skills or oral presentation, that are systematically built into project activities. They urged educators to focus on formative assessment, create simple scoring rubrics, and provide feedback to students as soon as possible after assessments are completed. We plan to heed this advice in our future research.

AUTHORS' NOTES

1. *The preparation of this manuscript was supported in part by Grant No. H180E30043 from the U.S. Department of Education, Office of Special Education Programs, Division of Innovation and Development.*

2. *The order of authorship is arbitrary.*

9. Computer-Based Study Strategies for Students with Learning Disabilities: Individual Differences Associated with Adoption Level

LYNNE ANDERSON-INMAN, CAROLYN KNOX-QUINN,
AND MARK A. HORNEY

The development of good study skills and study habits has become increasingly important for success in today's schools. Teachers are no longer viewed as the sole purveyors of academic information, and preparation for lifelong, independent learning is believed to be a fundamental goal of education. Acquisition of effective study strategies is consistently recommended by educational critics and curriculum developers who believe it is essential that students "learn how to learn" (Novak & Gowin, 1984). Sizer (1984), for example, recommended that schools take an active part in teaching students how to teach themselves, while at the same time enhancing student motivation to do so. The focus of this chapter is on innovative ways to use technology to support the efforts of students with learning disabilities (LD) to acquire and use effective study strategies.

Reprinted, with changes, from "Computer-based study strategies for students with learning disabilities: Individual differences associated with adoption level," by Lynne Anderson-Inman, Carolyn Knox-Quinn, and Mark A. Horney, *Journal of Learning Disabilities*, Vol. 29, 1996, pp. 461–484. Copyright © 1996 by PRO-ED, Inc.

Study strategies are the behaviors students employ, either singularly or in combination, to meet the academic expectations of school. In the act of studying, students need to perform various cognitive or procedural tasks in order to construct knowledge or develop skills (Loranger, 1994). The cognitive tasks relate primarily to information processing. For example, students who are effective studiers are good at accessing, analyzing, and synthesizing information in their efforts to turn that information into knowledge. To actually learn while studying, students need to be actively engaged in processing the information they are trying to learn, and cognitively manipulate it into something that is personally meaningful (Dansereau, 1985; Thomas & Rohwer, 1986). Studying is not a passive task: It requires effort and sustained attention.

The procedural tasks associated with studying are largely self-management activities—behaviors that students adopt in order to enhance the attention and effort that goes into studying (Thomas & Rohwer, 1986). For example, students might adopt such behaviors as underlining, outlining, and self-questioning in their efforts to enhance and facilitate the cognitive activities of reading and understanding a content area textbook. Students who are good at studying are skilled in analyzing the learning situation and selecting study strategies that meet the demands of the task at hand (Armbruster, Echols, & Brown, 1983; Brown, Campione, & Day, 1981). They are motivated to succeed and use strategies accordingly (Loranger, 1994). In short, effective studiers know how to take control of their learning.

Unfortunately, students with learning disabilities are often not very good at the skills required for effective studying. They frequently fail to understand what they read (Reid, 1988; Zigmond, Vallecorsa, & Leinhardt, 1980), have difficulty organizing and retaining information (Saski, Swicegood, & Carter, 1983), appear passive when faced with interpreting written material or copying notes from the chalkboard (Torgeson & Licht, 1983), and have difficulty integrating prior knowledge with new information (Reyes, Gallego, Duran, & Scanlon, 1989). Furthermore, many students with learning disabilities have some combination of auditory/receptive deficiencies, alternate learning styles, slow information-processing skills, poor handwriting and spelling, spatial organization problems, and distractibility that contributes to communication difficulties and inefficient study habits (McCrady, 1982; McGuire & O'Donnell, 1989).

Awareness of the importance of teaching study skills to adolescent and adult students with learning disabilities has emerged over the last decade (Anderson-Inman, 1992a; Bianco & McCormick, 1989; Deshler & Schumaker, 1986; Reith & Polsgrove, 1994; Zigmond, 1990). It is now generally recognized that "to be successful in academic settings LD students need to have a number of competencies (e.g., listening, note-taking, attending, problem-solving skills) in order to effectively manage the information-processing demands of the classroom" (Seidenberg, 1985). Unfortunately, the research literature provides very little guidance on how to help secondary students with learning disabilities meet the reading and studying demands of content area classrooms. In a review of the academic intervention research over a 10-year period (1978–1987), Lessen and colleagues (Lessen, Dudzinski, Karsh, & VanAcker, 1989) found only five studies that addressed advanced readings skills and only nine studies that examined the acquisition of content area information. Furthermore, their review underscores the need for more information about strategies that are effective for secondary-level students (only 22% of the studies researched academic interventions for secondary students).

STUDY STRATEGIES: TECHNOLOGY'S ROLE

At the Center for Electronic Studying at the University of Oregon, we have been exploring ways in which computer technology might help students with learning disabilities to acquire and use effective study skills and habits. We have adopted the term *electronic studying* to refer to the various ways in which computers and other forms of advanced technology can be used to enhance studying and learning across the curriculum. Our explorations suggest that there are at least three types of electronic studying, each with a different focus and a different goal. All three types are described below, and literature is cited where the approach was used to improve the academic performance of students with learning disabilities.

Guided Instruction

One of the first educational uses of computers for students with learning disabilities was to provide computer-assisted instruction, or CAI (MacArthur, Haynes, Malouf, Harris, & Owings, 1990; Malouf, Wizer, Pilato, & Grogan, 1990). This is a model in which the computer is programmed to present the learner with a sequence of academic tasks or problems, and the learner is expected to respond to each as a way of practicing familiar skills. When tutorials are added, the program might attempt to teach either new or missing skills. Building on the CAI model of using the computer to guide student learning, innovative examples of this approach to electronic studying have emerged in the literature. One example is the use of computer-based study guides to enhance acquisition of content area material from written texts. Lovitt and his associates have explored the use of computerized study guides for students with learning disabilities. They reported significantly higher performance by mainstreamed students with LD who used computerized study guides in a remedial world geography course than by comparable students who used a noncomputerized note-taking procedure (Horton, Lovitt, Givens, & Nelson, 1989). Higgins and Boone (1990) explored the use of a hypertext study guide for enhancing the social studies achievement of students with learning disabilities. In two related studies using a reversible baseline design, Higgins and Boone found that retention test scores were higher for students with learning disabilities when they used the hypertext study guides. The authors concluded that hypertext study guides were at least as effective as a well-prepared lecture.

A related effort is the development and use of electronic books (Yankelovich, Meyrowitz & Van Dam, 1985) that provide students with various resources designed to support and enhance their reading comprehension. Most of these electronic books present the user with a hypermedia interface, enabling various types of navigation throughout the electronic document (Anderson-Inman, Horney, Chen, & Lewin, 1994). The text (and therefore students' comprehension of the text) is supported by the addition of electronic resources in various media. Wise and Olson (1994), for example, found that inserting high-quality synthesized speech into electronic stories and books helped to improve the word recognition and phonological decoding of students with reading disabilities. Aweiss (1994–95) found that access to an electronic glossary enhanced reading comprehension for students learning to read a foreign language. MacArthur and Haynes (1995) described a software system for developing hypermedia versions of students' textbooks called SALT (Student Assistant for Learning from Text). Designed to help students with learning disabilities, the documents created using SALT provide students with three types of support: (a) *compensatory* support to improve reading fluency (e.g., glossary for definitions, speech synthesis for pronunciations etc.); (b) *strategic* support to guide students' use of cognitive and metacognitive reading strategies; and (c) *substantive* support of modifications that enhance comprehension of content. A test of the system with 10 adolescents with LD revealed significantly higher comprehension scores when the enhanced electronic text was used. These and similar efforts provide students with "supported text" (Horney & Anderson-Inman, in press)—text that has been electronically enhanced in an effort to promote and guide students' comprehension while they read and study.

Assignment Production

Secondary-level students with learning disabilities often have a difficult time completing assignments on time and in a manner that is legible to their teachers. Failure to turn in acceptable assignments when required usually results in poor grades and considerable frustration with the education system. Student difficulties related to assignment production can arise from a variety of interrelated factors: severe reading and writing deficits, poor organizational skills, deficient study skills, a passive attitude toward school, and a lack of motivation for academic tasks (Reith & Polsgrove, 1994). The negative impact of these factors is magnified when you take into consideration the increased time required by even the most motivated student with learning disabilities to do what nondisabled students can often do quite quickly. Teaching word processing to students with learning disabilities has long been utilized as an effective way to improve their writing skills and enhance their abilities to produce acceptable assignments more efficiently (Arms,1984; Jacobi,1986; Outhred, 1989). These effects are most pronounced when students with learning disabilities learn to use a word processor within an instructional context that focuses on writing as a process and when they are specifically taught how to improve their papers using the various types of revision mechanisms facilitated in a word processing environment (Graham & MacArthur, 1988; Kerchner & Kistinger, 1984; Schwartz & MacArthur, 1990).

Word processors are not the only tool available to students with learning disabilities when using computers for assignment production. For example, the power of word processing for assignment production is further enhanced when students are able to access assistive writing tools, such as spell checkers and grammar checkers, and electronic references materials, such as dictionaries and encyclopedias. Spell checkers alone greatly improve a paper's legibility as well as alter a teacher's perception of student competence and intelligence. It is extremely important, however, that students with learning disabilities be taught strategies for using a spell checker effectively. To students with learning disabilities it is not always apparent which of the several alternatives suggested by a spell checking program is the correct one (if indeed, any of the alternatives is correct) (Fais & Wanderman, 1987). Strategies for narrowing down the options and/or using computer-based speech to point out the correct alternative can make the use of such writing tools less frustrating and more efficient for students with severe spelling difficulties (Anderson-Inman & Knox-Quinn, 1996). In short, word processing and other writing aids allow students with learning disabilities to "take control of the page" (Sullivan, 1991), using it to show their strengths instead of their deficits.

Information Processing

The third form of electronic studying is the use of computers to enhance meaningful understanding of content area material by facilitating students' abilities to process the information they are trying to learn. The recognition that poor information-processing skills are frequently associated with learning disabilities (Reyes et al., 1989; Saski et al., 1983) has led to various suggestions and programs for improving the information-processing skills of such students (Borkowski, Schneider & Pressley, 1989; Deshler & Lenz, 1989).

Numerous applications of computer technology make it an ideal environment for supporting information-processing efforts. In the current vernacular, the computer can be a "cognitive tool" (Lajoie, 1993; Pea, 1985; Perkins, 1985; Salomon, Perkins, & Globerson, 1991), one that enhances cognitive activity by either supporting cognitive processes or sharing the cognitive load (i.e., performing some of the tasks the learner would ordinarily have to do). Common computer applications that can be used as cognitive tools include databases that can be used to record and search for information, outlining programs that can be used to record and synthesize information, and concept-mapping programs that can be used to record and visualize the interrelationship of ideas. These types of programs are

> *tools* inasmuch as their operation depends on the learners' operations; they are *cognitive* inasmuch as they serve to aid students in their own constructive thinking, allowing them to transcend their cognitive limitations and engage in cognitive operations they would not have been capable of otherwise. (Salomon, 1993, p. 180)

Anderson-Inman and colleagues at the University of Oregon have been researching the use of cognitive tools to improve student understanding of content area texts and lectures. Results from a series of studies indicate that computer-based outlining programs can be powerful tools for improving the text comprehension of average and below-average students (Anderson-Inman, Redekopp, & Adams, 1992; Anderson-Inman & Tenny, 1989; Tenny, 1988). Furthermore, there is preliminary evidence that using computer-based outlining programs as study tools is effective in improving the test performance of students with learning disabilities, even when the studying is conducted outside the general education classroom (Adams, 1992; Adams & Anderson-Inman, 1991). Observations of teachers who are integrating computer-based outlining programs into their curriculum suggest that the programs are easily implemented and widely effective across varying conditions (Anderson-Inman, 1991; Anderson-Inman, 1992b). Research on the use of computer-based concept-mapping tools to enhance learning suggests similar results. For example, Zeitz and Anderson-Inman (1992) reported that students in a high school science class were successful in learning to use a computer-based concept-mapping program as a vehicle to synthesize information across 7 days of reading and lectures. As evidenced by performance on curriculum-embedded quizzes, the more complex their maps, the more they learned.

This chapter describes current research at the Center for Electronic Studying on the use of computer-based study strategies to enhance the academic success of secondary-level students with learning disabilities. The computer-based study strategies under investigation combine elements of the second and third types of electronic studying described above: assignment production using computers and information processing using computers. Specifically, this chapter presents the context within which the research on computer-based study strategies has been conducted, and reports data on learner characteristics found to be associated with the extent to which students adopted and applied the computer-based study strategies they had been taught.

METHOD

Preliminary data on individual differences associated with the adoption of the computer-based study strategies by students with learning disabilities have emerged from our work in Project SUCCESS. Project SUCCESS was a 3-year, federally funded research effort designed to investigate and evaluate the extent to which computer-based study strategies enhance the academic performance of secondary students with learning disabilities in general education content area classes. The project involved working with students and teachers at three demonstration sites in the state of Oregon (two middle schools and one high school) to explore the efficacy of computer-based information organizers as tools for studying and learning across the curriculum. Participating students were each provided with a laptop computer (Macintosh PowerBook 145) and taught a variety of computer-based study strategies using software designed to facilitate information recording, organization, and manipulation. It was expected that students would use their portable computers to take notes in class, complete assignments, record and organize information from reading materials, and study for tests. To enhance their organization skills and promote effective studying, students were taught to use an array of computer-based information organizers (word processing, outlining, and concept-mapping programs) as well as various electronic reference materials (dictionaries and encyclopedias).

Project SUCCESS had three major goals: (a) to investigate the effects of electronic studying on participating students' academic performance, study skills, content area knowledge, motivation, self-concept, and school satisfaction; (b) to explore the impact of electronic studying on teacher/student roles and classroom activities; and (c) to identify the implementation factors affecting the use of electronic study strategies by students with learning disabilities in middle school and high school. To accomplish these goals, project activities were divided into three phases, each of which was designed to provide information useful for planning and decision making in the subsequent phase. The following paragraphs provide a brief overview of the major project activities for each of these three phases.

During Phase 1, research staff identified schools to participate in the project and developed site-specific implementation plans for introducing computer-based study strategies to students with learning disabilities at each school. The schools selected were already committed to the integration of technology for instructional purposes, had already invested in an array of hardware and software that could be used to support the project, and were staffed by computer-literate special education teachers willing to invest time and effort in the project (referred to as "project liaisons" in the remainder of this chapter).

Phase 2 of the project comprised three major activities: student selection, pilot projects, and preparation of students for Phase 3. During Phase 2, research staff developed and implemented plans at each school for selecting students to participate in the project. In addition, the staff conducted exploratory pilot studies with 3 students at two of the schools (one middle school and one high school). The purpose of these six pilot studies was to gather data about the use of computer-based study strategies with students with LD that would be helpful during the more large-scale implementation planned for Phase 3. The third major activity for Phase 2 was preparing participating students with the skills believed to be necessary in order for them to benefit from instruction on computer-based study strategies. In general, preparation focused on improving students' keyboarding skills and ensuring familiarity with computers and basic computer applications, such as word processing. At one of the middle schools, this type of preparation was not possible because the school consisted of only two grades and participating students had been selected at their elementary schools prior to attending the middle school.

Observations and data from the pilot studies were used to refine the implementation plans at each school in preparation for implementing Phase 3. Phase 3 was a full-scale implementation of the intervention and was designed to last for 2 full academic years. Implementation began at all three schools during the first week of September 1993 and continued through June 1995. Ongoing data collection during Phase 3 included (a) student assessments, observations, and interviews; (b) teacher observations and interviews; (c) permanent products in the form of electronically produced assignments and study aids; and (d) weekly contact reports describing instructional efforts, technical assistance needs, student activities, teacher concerns, and plans for the future. These data were examined as they emerged and used to refine the curriculum and instructional procedures at each school.

Settings

Ware Middle School.   Ware Middle School is a 2-year middle school (seventh and eighth grades) in an outlying urban neighborhood with homes that are generally below average in value. The school serves approximately 932 students and has a staff of 56 teachers. During the second year of implementation, students and teachers were reorganized into three "Houses," or schools within a school, with each "House" having 10 to 15 teachers. Students at Ware now receive all instruction on academic subjects from their House teachers and remain with the same group of teachers for both years at the school. Ninety students in the school receive special education services, and although most of these are identified as students with learning disabilities, 15 have more severe disabilities. Ware employs four certified special education teachers who share positions totaling 2.5 full-time equivalent (FTE). The school also employs two full-time and two part-time teacher aides to work with students having special needs, and five foster grandparents who volunteer to work with students on an individual basis. The school has adopted an inclusion model for students with learning disabilities. This means that they all attend general education classes most of the day, with some of the students receiving support from the resource room. A few students with learning disabilities receive no special education support and are simply monitored as they progress toward termination from special student services.

Piper Middle School.   Piper Middle School is a 3-year middle school (sixth through eighth grades) in a small, urban neighborhood setting with homes of average to below-average value. The school serves approximately 750 students and has a staff of 55 teachers. Students and teachers here are also organized into three "Houses," each having 10 to 15 teachers. Students receive all instruction on academic subjects from these teachers and remain with the same teachers for all 3 years at the school. Various elective courses, including instruction from special education teachers, are taken outside the House. Piper Middle School currently has 100 students identified as needing special education services, and a special education staff of four teachers. The students with learning disabilities are randomly assigned to each of the three Houses but receive their special education services in combination. Special education services for students with learning disabilities include part-time assistance in a resource room, and self-contained classes for specific subjects (e.g., language arts, math).

Riverview High School.   Riverview High School is a 4-year comprehensive high school (9th through 12th grades) located in a low-income suburban neighborhood of shopping malls, office buildings, and apartments. The school serves approximately 988 students and has a staff of 85 teachers. The school has recently experienced major school reform and restructuring. Students now attend four 90-minute classes each day, with what used to be year-long classes now lasting only a semester. There are two certified special education teachers and instructional assistants who share 3.5 FTE. The school serves approximately 75 students with Individualized Education Programs (IEPs), most of whom have been determined eligible for special education services as learning disabled. All students with learning disabilities attend general education classes most of the day and receive special education support through a one-period resource room. Special sections of some classes have been developed to meet the needs of students unable to succeed in the general education program.

Participants

The number of students selected to participate in Project SUCCESS was determined, in large part, by the number of portable computers we could afford to purchase for their use. Thus, it was decided that 32 students with learning disabilities would be selected to participate in Project SUCCESS, distributed more or less equally across the three participating schools. The same set of selection criteria was used at each school and included the following:

1. Identification as a student with a specific learning disability using the eligibility criteria established by the state of Oregon (see Note 1);

2. Ability to participate in the project for at least 2 academic years;

3. Learning skills that made integration into the general academic curriculum a realistic expectation;

4. No major (disruptive) behavioral problems;

5. Scheduled to receive part-time instructional assistance from the participating special education teacher;

6. An interest in participating on the part of both the student and his or her parent/guardian.

The actual selection procedures differed slightly across the three schools. At Ware Middle School, the special education teacher serving as project liaison worked with all feeder elementary schools in the spring of 1993 to identify appropriate students who would be attending the school the following year as seventh graders. Invitations were extended, and 10 students were selected from those who responded favorably. At Piper Middle School, the special education teacher serving as project liaison identified potential students from the school's pool of sixth-grade students with learning disabilities. Research staff provided a brief orientation for interested parents and students in the winter of 1993, after which students were asked to volunteer if they wished to participate. Files for those students who volunteered were reviewed and 10 students were selected to participate. At Riverview High School, 2 of the 3 sophomores participating in the pilot studies at that school during Year 1 elected to continue with the project as juniors; the remaining 10 students were selected from those who volunteered for the project after a brief orientation meeting in the spring of 1993 (to which mostly ninth-grade students with learning disabilities, meeting the general criteria, were invited). Nine of these 10 students began the project as sophomores, 1 as a junior.

Research staff, in collaboration with special education teachers at the schools, selected a total of 32 students to participate in Phase 3 of the project—10 from each of the two middle schools and 12 from the high school. This original configuration of students comprised 23 boys and 9 girls. Although considerable effort was expended trying to make the gender balance more equitable, this proved to be impossible: Each school had fewer girls with learning disabilities than boys, and many of the girls were not interested in joining a technology-based project. By the end of the first year, 7 students had dropped out of the program for various reasons. Three students moved away (1 boy and 2 girls), 2 students decided they no longer wanted to participate (both boys), and 1 student was eliminated due to serious behavioral problems at the school (also a boy). As soon as possible, these students were replaced by alternates from the same school, selected using the same criteria.

Table 9.1 provides demographic data on 30 of the 31 students participating in Project SUCCESS during the second year of Phase 3, arranged by school (see Note 2). Under each school, students are listed by their self-selected pseudonyms (column 1) in order of their "start date" (the date on which their participation in the project began; column 3). Following this column are data that describe students' ages and grades at the time they joined the project (columns 4 and 5). Column 6 provides overall IQ scores for as many students as possible, taken from tests administered prior to their involvement with Project SUCCESS. The only exception to this is the IQ score for Felix (Piper Middle School), which

TABLE 9.1
Demographic and Achievement Data on Students in Project SUCCESS

Student	Gender	Start data			IQ		Years from start date	Reading level		
		Date	Age	Grade	Score	Test		Grade equivalent score	Test	Grade when tested
Ware Middle School										
Lee	M	09/01/93	12.8	7	118	WISC-R	2.9	1.6	K-TEA	4.1
Rick	M	09/01/93	12.1	7				6.2	K-TEA	4.1
Brian	M	09/01/93	13.3	7	89	WISC-R	6.7	4.2	WJ-R	7.2
Ryan	M	09/01/93	13.2	7	98	WISC-R	5.6	4.9	K-TEA	5.5
Jeff	M	09/01/93	12.7	7	94	WJ-PB	4.9	4.0	WRMT	5.2
Butch	M	09/01/93	13.4	7	107	WISC-R	1.5	4.0	K-TEA	5.7
Duane	M	09/01/93	13.6	7	81	WISC-R	2.3	1.3	K-TEA	6.7
Avon	M	09/01/93	12.2	7	96	WISC-R	5.3	2.8	WJ-R	7.9
Piper Middle School										
Brady	M	09/01/93	12.2	7	93	K-BIT	0.3	2.8	WJ-R	5.3
Grace	F	09/01/93	12.2	7	105	K-BIT	0.9	4.6	WJ-R	6.8
Sady	F	09/01/93	12.3	7	77	K-BIT	0.9	3.4	WJ-R	6.1
Ed	M	09/01/93	13.2	7	86	K-BIT	1.5	2.8	WJ-R	6.1
Susie	F	09/01/93	13.4	7	119	K-ABC	3.3	4.3	WJ-R	5.6
Thor	M	09/01/93	12.6	7	91	K-BIT	0.3[a]	6.2	WJ-R	6.8
Felix	M	02/01/94	13.1	7.5	95	WISC-R	4.8	6.7	WJ-R	7.8
Shelby	F	09/01/94	13.0	8	88	WISC-R	4.5	2.5	WJ-R	5.3
Mike	M	09/01/94	14.4	8	97	K-BIT	0.8	6.0	WJ-R	6.3
Brittany	F	09/01/94	13.0	8	78	WISC-R	3.9	7.0	WJ-R	7.3
Reuban	M	09/01/94	13.6	8				3.1	WJ-R	5.2

Table continues

TABLE 9.1 (cont.)

Student	Gender	Start data			IQ			Reading level		
		Date	Age	Grade	Score	Test	Years from start date	Grade equivalent score	Test	Grade when tested
Riverview High School										
Bud	M	05/01/93	16.8	10				2.2	WJ-R	3.6
Rebecca	F	05/01/93	15.5	10						
Veronica	F	09/01/93	15.7	10	117	WISC-R	5.9	4.8	WJ-R	7.5
William	M	09/01/93	15.4	10	105	WISC-R	1.3	10.0	WJ-R	8.8
Chad	M	09/01/93	16.2	11				5.7	WJ-R	8.7
Cindy	F	09/01/93	15.6	10				5.6	WJ-R	6.7
Harry	M	09/01/93	16.8	10				8.0	WJ-R	9.6
Mickey	M	09/01/93	15.0	10				5.2	WJ-R	7.6
Sara	F	09/01/93	15.3	10	100	WISC-R	5.6	5.8	WJ-R	4.5
Chico	M	01/01/94	15.6	10.5				4.3	WRMT	7.5
Don	M	01/01/94	16.2	10.5				8.0	WJ-R	8.8

Note. K-ABC = Kaufman-Assessment Battery for Children (Kaufman & Kaufman, 1987); K-BIT = Kaufman Brief Intelligence Test (Kaufman & Kaufman, 1987); K-TEA = Kaufman Test of Educational Achievement (Kaufman & Kaufman, 1985); WISC-R = Wechsler Intelligence Scale for Children–Revised (Wechsler, 1974); WJ-PB = Woodcock Johnson Psycho-Educational Battery/Tests of Cognitive Ability (Woodcock & Johnson, 1977); WJ-R = Woodcock Johnson–Revised (Woodcock & Johnson, 1989); WRMT = Woodcock Reading Mastery Test (Woodcock, 1987).
[a]This student was tested at 0.3 months after (rather than before) the project start date.

was taken from a test administered 3 months after his start date. Information about the tests from which these IQ scores were derived and the time of administration (in terms of years before or after a student's start date) can be found in columns 7 and 8.

IQ data reported in Table 9.1 were taken from the students' cumulative folders at their respective schools or from information at the school district's central office. Because the students attended different schools in different districts, there was no consistency to the tests selected, the procedures adopted by test administrators, or the dates on which evaluations were made. In cases in which multiple evaluations resulted in students' having more than one IQ score recorded in their files, the most recent score was selected for Table 9.1. Although every effort was made to find a valid IQ score for each participating student, we were not successful for some of the students participating in the project. Gaps existed where files had been lost or parents had elected to purge files of these data. When questioned about these gaps in data, school district administrators and school psychologists told research staff that students who qualify to receive services as learning disabled based on IQ and other test scores during their elementary years are "grandfathered" into the service delivery system when they reach the secondary level. This apparently eliminates the need to retest or even retain IQ test scores.

The last three columns in Table 9.1 present information about students' reading abilities when last tested by the school district. Column 9 provides a grade-level equivalent for the scores obtained on the test listed in column 10. So that these scores can be interpreted in light of a student's age at the time tested, the last column indicates what grade the student was in when the reading evaluation was conducted. As with the IQ test scores described above, these reading scores were taken from students' files, and the tests listed were administered under various conditions and at various times. By comparing this information with that in column 5, it is possible to ascertain the time gap between this test date and when a student started in the project.

As can be seen from Table 9.1, 25 of the students had been involved with Phase 3 of Project SUCCESS for all or part of the previous year, and 5 were new to the project beginning in the fall of 1994. Eight of the students who participated during this second year of Phase 3 were girls, 22 were boys. Most of the middle school students started the project during seventh grade and almost all of the high school students began their involvement as sophomores (10th grade). Students' IQ scores ranged from 77 (considered borderline average) to 119 (considered high average). Students' reading scores ranged from a grade-level equivalent of 1.3 (for a student tested as a sixth grader) to a grade equivalent of 10.0 (for a student tested as an eighth grader). For some of the students in the project, reading scores were not the best indicator of their problems in school or their learning disabilities. For example, many of the students whose reading scores were either at grade level or above, scored extremely low on standardized tests of writing and/or spelling. Furthermore, some of the students also scored very low on a standardized test of math skills (one as low as the 4th percentile).

Implementation Procedure

As described above, research staff worked with the special education project liaisons at each school to develop an implementation plan that made sense for that school. The initial implementation plans at each school varied along a number of dimensions because they took into consideration the following features: (a) number of grade levels at the school, (b) existing procedures for developing computer literacy skills, (c) the school's daily schedule, (d) curriculum expectations within the general education program, (e) curriculum expectations within the special education program, (f) student characteristics, (g) the special education staff's technological skills, and (h) the distribution of existing technology resources. It was anticipated that these initial implementation plans would be altered over time as research staff worked with teachers and students at each school. This proved to be the case, and modifications occurred as data and feedback were used to refine procedures at each site.

At the two middle schools, the special education teachers worked with research staff to design and implement a technology-based study skills class in which all participating students were scheduled together for one period. This enabled the special education teachers and research staff to provide direct instruction to the students as a group and support their use of electronic study strategies in general classes on a daily basis. Because students at Ware Middle School had little prior experience with the computer, they were also scheduled into a regular computer literacy class during their first 9 weeks at the school.

Implementation plans at the two middle schools also differed in the extent to which the instruction provided in the technology-based study skills classes was coordinated with the general education teachers' expectations. At Ware Middle School, the special education teacher tried to be responsive to the daily expectations of general education teachers and coordinated at least part of his instruction with the skills students needed for their content area assignments. Participating students were also scheduled into content area classes (English, science, and social studies) with as few different general education teachers as possible, in order to facilitate this coordination. At Piper Middle School, such coordination was more difficult, due to the school's structure and the larger number of teachers involved; therefore, a parallel curriculum was developed to teach students the electronic study strategies felt to be maximally useful in the general education curriculum, and efforts were made to promote student application of these strategies in their content area classes.

At Riverview High School, project students were scheduled into one of three 90-minute study halls provided specifically for students with learning disabilities. During the first year, the study halls were supervised by an experienced, full-time instructional assistant who was very skilled in using the computer. Research staff and the instructional assistant provided participating students with direct instruction on electronic study strategies, individually or in small groups, and also spent time with students meeting their individual needs for technical support. The focus in the study halls was on electronic study strategies appropriate for learning information and accomplishing class assignments in students' general education courses.

This very individualized approach was adopted because students selected content area courses from a large array of possibilities, resulting in little congruency in general education teachers' expectations for participating students at any given time. To provide focus for the instruction, a contract was developed with each student. These contracts included plans for developing and using the electronic study strategies most relevant for one or two specific courses in each student's schedule. The contracts were then revised as courses changed and as students became more proficient at using the computer for studying. During the second year of Phase 3, the students worked more independently. For part of the year, most of them were able to get together as a group during a study hall to collaborate and share what they were doing. Research staff visited them once a week to solve any technical problems and bring in new software as needed. A modest amount of new instruction was provided, but, for the most part, the students worked independently to apply the electronic study strategies they already knew to meet the academic expectations in their various courses.

Computer-Based Study Strategies

Students at each school were taught a repertoire of computer-based study strategies applicable for learning and studying content area material at the secondary level. Some of these study strategies were refinements of strategies already in the literature (e.g., Anderson-Inman et al., 1992; Anderson-Inman & Tenny, 1989; Anderson-Inman & Zeitz, 1994; Horney, Zeitz, & Anderson-Inman, 1991); other strategies had emerged as solutions to specific academic tasks that participating students found to be problematic. Underlying all of the strategies was an emphasis on active mental engagement, supported by software for information access, organization, and manipulation. Overall, there was an emphasis on using the power of the computer to minimize the negative effects of students' learning disabilities and to enhance their sense of personal responsibility for school performance.

Described below are three of the computer-based study strategies taught to students participating in Project SUCCESS. In the interest of simplicity, all three of the study strategies described below can be implemented using only one piece of software, Inspiration 4.0 (Inspiration Software, Inc., 1994). Inspiration is a computer-based information-organizing program that allows its users to create electronic outlines and diagrams. Although the program was originally designed for planners and writers in the world of business, computer-using educators have found an array of uses for the flexible "thought processor" (Tenny, 1990). There are many other good electronic outlining programs on the market, but Inspiration is unique in that its outliner is fully integrated with a graphics component, thereby enabling students to change outlines into diagrams and vice versa. Furthermore, Inspiration's graphical interface is so flexible that (a) diagrams of various types can be created (e.g., concept maps, semantic webs, flow charts, etc.); (b) diagrams can be individualized to present information in uniquely personal ways; and (c) information (in the form of text and/or graphics) can be attached to any symbol in the diagram. Taken together, these features provide teachers and students with a wealth of options for using the software as a tool for studying and learning content area material. The following three strategies illustrate some of the options we found to be particularly effective for students with learning disabilities.

Real-Time Note Taking.   Being able to take meaningful notes in lecture-type classes is an important survival skill at the secondary level. Unfortunately, students with learning disabilities often have trouble taking notes and then using those notes to study for tests or complete an assignment. Poor organizational skills, distractibility, spelling problems, and illegible handwriting frequently combine to sabotage successful note taking for this population (McGuire & O'Donnell, 1989; Reid, 1988). One of the computer-based study strategies introduced to students in Project SUCCESS was "real-time note taking," a strategy in which they learned to use their portable computers and Inspiration to record and organize information presented in class by the teacher or other students.

Figure 9.1 presents a sample of the notes generated by a seventh-grade student at Ware Middle School. The electronic outline contains main ideas and details that the student gleaned from watching two episodes of Channel One, a 10-minute news program designed specifically

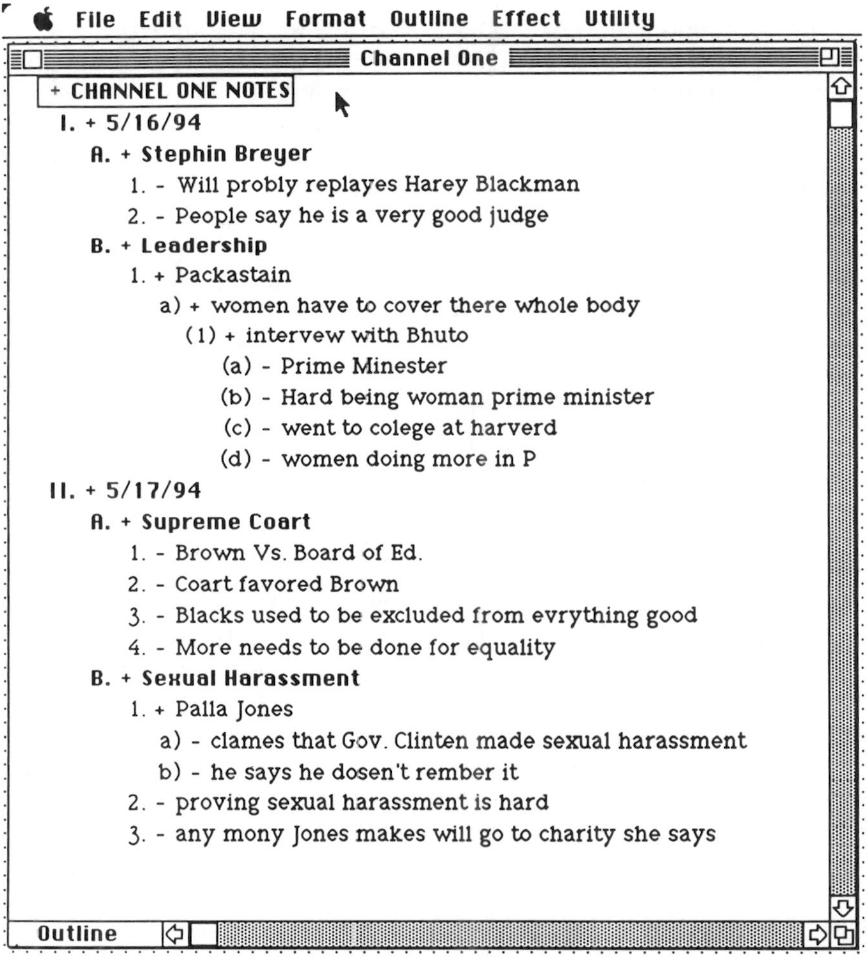

File   Edit   View   Format   Outline   Effect   Utility

Channel One

+ CHANNEL ONE NOTES

I. + 5/16/94
   A. + Stephin Breyer
      1. - Will probly replayes Harey Blackman
      2. - People say he is a very good judge
   B. + Leadership
      1. + Packastain
         a) + women have to cover there whole body
            (1) + intervew with Bhuto
               (a) - Prime Minester
               (b) - Hard being woman prime minister
               (c) - went to colege at harverd
               (d) - women doing more in P
II. + 5/17/94
   A. + Supreme Coart
      1. - Brown Vs. Board of Ed.
      2. - Coart favored Brown
      3. - Blacks used to be excluded from evrything good
      4. - More needs to be done for equality
   B. + Sexual Harassment
      1. + Palla Jones
         a) - clames that Gov. Clinten made sexual harassment
         b) - he says he dosen't rember it
      2. - proving sexual harassment is hard
      3. - any mony Jones makes will go to charity she says

Outline

Figure 9.1   Class notes using electronic outliner.

for adolescents. Because students in the school watch the program every day and because the format is relatively consistent, it was an ideal forum for teaching students real-time note taking and provided an excellent opportunity for daily practice of their note-taking skills. Misspellings in the Figure 9.1 outline reveal that this is the type of work the student can produce "on the fly" and without accessing the spell checker provided with Inspiration. The notes are clearly readable and take advantage of the hierarchical structure inherent in an outline. One of the benefits of using an electronic outlining program for this type of activity is that the notes are automatically formatted into an outline. Headings and subheadings can be manipulated as needed to reflect the organizational structure of the material being recorded. Details can be easily distinguished from main ideas, and multiple details can be inserted in such a way that they are easily separated from each other.

Figure 9.2 presents a concept map generated by a seventh-grade student at Ware Middle School as he listened to a debate in English class. The debate topic was "Students should not have to go to school." The map clearly distinguishes between arguments that agree and disagree

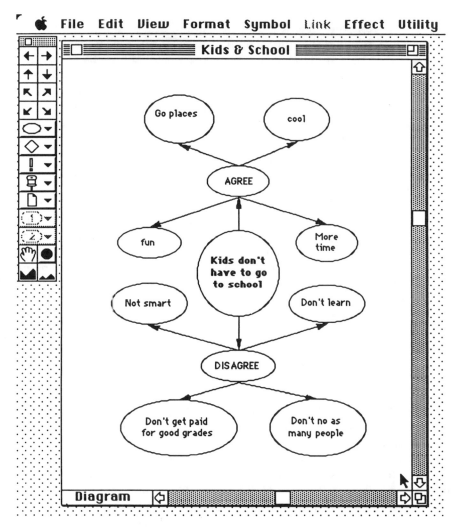

Figure 9.2   Class notes using electronic concept mapper.

with the topic and provides a concise summary of the ideas presented. Although the same information could have been recorded in outline form, this student's tool of choice was the portion of Inspiration that allowed him to create concept maps. We found that for some students with learning disabilities, the graphic nature of concept mapping was friendly and facilitating. By definition, there is a reduced need to generate text and the resulting product can be reviewed quickly.

Studying a Textbook.   A common expectation for students at the secondary level is the reading and studying of information presented in content area textbooks. Students with learning disabilities, however, are often unsuccessful in meeting this expectation due to poor reading skills and organizational difficulties. To help students with this type of activity, we taught them a study process that takes advantage of the structured yet flexible nature of computer-based information organizers. Although students were initially taught the strategy using an electronic outlining program, they also learned to implement the process using a concept-mapping program. (For a more detailed description of the process, the reader is referred to Anderson-Inman, 1995/1996, or Anderson-Inman and Tenny, 1989.)

Research staff taught participating students that studying a textbook chapter using electronic outliners or concept-mapping programs is a three-step process. First, each student was taught to create a skeleton of a chapter by typing in the chapter's headings and subheadings. This gave him or her an overview of the chapter's structure and its major topics. For example, the outline to the left in Figure 9.3 shows the headings and subheadings from a section of text in a book on American government. The computer was helpful in this process because subheadings were indented a standard amount and all headings/subheadings were labeled (numbered) automatically. The concept map to the left in Figure 9.4 shows the three major headings in a section of text on agricultural water pollution.

Second, students were taught to read each paragraph in a section carefully and record key words or phrases of its main ideas. If creating an outline, students were taught to insert these ideas into the skeleton under their appropriate headings or subheadings (see Figure 9.3). If creating a concept map, they were taught to insert them as informational nodes linked to a major heading node. Note that Inspiration allows users to individualize the shape of the nodes in a concept map, making it easy for students to clarify which nodes are headings and which nodes are summarized details (see Figure 9.4). This crystallization of the chapter's content into key words and phrases requires active processing of the text and manipulation of the information into something that is personally meaningful to the student.

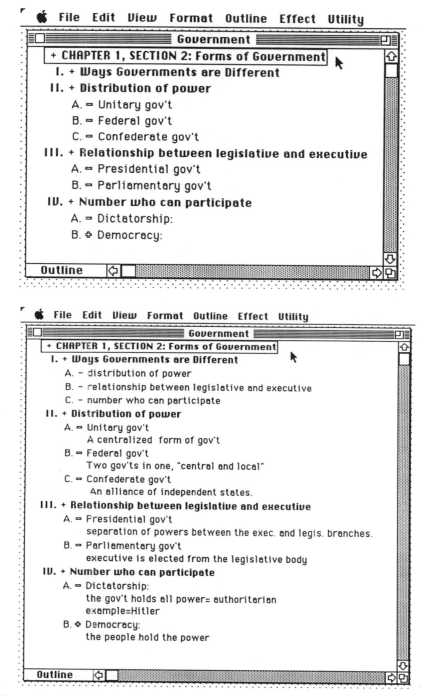

Figure 9.3   Studying a textbook using electronic outliner.

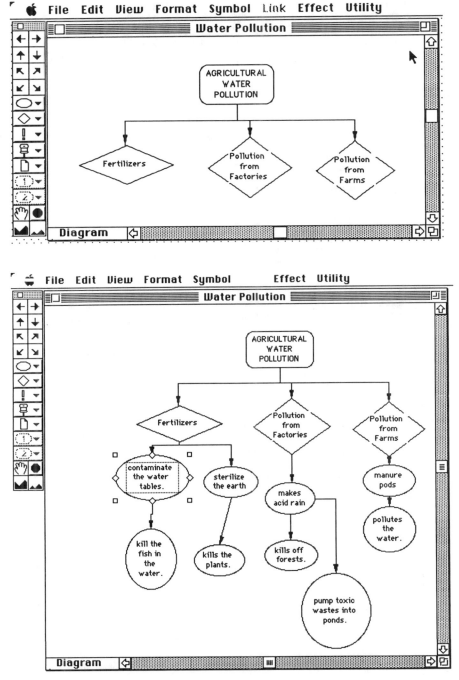

Figure 9.4   Studying a textbook using electronic concept mapper.

And third, students were taught to systematically self-test their knowledge of the information in the outline or concept map. Self-testing with an electronic outline is accomplished by expanding and contracting portions of the outline to hide or show material under each heading. Students were coached to ask themselves (a) How many? (b) What are they? and (c) What more do I know? When using a concept map, self-testing is accomplished by (1) electing to show only the nodes up to a certain level or (2) opening and closing a window for notes that can be attached to any node. With either procedure the student is taught to use the same self-testing questions to rehearse the content in the unseen levels or in the unseen notes. This self-testing gives students an opportunity to monitor their comprehension of the chapter and direct their study efforts to the most troublesome topics. Self-monitoring of study progress is a particularly important concern for students with learning disabilities, as they are frequently out of touch with what they know and do not know.

This three-step study process provided participating students with the structure they needed to identify and learn important information from text-based materials. The act of creating a hierarchical framework and then summarizing text to add to that framework requires learners to organize and synthesize the information they are trying to learn. The process of self-testing provides feedback to students on how well they comprehend and remember what is being studied. Self-testing has long been recommended as a study procedure because it strengthens the students' ability to reconstruct a mental representation of newly learned material. When students can correctly and consistently identify the material under any given heading without expanding the outline (or showing more nodes) to prompt their responses, that information can be considered "learned." In a quantitative synthesis of research on the effects of metacognitive strategies for reading comprehension, Haller, Child, and Walberg (1988) found that teaching students to use self-questioning strategies was one of the most effective ways to increase text comprehension.

Synthesizing Materials.   Writing papers and reports that require the synthesis of information from a variety of sources is another common expectation for students in secondary-level content area classes. Unfortunately, students with learning disabilities often experience frustration and failure when asked to (a) locate multiple sources on a topic, (b) read and extract important facts/ideas from each source, (c) record key pieces of information so they can be retrieved at a later time, and (d) synthesize this information into an original document that illustrates understanding of the topic. To help Project SUCCESS students accomplish this array of tasks with a minimum of trouble, research staff developed a strategy for using electronic outlining or concept mapping as a vehicle for recording and synthesizing information from multiple sources. The process includes three basic steps: (1) creating a topical outline or concept map, (2) reading and inserting information, and (3) organizing the information into conceptual units. (For a detailed description of this process, the reader is referred to Anderson-Inman and Zeitz, 1994).

Figure 9.5 presents an electronic outline developed by Veronica, a high school student at Riverview. In her class on criminal law she had been assigned to write a profile of a specific type of criminal, using a real

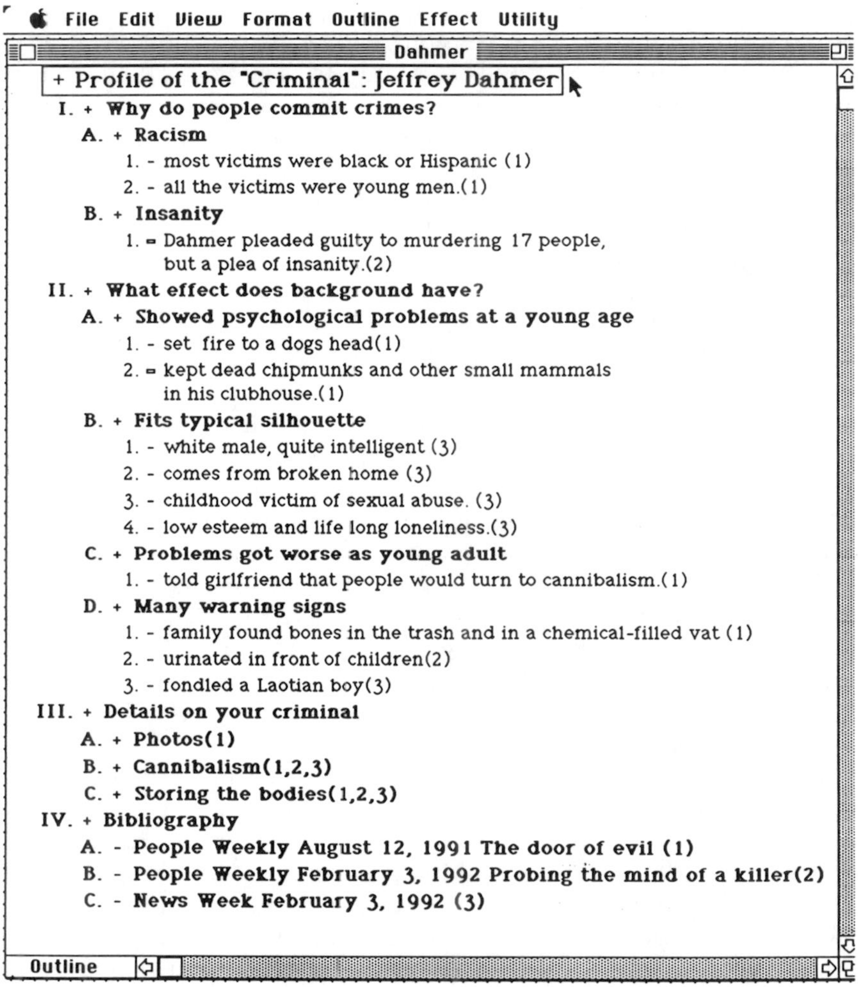

```
 ⬛  File  Edit  View  Format  Outline  Effect  Utility
═══════════════════════════ Dahmer ═══════════════════════
 + Profile of the "Criminal": Jeffrey Dahmer ▲
   I. + Why do people commit crimes?
      A. + Racism
         1. - most victims were black or Hispanic (1)
         2. - all the victims were young men.(1)
      B. + Insanity
         1. = Dahmer pleaded guilty to murdering 17 people,
            but a plea of insanity.(2)
  II. + What effect does background have?
      A. + Showed psychological problems at a young age
         1. - set fire to a dogs head(1)
         2. = kept dead chipmunks and other small mammals
            in his clubhouse.(1)
      B. + Fits typical silhouette
         1. - white male, quite intelligent (3)
         2. - comes from broken home (3)
         3. - childhood victim of sexual abuse. (3)
         4. - low esteem and life long loneliness.(3)
      C. + Problems got worse as young adult
         1. - told girlfriend that people would turn to cannibalism.(1)
      D. + Many warning signs
         1. - family found bones in the trash and in a chemical-filled vat (1)
         2. - urinated in front of children(2)
         3. - fondled a Laotian boy(3)
 III. + Details on your criminal
      A. + Photos(1)
      B. + Cannibalism(1,2,3)
      C. + Storing the bodies(1,2,3)
  IV. + Bibliography
      A. - People Weekly August 12, 1991 The door of evil (1)
      B. - People Weekly February 3, 1992 Probing the mind of a killer(2)
      C. - News Week February 3, 1992 (3)

 Outline
```

Figure 9.5 Materials synthesis using electronic outliner.

person for illustration. She chose to examine the profile of serial killers and selected Jeffrey Dahmer as her example. The first step was to create a topical outline, in this case using the topics assigned by the teacher. Hence, her outline contained three major topics: (a) why people commit crimes, (b) the effect of background, and (c) details about her criminal. The fourth major heading, bibliography, was included so that information about her sources could be integrated into the outline. The second step was to read and insert information into the outline from each of her three sources. Each detail that she thought might be relevant was inserted under the appropriate topic and labeled with a number indicating the source in which she found the information.

At various points in the process, Veronica combined the details she had inserted into conceptual units. For example, the details about Jeffrey Dahmer that she listed under the first topic, why people commit crimes, suggested two possible motivations: racism and insanity. Because the student was using an electronic outliner instead of doing this on paper, she could easily insert the subheadings and arrange the details under them accordingly. The student used a similar process to organize information under the second and third topics. The resulting product is an outline that (a) shows the student can synthesize information from a variety of sources and (b) serves as a good starting point for writing her report. By having the bibliographic references included in the outline and cross-referenced with the information under each heading, Veronica could easily document where her information came from and recheck it if discrepancies arose during the process.

Figure 9.6 presents a concept map that was constructed in much the same way. The report was to be written about Kublai Khan, grandson of the great Genghis Khan. The five major topics to be addressed were Life Style, Appearance, Accomplishments, Family, and Palaces. Under each major topic the student entered various details gleaned from reading multiple sources To indicate which source provided which details, the student altered the shape of the node. The key for these sources was attached to the bibliography node, and the details about each source were written into a notes window. The full bibliographic reference for the student's second source is displayed in Figure 9.6, as are the notes for the node "paper money." Once such a detailed concept map was created, the student was ready to start writing the report. The fact that the concept map is electronic means it was easily modifiable during this process of information gathering and organization. Details could be inserted anywhere and the system would automatically rearrange itself to accommodate the new information. This flexibility appeared to be extremely helpful to students with learning disabilities, as there was minimal need for advance planning and lots of opportunity for revision.

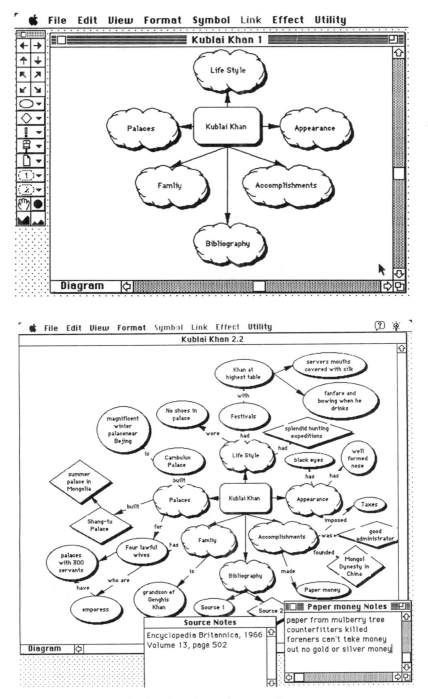

Figure 9.6   Materials synthesis using electronic concept mapper.

Instrumentation and Data Collection

Information on the learning characteristics of participating students was collected at various times throughout the project. Because much of the preexisting data on students had been acquired using a variety of standardized tests, administered under various conditions at uncontrolled times in the students' school careers, time and energy was committed to acquiring up-to-date information on various dimensions of student learning felt to be relevant to the project. An educational psychologist specializing in diagnostic procedures for adolescent and adult students with learning disabilities was hired to administer a battery of intelligence and literacy tests to all participating students. In addition, research staff collected information about study skills, handwriting speed, and keyboarding fluency. Each of the instruments used is described below, along with details concerning its administration and the type of data that emerged. Also described are the more informal data-collection procedures that were instituted throughout the 2 years of full-scale project implementation: student observations, student and teacher interviews, as well as the collection of student assignments and study materials.

Intelligence Tests. A standardized intelligence test was administered to each participating student by a licensed educational psychologist 4 to 5 weeks into the project's second implementation year. For 23 of the students, this was at the beginning of their second full year in the project. Three of the remaining students had been in the project for a portion of the previous year, and 4 students had just started their involvement in the project. Students were tested individually in private conference rooms at their respective schools. The Wechsler Intelligence Scale for Children–Third Edition (WISC-III; Wechsler, 1991) was administered to students under the age of 17. All subtests were administered. The WISC-III includes six verbal subtests and seven performance subtests (although only five of the latter are used in the calculation of students' intelligence scores). Three composite scores are derived from the data: a Verbal IQ, a Performance IQ, and a Full Scale IQ. In addition, the WISC-III provides diagnostic information leading to an assessment of four factors related to cognitive ability: verbal comprehension, perceptual comprehension, freedom from distractibility, and processing speed. The Wechsler Adult Intelligence Scale–Revised (WAIS-R; Wechsler, 1981) was administered to participating students who were 17 years of age or older. Again, all subtests, including six verbal subtests and five performance subtests, were administered. Raw scores were used to calculate a Verbal IQ, Performance IQ, and Full Scale IQ for each student.

Literacy Tests. Two types of literacy tests were administered to participating students: a measure of reading and a measure of writing. The

Woodcock Reading Mastery Tests–Revised, Form H (WRMT-R; Woodcock, 1987), were used to assess students' reading skills on four dimensions: word identification, word attack, word comprehension, and passage comprehension. The Word Identification test requires students to recognize (read aloud) individual words, presented in isolation. The Word Attack test assesses a student's ability to use phonic and structural analysis skills to decode nonsense words. The Word Comprehension test includes three subtests: an Antonyms subtest, which asks a student to provide a word that means the opposite of a target word; a Synonyms subtest, which asks a student to provide a word that means the same as a target word; and an Analogies subtest, which requires a student to state the relationship between two pairs of words. Each test and subtest were individually administered to participating students under the same conditions as the IQ tests described above and by the same educational psychologist. The tests were administered during the students' fifth or sixth week of school during that academic year. As described above, for most students this was at the beginning of their second year in the project. Raw scores were converted into standard scores that have a mean of 100 and a standard deviation of 15. Percentile ranks and grade-level equivalents were also calculated for each test and for the battery as a whole (a score of "Total Reading").

To assess students' writing abilities, two subtests from the Diagnostic Achievement Test for Adolescents (DATA-2; Newcomer & Bryant, 1993) were administered. The DATA-2 is a reliable, valid, and nationally standardized measure of academic achievement for students between the ages of 12 and 18. Of its 13 subtests, 2 were administered to participating students—a test of spelling and a test of written composition. Using a standard spelling dictation format (word, sentence, word repeated), the Spelling subtest determines spelling aptitude by requiring students to write words that follow both regular and irregular phonetic rules. The Spelling subtest was administered to participating students individually by the same educational psychologist who administered the IQ and reading tests described above. It was administered during the same testing session as the WRMT-R. The Written Composition subtest is designed to measure written expressive language by asking students to compare a short story based on three stimulus pictures. It was administered by the project's research staff to students at each school as a group, approximately 1 month after the Spelling subtest. For both subtests, raw scores were converted to standard scores that have a mean of 10 and a standard deviation of 3. In addition, standard scores for the two subtests combined were used to compute a "composite quotient." The composite score was derived by adding students' standard scores for the two subtests and converting the sum to a quotient having a mean of 100 and a standard deviation of 15.

Study Skills Tests.   To assess students' study skills, research staff administered the Learning and Study Strategies Inventory–High School Version (LASSI-HS; Weinstein & Palmer, 1990). The LASSI-HS contains 76 self-report items designed to measure the thought processes and behaviors associated with studying and learning at the secondary level. The test items cover 10 scales: Attitude, Motivation, Time Management, Anxiety, Concentration, Information Processing, Selecting Main Ideas, Study Aids, Self Testing, and Test Strategies. Test items are presented as either positive or negative statements, and students must decide whether a statement is *not at all like me, not very much like me, somewhat like me, fairly much like me,* or *very much like me.* Student responses are rated on a 5-point Likert scale. Raw scores for each scale are the total of all points earned on items included in that scale and can be converted to percentiles. The LASSI-HS was administered by research staff to participating students either individually or in small groups at their respective schools. The test was administered during the second or third week of their participation in the project. For most students, the test took 15 to 20 minutes to complete.

As a supplement to the study skills assessment, research staff measured student's handwriting and keyboarding speeds three times throughout the 2-year implementation period: once in the spring of the first year and twice in the second year (fall and spring). Students were provided with 5" × 7" cards containing passages written at the seventh-grade level. These were developed using passages that appeared in the Ekvall Reading Inventory (Ekvall, 1986). One card contained a 142-word passage about spiders and the other card contained a 157-word passage about cats. Both passages were expository in tone and straightforward in content. Either individually or in small groups, students were presented with one of the cards and asked to copy, writing by hand on paper, as much as possible in a 5-minute period. Students were then presented with the other card and asked to copy, typing on their portable computers, as much as possible in 5 minutes. Research staff counted the number of words copied under each condition and then computed the words per minute (WPM) written by hand and written using the computer. No adjustment was made for spelling errors.

Student Activities and Products.   Throughout the duration of the implementation period, a variety of procedures was used to monitor student activities, reactions, and products. Research staff met with participating students at their schools approximately once each week to provide instruction on electronic study strategies and technical assistance on using the computer. At periodic intervals, these visits were used to conduct informal interviews with the students or their teachers. These interviews were either audiotaped or videotaped and later transcribed or logged. Transcriptions resulted in a verbatim record of the taped interview; logging resulted in a more rough record of what was discussed, divided into conceptual chunks and demarcated by time. The purpose of the logs was to provide research staff with easy access to material on the audio- or videotape, without the labor-intensive process of creating verbatim transcripts.

Research staff also conducted periodic observations of participating students in their general education classes. Field notes of these observations were recorded in real time using an electronic outlining program on portable computers. These were combined with "contact reports" (typed summaries of each visit to a school), to provide research staff with ongoing information about what students were doing to learn and apply computer-based study strategies for the purposes of completing school assignments and meeting the expectations of their content area classes. In addition, research staff regularly collected electronic copies of students' study materials and assignments, as well as paper copies of teachers' syllabi, assignment descriptions, and tests taken by students. These paper and electronic products were organized chronologically by student and school and used to monitor student success in the program, as well as to identify individual needs for instruction or technical assistance.

Data Analysis

For the purpose of understanding observed differences in how students used and applied their knowledge of computer-based study strategies, we adopted a four-step data analysis process. First, research staff created three categories representing different adoption levels. These categories reflected the general differences observed by research staff when working with students at their schools. Research staff then assigned a label to each category and developed a list of descriptors for the behaviors that would help to distinguish among the three adoption levels. Second, research staff reviewed each student's file (observations, interviews, activities, and products) and placed him or her into one of the three categories, using the descriptors as decision guidelines. This process was conducted during the seventh month (March) of the second implementation year (1994–95).

Third, data from students' intelligence tests, literacy tests, and study skills tests were subjected to statistical analyses to determine the extent to which any of these variables were correlated with group membership. One-way ANOVAs were conducted to test for differences in mean scores across the three groups on each test or subtest. Because of the large number of tests conducted at one time (25), the data were subjected to a Bonferroni adjustment to control for inflated Type I error. Fourth, all quantitative and qualitative data on participating students were examined to help understand the statistical results. Due to the small sample size, unequal numbers in each group, and failure to meet the criteria for conducting an analysis of variance, the study must be viewed as exploratory and the results as only suggestive of possible trends.

RESULTS

Adoption Levels

Students participating in Project SUCCESS differed greatly in the extent to which they adopted the computer-based study strategies taught to them. Three types of students were found: (a) Power Users, (b) Prompted Users, and (c) Reluctant Users. Described below are the distinguishing characteristics of each adoption group.

Power Users. Students in this group became very skilled in using their portable computers and used the technology to complete as much of their schoolwork as possible. The students developed extensive repertoires of computer-based study strategies from which to choose, and they learned to select appropriate strategies for the academic tasks expected of them. Power Users showed considerable independence and skill in using the technology and applying various electronic study strategies. In some cases, students in this group even developed their own electronic study strategies to meet novel academic demands or to move beyond the suggestions made by research staff. Their willingness to use the computer and accompanying study strategies appeared to be intrinsically motivated, independent of teacher support or input from research staff. When obstacles arose, these students had the persistence to find solutions or the willingness to work around the inconvenience. Sometimes this meant teaching themselves new things about the computer or being proactive in obtaining better access to scarce resources, such as printers. In short, Power Users completely "partnered" with their computer (Salomon et al., 1991), relying on it to assist them in performing up to their full academic potential in school. At the time that we identified students with adoption levels, there were 7 students who fell into this category.

Prompted Users. Students in this group developed moderate to excellent skills in using the computer. They learned to use a variety of computer-based study strategies and applied what they had learned to complete many of their school assignments. Although Prompted Users could use the computer more or less independently for assignment production, they continued to need prompting and assistance to move beyond these basic applications. For example, most students in this group saw the computer as their tool of choice when expected to write something for a class assignment, using both a word processor and spell checker to produce a legible product. None, however, used the computer on a regular basis to take notes in class or develop outlines for studying the material in a textbook chapter unless specifically asked to do so. Furthermore, Prompted Users were unlikely to generate new uses of the computer for studying and were not very proactive in seeking out new ideas from research staff. Nonetheless, these students had a positive attitude about using the computer for school and would not want it to be taken away. At the time that we identified students with adoption levels, there were 16 students who fell into this category.

Reluctant Users.   Students in this group had basic to moderate skills in using the computer. Although they used their laptops for some school assignments, students in this group developed only limited knowledge of computer-based study strategies and rarely used what knowledge they had except under direct teacher supervision. Reluctant Users remained quite dependent in their use of the technology, failing to apply what they knew, even when there was evidence that such application would result in better grades. Some of the students in this group liked the computer but failed to use it for academic purposes; other students in this group demonstrated a distaste for the computer that seemed to mirror their distaste for school. Some of the students in this group moved in and out of Project SUCCESS based on their willingness to participate in school and abide by school rules. Others just seemed to drift away from the project. Clearly, having access to portable computers and knowledge of electronic study strategies was not a powerful enough intervention for these students to overcome the many barriers that plagued their road to school success. At the time that we identified students with adoption levels, there were 7 students who fell into this category. It would be appropriate, however, to also consider the 3 students who voluntarily dropped out of the program during or after the first year as Reluctant Users.

Learner Characteristics Associated with Adoption Level

Intelligence.   Table 9.2 presents scores from the intelligence tests administered under the auspices of Project SUCCESS (i.e., not the scores administered by school district personnel to determine eligibility for special education services). Students (using pseudonyms) are arranged

TABLE 9.2
Intelligence Test Scores for Students, by Adoption Level

Student	Full Scale IQ	Verbal IQ	Performance IQ
Power users			
Lee (W)	108	115	99
Rick (W)	117	123	108
Veronica (R)	113	101	125
William (R)	116	110	121
Chad (R)	109	97	128
Bud (R)	107	102	112
Rebecca (R)	102	101	102
Prompted users			
Brian (W)	77	82	77
Ryan (W)	91	90	94
Jeff (W)	93	90	99
Butch (W)	89	88	94
Brady (P)	96	95	98
Felix (P)	108	93	113
Grace (P)	90	89	94
Sady (P)	95	87	103
Thor (P)	110	108	111
Shelby (P)	88	88	91
Cindy (R)	86	81	95
Harry (R)	84	97	73
Mickey (R)	95	90	102
Chico (R)	94	85	108
Sara (R)	92	87	99
Don (R)	83	82	87
Reluctant users			
Duane (W)	84	81	90
Avon (W)	85	81	93
Mike (P)	99	97	102
Brittany (P)	88	81	99
Ed (P)	86	81	74
Reuban (P)	73	76	74
Susie (P)	64	67	66

Note. W = Ware Middle School; P = Piper Middle School; R = Riverview High School.

by adoption level, with an initial following each name to show which school the student attended. For each student, three IQ scores are provided: a Full Scale IQ, a Verbal IQ and a Performance IQ. As noted previously, these scores were derived from the WISC-III for students under the age of 17 and the WAIS-R for students 17 and older. Scores of 80 to 119, inclusive, are considered to be in the average range (on a continuum of low average to high average), whereas scores of 120 and above are judged to reflect intelligence that is either superior or very superior. Based on Full Scale IQ scores in Table 9.2, it is clear that all but 3 of the students were tested as having average or above-average intelligence. Of the 3 exceptions, one was a Prompted User and 2 were Reluctant Users. From examining Performance IQ scores, it is clear that at least 3 of the students were tested as having superior intelligence in that domain and that all three were Power Users. An additional Power User tested in the superior range of the Verbal IQ scale.

To gain preliminary insight into whether intelligence scores could be used to predict who might benefit the most from the combined intervention of portable computers and electronic study strategies, we compared adoption group means using one-way analyses of variance. Table 9.3 presents the mean IQ scores and standard deviations for students at each of the three adoption levels. Statistical analyses revealed that F ratios for all three measures of intelligence were significant: Full Scale IQ, $F(2, 27) = 19.83$, $p < .001$; Verbal IQ, $F(2, 27) = 20.92$, $p < .001$; and Performance IQ, $F(2, 27) = 10.36$, $p < .001$. In addition, mean scores on all three measures favored the Power Users, with a consistent trend of decreasing IQ associated with decreased use of the computer for purposes of electronic studying. These results suggest that intelligence, as measured by IQ tests, is positively associated with adoption level.

Literacy.   Table 9.4 presents scores from two types of literacy tests, one that measures reading achievement (WRMT-R) and one that measures writing achievement (DATA-2). Students are arranged by adoption level, followed by standard scores for each test and subtest. Also included are grade-level equivalents for the WRMT-R and percentile rankings for the two DATA-2 subtests and composite score. From Table 9.4 it is clear that the literacy skills of students in Project SUCCESS varied considerably. Most of the students in the Power User group appeared to be reading at the ninth-grade level or above (as judged by grade-level equivalents

TABLE 9.3
Mean IQ Scores of Students, by Adoption Level

	Adoption level					
	Power users[a]		Prompted users[b]		Reluctant users[a]	
Test	$\overline{X}$	(SD)	$\overline{X}$	(SD)	$\overline{X}$	(SD)
Full Scale IQ	110.29	(5.35)	91.94	(8.39)	82.71	(11.22)*
Verbal IQ	107.00	(9.36)	89.50	(6.65)	80.57	(8.90)*
Performance IQ	113.57	(11.36)	96.13	(10.87)	85.43	(14.00)*

[a]$n = 7$. [b]$n = 16$.
*$p < .001$.

TABLE 9.4
Literacy Test Scores for Students, by Adoption Level

Student	WRMT-R					DATA-2		
	WI	WA	WC	PC	TR	Spell	WC	CQ
	(Grade equivalents)					(Percentiles)		
Power users								
Lee (W)	3.3	1.6	3.7	6.4	3.3	2	16	73
Rick (W)	7.7	6.7	11.3	16.5	10.5	16	75	42
Veronica (R)	7.7	4.1	10	15.6	9.2	9	25	12
William (R)	10.1	16.9	14.4	16.9	14.3	37	50	42
Chad (R)	6.6	2.9	7.9	4.9	5.6	2	25	5
Bud (R)	10.1	4.6	16.6	13.8	12.4	9	<1	<1
Rebecca (R)	7.4	5.9	9.3	16.5	9.7			
Prompted users								
Brian (W)	4.9	3	2.6	2.9	3.4	1	63	12
Ryan (W)	6.3	16.9	3.8	7.3	6.4	9	16	8
Jeff (W)	4.8	2.8	4.8	4.2	4.4	2	50	12
Butch (W)	3.9	2	4.1	6	3.7	2	16	<1
Brady (P)	4.9	4.1	4.4	6	5			
Felix (P)	4.7	3.7	4.2	2.9	3.8	5	5	2
Grace (P)	4.8	3.2	4.8	3.9	4.4	9	50	21
Sady (P)	3.8	3	4.4	7.8	4.4	9	25	12
Thor (P)	5.3	1.9	7	9	5.2	9	50	21
Shelby (P)	4.8	2.8	3.5	3.1	3.6	2	37	8
Cindy (R)	9.7	12.7	5.4	16.9	10.1	25	75	50
Harry (R)	5.5	5.9	10	5.6	6.4	9	25	12
Mickey (R)	5.3	5.2	7.5	10.7	6.6	9	50	21
Chico (R)	5.7	2.9	5.4	12.9	6	5	1	<1
Sara (R)	16.9	16.9	10.8	16.9	16.9	63	1	12
Don (R)	15.3	16.9	10.4	16.9	14.8	25	25	21
Reluctant users								
Duane (W)	1.6	1.4	1.6	1.2	1.5	1	<1	<1
Avon (W)	2.1	1.4	2.2	2	2.1	2	16	3
Mike (P)	7.4	16.9	5.2	4.5	6.8	9	25	12
Brittany (P)	6	7.9	4.9	6.4	6	9	50	21
Ed (P)	3.3	1.8	3	2.9	2.8	2	25	5
Reuban (P)	3.9	4.6	3	4.9	3.7	1	9	1
Susie (P)	5.2	4.1	3.9	4.2	4.6	2	9	2

Note. W = Ware Middle School; P = Piper Middle School; R = Riverview High School. WRMT-R = Woodcock Reading Mastery Test–Revised; WI = Word Identification; WA = Word Attack; WC = Word Comprehension; PC = Passage Comprehension; TR = Total Reading; DATA-2 = Diagnostic Achievement Test for Adolescents (2nd ed.); Spell = Spelling; WC = Written Composition; CQ = Composite Quotient.

on the WRMT-R score for "Total Reading," or TR). The two exceptions were Chad and Lee. By comparison, most students in the Reluctant User group appeared to be reading below the fifth-grade level, with the two exceptions being Mike and Brittany.

The standard scores from both the WRMT-R and the DATA-2 were submitted to one-way ANOVAs to test for significant differences in means across groups. Table 9.5 presents the mean standard scores and standard deviations for each test and subtest on the two measures of literacy. Due to the Bonferroni adjustment, only p values of .002 or lower can be considered to indicate statistically significant F ratios. Given this criterion, differences in mean scores on the Word Identification subtest of the WRMT-R were not statistically significant. They were, however, suggestive, and in the direction predicted by visual analysis—$F(2, 27) = 3.472, p < .05$. Differences in mean scores on the Word Attack subtest were also not significant. F ratios for the Word Comprehension subtest were significant; $F(2, 27) = 9.953, p < .002$, and met the criterion established by the Bonferonni adjustment. F ratios for the Passage Comprehension subtest were not significant, given this criterion, but were close, $F(2, 27) = 6.895, p < .005$. Because the mean scores for Total Reading were a composite of all subtests, it is understandable that they were not statistically significant at the high level of confidence required by the Bonferonni adjustment. They were, however, suggestive and followed the same trend established by three of the reading subtests. In summary, results from Table 9.5 suggest that some reading skills varied systematically by adoption level and that the highest reading skills, on average, were associated with students in the Power User group.

Table 9.5 also presents means and standard deviations for two subtests from the DATA-2, as well as a composite quotient reflecting performance on both subtests combined. F ratios for the two subtests and the composite score for writing were not significant. Although a visual examination of the subtest means for spelling and written composition reveals the same trend in variance across groups as found in the reading scores, these differences were not found to be statistically significant. This is possibly because students in all three groups scored quite low, especially on the spelling subtest, leaving little room for significant variance in mean scores.

Study Skills.   Table 9.6 presents raw scores for students by adoption level on all 10 subtests of the LASSI-HS. The LASSI-HS was administered in the fall of the first full-scale implementation year. Students for whom there are no scores on the LASSI-HS in Table 9.6 started the program during the second full-scale implementation year so did not participate in this administration of the study skills tests. In addition, the table contains information about students' writing speed in words per minute

TABLE 9.5
Mean Literacy Test Scores of Students, by Adoption Level

Test	Adoption level					
	Power users[a]		Prompted users[b]		Reluctant users[a]	
	$\bar{X}$	(SD)	$\bar{X}$	(SD)	$\bar{X}$	(SD)
WRMT-R						
Word Identification	87.00	(11.48)	85.75	(11.85)	68.00	(25.81)**
Word Attack	87.43	(13.90)	89.31	(13.37)	80.71	(22.51)
Word Comprehension	100.57	(14.13)	86.13	(8.65)	72.00	(16.10)****
Passage Comprehension	104.29	(14.66)	91.75	(16.89)	67.57	(26.35)***
Total Reading	93.57	(13.81)	87.06	(11.64)	68.43	(24.72)*
DATA-2						
Spelling	6.00	(1.90)	5.60	(2.47)	4.29	(1.25)
Written Composition	10.46	(4.24)	5.82	(2.57)	3.40	(1.34)
Composite Quotient	81.00	(14.16)	81.00	(9.93)	71.43	(14.05)

Note. Homogeneity of variance assumption violated for WRMT-R–Word Identification.
[a] $n = 7$. [b] $n = 16$.
$*p < .02$. $**p < .05$. $***p < .005$. $****p < .002$.

TABLE 9.6
Study Skills Test Scores for Students, by Adoption Level

Student	ATT	MOT	TMT	ANX	CON	INP	SMI	STA	SFT	TST	HW	KB
					LASSI-HS						Writing speed (wpm)	

Student	LASSI-HS										Writing speed (wpm)	
	ATT	MOT	TMT	ANX	CON	INP	SMI	STA	SFT	TST	HW	KB
Power users												
Lee (W)	35	39	34	33	40	13	24	29	29	39	22	16
Rick (W)	21	21	13	26	18	26	18	18	16	29	19	22
Veronica (R)	31	27	13	13	17	21	11	18	26	28	18	13
William (R)	32	30	19	35	36	24	21	23	23	34	31	24
Chad (R)	21	25	12	15	18	19	9	16	16	18	17	35
Bud (R)	26	25	19	32	31	26	11	18	16	30	12	18
Rebecca (R)	33	37	26	29	26	25	20	25	28	25	28	38
Prompted users												
Brian (W)	23	26	20	27	21	22	15	14	11	26	18	13
Ryan (W)	25	26	21	22	16	27	9	25	18	22	17	27
Jeff (W)	26	30	25	29	27	28	19	31	32	21	23	11
Butch (W)	15	21	22	23	27	23	19	17	16	20	9.6	7.8
Brady (P)	28	21	19	22	21	26	13	21	19	24	16	24
Felix (P)											23	25
Grace (P)	29	33	21	20	22	7	10	14	22	16	15	23
Sady (P)	30	20	19	36	27	21	15	23	16	28	22	31
Thor (P)	30	23	18	28	26	23	16	19	20	31	16	11
Shelby (P)											23	12
Cindy (R)	37	32	23	33	29	22	18	22	23	29	29	22
Harry (R)	30	28	23	23	28	30	15	26	28	35	15	6
Mickey (R)	33	29	26	31	28	23	20	20	22	31	20	16

Table continues

TABLE 9.6. (cont.)

Student	LASSI-HS										Writing speed (wpm)	
	ATT	MOT	TMT	ANX	CON	INP	SMI	STA	SFT	TST	HW	KB
Chico (R)	26	23	17	20	18	17	11	18	17	20	17	17
Sara (R)	40	36	34	36	40	40	25	30	40	36	10	18
Don (R)											19	26
Reluctant users												
Duane (W)	29	24	13	20	23	23	10	26	26	25	22	11
Avon (W)	21	23	25	17	18	20	10	26	23	21	14	10
Mike (P)											23	13
Brittany (P)											16	15
Ed (P)	38	30	29	35	36	23	12	27	27	26	11	11
Reuban (P)												
Susie (P)	24	21	25	23	15	23	11	30	22	21	14	15

Note. W = Ware Middle School; P = Piper Middle School; R = Riverview High School. LASSI-HS = Learning & Study Skills Inventory–High School Version; ATT = Attitude; MOT = Motivation; TMT = Time management; ANX = Anxiety; CON = Concentration; INP = Information processing; SMI = Selecting main ideas; STA = Study aids; SFT = Self-testing; TST = Testing strategies; HW = handwriting; KB = keyboarding.

(WPM) under two conditions: writing by hand and keyboarding. The latter two tests were administered at the time that students were assigned to adoption levels and so are an indication of keyboard familiarity after participation in the program for a period of time ranging from 7 to 16½ months. (It should be remembered that all students, including those who joined the program late, had keyboarding experience prior to their participation in Project SUCCESS.) An examination of students' writing speeds reveals that some of the students had learned to keyboard faster than they could write by hand. This was true for 4 students in the Power User group, 7 students in the Prompted User group, and 1 student in the Reluctant User group. For another 6 students, keyboarding speed was above 15 words per minute: 2 students in the Power User group, 3 students in the Prompted User group, and 1 student in the Reluctant User group. These are the two criteria suggested in the literature as indicative of sufficient keyboarding speed to make word processing a useful mode for writing. In total, 18 of the 30 students had keyboarding speeds that met one or more of these criteria.

Table 9.7 presents mean scores and standard deviations by adoption level for all 10 subtests on the LASSI-HS and for the tests of writing speed. One-way ANOVAs on all subtests of the LASSI showed that none of the F ratios were significant. This suggests that students' study skills, at least as measured by the LASSI, did not vary systematically across adoption groups. Power was very low in this analysis, due to the missing scores for students who started the program during its second year. If this study is replicated in the future with a larger population of similar students, two subtests to watch are those labeled Selecting Main Ideas (SMI) and Study Aids (STA). F ratios were stronger for these two subtests than for any of the others. One-way ANOVAs on the two tests of writing speed revealed that keyboarding speed varied systematically across adoption level and was statistically significant at the .05 level of confidence, $F(2, 26) = 3.689$, $p < .05$. The importance of this finding is restricted by the fact that the data violate the homogeneity-of-variance assumption and that the confidence level does not meet the conservative criterion set by the Bonferonni adjustment ($p < .002$). Nonetheless, the data suggest that Power Users are generally better at keyboarding than students in either of the other two groups and that the differences across groups follow the trend suggested by students' scores on measures of intelligence and reading ability.

DISCUSSION

In summary, the data suggest that at least two learner characteristics are associated with adoption level in a systematic and statistically signifi-

TABLE 9.7
Mean Study Skills Test Scores, by Adoption Level

| | Adoption level | | | | | |
| Test | Power users[a] | | Prompted users[b] | | Reluctant users[a] | |
	$\overline{X}$	(SD)	$\overline{X}$	(SD)	$\overline{X}$	(SD)
LASSI-HS						
Attitude	28.43	(5.77)	28.62	(6.25)	28.00	(7.44)
Motivation	29.14	(6.64)	26.77	(5.09)	24.50	(3.87)
Time management	19.43	(8.10)	22.15	(4.43)	23.00	(6.93)
Anxiety	26.14	(8.80)	26.92	(5.77)	23.75	(7.89)
Concentration	26.57	(9.38)	25.39	(6.06)	23.00	(9.27)
Information processing	22.00	(4.76)	23.77	(7.52)	22.25	(1.50)
Selecting main ideas	16.29	(5.88)	15.77	(4.48)	10.75	(0.96)
Study aids	21.00	(4.76)	21.54	(5.41)	27.25	(1.89)
Self-testing	22.00	(5.92)	21.85	(7.68)	24.50	(2.38)
Testing strategies	29.00	(6.63)	26.08	(6.20)	23.25	(2.63)
Writing Speed						
By hand	21.04	(6.48)	18.15	(5.10)	16.97	(4.83)
Keyboarding	23.70	(9.55)	18.12	(7.58)	12.50	(2.21)*

[a] $n = 7$. [b] $n = 16$.
*$p < .05$. Homogeneity of variance assumption violated.

cant way: intelligence test scores and reading test scores. Specifically, the mean test scores for Power Users were consistently higher than those for either of the other two adoption levels on all three IQ scales, followed by mean scores for Prompted Users. The differences in mean scores across groups were statistically significant at the .001 level of confidence. This suggests that IQ may be a good predictor of students who will adopt and effectively use instruction on computer-based study strategies when provided with the opportunity and technology to do so.

Another good predictor may be students' achievement in reading. Differences in mean scores across groups for specific subtests of the WRMT-R were found to be statistically significant. Particularly interesting as possible predictors were students' scores on the Word Comprehension and Passage Comprehension subtests. The statistical analyses of reading achievement must be viewed with considerable caution, however. Because there is an unequal distribution of students by age across the three adoption levels, the differences in reading achievement may be more a reflection of student grade level than student ability in reading. On average, the high school students read at a higher level than the students from the two middle schools. As there were proportionately more high school students in the Power User group (71%) than in either of the other two groups (37.5% and 0%, respectively), the differences in mean scores on tests of reading achievement were probably a function of students' ages, not their relative success with reading.

Results also suggest that students' writing skills and study skills, at least as measured by the DATA-2 and the LASSI-HS, would not make good predictors of who might fully adopt a program of technology-supported studying using laptop computers and information-organizing software. Because the data are hampered by a small sample size and unequal groups, there is very little power to detect differences in mean scores. Replication of this study with a much larger population and additional tests of writing and study behavior would be advised before ruling out the possible utility of writing and study skills performance for predicting a student's likelihood of benefiting from a program of instruction on electronic study strategies.

IMPLICATIONS AND RECOMMENDATIONS

Results from this study are preliminary in nature and should be viewed as suggestive only. Nonetheless, it might be illustrative to imagine a scenario in which the conclusions from this study (and future replications) could be useful. The intervention described above is fairly expensive to implement. A portable computer must be purchased for each participating student, and instructional time must be devoted to teaching specific ways in which to use the computer for enhancing student success across the curriculum. If resources are limited (e.g., if a school has 10 computers for 25 students with learning disabilities), it would be important to deploy these resources to maximum advantage. Based on results from this exploratory study, we recommend that student selection focus on those with above-average intelligence and reading skills that are as close to grade level as possible. Results also suggest that if students are selected who do not meet these criteria, a more powerful intervention than the one described here should be considered.

Some suggestions for a successful program of instruction on computer-based study strategies also emerge from the data. First, good keyboarding skills seem to be associated with higher levels of adoption. Unfortunately, it is impossible to tell from these data which came first, good keyboarding skills or a willingness to use existing keyboarding skills in the interest of electronic studying and thereby improving keyboarding skills through practice. The data suggest, however, that students might be well served by instruction on, and lots of practice in, computer keyboarding. Student interviews support this focus, as many commented on the need to develop faster keyboarding skills in order to apply some of the study strategies they were learning in class (most specifically, in-class note taking). Many of the students, however, never perceived keyboarding speed to be important. The ability to produce legible assignments for class far outweighed any frustration that slow keyboarding may have brought to the process. This finding is consistent with work by Fais and Wanderman (1987), who found that although some students with learning disabilities were frustrated by slow keyboarding, for the vast majority, keyboarding was "a non-issue. As long as they didn't have to do the writing by hand, dysgraphic students weren't at all bothered by how long it took them to peck out their thoughts" (p. 14).

A successful electronic study skills program should also recognize that amount of instruction seems to be positively correlated with adoption level. Support for this conclusion can be seen from the data: More than half of the students in the Reluctant User group were new to the program during its second implementation year. These students may not have had the time to develop a wide range of computer-based study strategies or develop a real vision of how what they had learned would help them be better students in their classes. Supporting this conclusion is a comparison of the different implementation plans at the two middle schools. Implementation at Ware Middle School was much more intensive and more closely tied to the general education curriculum than that at Piper Middle School, at least during the first year. On average, this level of intensity in the instructional portion of the program seemed to boost students at Ware into adoption groups portraying a higher level of independence and application. Perhaps these students were better able, as a function of their more integrated instructional experiences, to see the utility of what they were learning and therefore to take it seriously.

Overall, we were both surprised and pleased to see students fall into different adoption groups. We were surprised because our previous experience had suggested that using the computer as a study tool would be a wonderful way to help all students with learning disabilities compensate for skill deficits that seemed to impinge on their chances for school success, and pleased because the differences help us to understand what might be needed to make the program even more successful than it was. Both the Power Users and the Prompted Users should be considered successful participants in the project, able to model what we tried to teach and currently on the road to being even more successful as students. Students in the Reluctant User group, however, could be considered our failures. For some, no matter what we tried, the combined use of portable technology and computer-based study strategies was not enough to overcome the many personal and environmental inhibitors they encountered on a day-to-day basis. Further research is needed to understand how to intervene with these students in a way that will make a significant difference in their lives.

AUTHORS' NOTE

The research reported in this chapter was funded by a grant from the Office of Special Education Programs, U.S. Department of Education (Award No. H180E20039).

NOTES

1. *Oregon's Administrative Rules (July 1994) state that for a child to be eligible for services as having a specific learning disability, a multidisciplinary team must determine that "the child has a severe discrepancy between achievement and intellectual ability in one or more of the following areas: (a) oral expression, (b) listening comprehension, (c) written expression, (d) basic reading skills, (e) reading comprehension, (f) mathematics calculation, or (g) mathematics reasoning"; that there is a "deficit in perception, conceptualization, language, memory, motor skills or control of attention" severe enough to require special education; and that the problems identified above are not the result of a sensory impairment, mental retardation, emotional disturbance, or socioeconomic disadvantage (8-Div. 15).*

2. *The missing student was unavailable for the testing presented as results later in this chapter and so was not included in this table.*

10. Assistive Technology for Postsecondary Students with Learning Disabilities

SHERYL L. DAY AND BARBARA J. EDWARDS

Assistive technology is defined by the Technology-Related Assistance Act of 1988 (P.L. 100-407) as any technology used to increase, maintain, or improve the functional capabilities of individuals with disabilities. Although assistive technology is recognized in the area of rehabilitation as a means to improve the quality of life for persons with physical disabilities, it has received little attention as a tool for helping individuals with learning disabilities (LD) to compensate for specific cognitive deficits. In the field of education, reports addressing the benefits of using assistive technology to compensate for specific learning disabilities have been generated primarily by professionals at the postsecondary level attempting to meet the needs of increasing numbers of students with learning disabilities attending college (Raskind, 1994).

As noted, an increasing number of students with learning disabilities are enrolling in and graduating from postsecondary institutions (Adelman & Vogel, 1992; Fairweather & Shaver, 1991; Henderson, 1992). In 1991, 8.8% of full-time college freshmen reported having some form of disability, compared with 2.6% in 1978. Of the types of disabilities reported, learning disabilities were the fastest growing group, increasing from 15% to 25% of all students with disabilities over the 13-year period (Henderson, 1992). A number of researchers (Rothstein, 1993; Shaw, McGuire, & Brinckerhoff, 1994; Vogel, 1993) have pointed to factors that result in increased numbers of individuals with disabilities attending postsecondary institutions:

1. The passage of Section 504 "E" of the Rehabilitation Act of 1973 mandated accessibility to postsecondary education for students with disabilities and required postsecondary institutions to provide "auxiliary aids," such as taped texts, to students with disabilities.

2. P.L. 94-142 and P.L. 101-406 mandated special education programs and services for elementary and secondary students with disabilities; as a result, more of these students are completing high school and view attending college, with the assistance of support services, as the next logical and viable step.

3. As a result of being placed in least restrictive environments, many students with disabilities have taken sufficient academic course work prerequisite to attending college.

4. Students with disabilities have become increasingly attractive to college admissions officers as a viable student market.

5. Advocacy groups and postsecondary guidebooks (e.g., Peterson's, Lovejoy's) have made these students aware of both their needs and their rights in regard to college options.

6. The increased availability of computers and other compensatory technology has resulted in greater student independence and access in the college setting.

   As students with learning disabilities attend college in increasingly large numbers, the impact of assistive technology on their ability to successfully complete postsecondary education is being recognized (Raskind, 1994; Raskind & Scott, 1993). Educational support service providers, in meeting the demands of these students, will likely rely on assistive technology. What do educational service providers need to know in order to provide effective assistive technology services to students with learning disabilities at the postsecondary level? The purposes of this chapter are to present types of assistive technologies appropriate for postsecondary students with learning disabilities, discuss ways in which assistive devices enhance learning, provide an overview of legislation affecting assistive technology at the postsecondary level, and present issues involving assistive technology at that level. Additionally, this chapter presents postsecondary assistive technology program components and provides guidelines on device selection and training.

Devices and Their Effect on Learning Abilities

Difficulties experienced by postsecondary students with learning disabilities include reading, organization, memory, listening, math, and written language. The majority of reports involving students with learning disabilities using assistive technology have investigated written language difficulties (e.g., Collins, 1990; Cutler, 1990; Primus, 1990; Raskind, 1994). This is not surprising, as estimates of the number of adults with learning disabilities who exhibit written language disorders range from 80% to 90% (Blalock, 1981).

For students with learning disabilities, the technologies available include word processors with spell checking, proofreading, abbreviation expanders (programs that allow students to type abbreviations for frequently used words or phrases and press the space bar to produce the complete word or phrase), and outlining software programs. Also available are variable speech-control tape recorders, optical character recognition systems (reading machines), listening aids (systems that use a microphone and headset designed for students with auditory deficits), speech-synthesis/screen-review systems (voice output systems that read back text displayed on the computer screen), speech-recognition systems (systems that allow the user to operate the computer by speaking to it), data managers (technologies that store personal information for students with organization and memory difficulties), and talking calculators.

These devices can enhance the individual's learning abilities by circumventing deficits. According to Garner and Campbell (1987), circumventing deficits is one of the two major purposes of assistive devices and is referred to as the *compensatory* approach. In this approach, an individual is helped to perform a specific task using assistive technology. For example, when a student acquires and listens to a taped version of the book that is to be read for English class in order to correctly answer comprehension questions about the material, his or her aim is to bypass a reading disability, not to learn to read. If, instead, the student wishes to improve his or her reading, the student might use a computer program to practice phonics skills. In this example, using assistive technology to learn to read exemplifies the second major purpose of assistive technology and is referred to as the *remedial* approach (Garner & Campbell, 1987). The purpose of this approach is to improve areas of deficiency. Of course, the two purposes may overlap. The compensatory strategy in which the student utilizes a taped book could possibly have remedial results if, while listening to the tape, the student follows along in the print version of the book, attempting to learn unfamiliar words.

Raskind (1994) suggested that although both remedial and compensatory approaches are beneficial for adults with learning disabilities, the compensatory approach "may offer the most expeditious means of addressing specific difficulties within particular contexts" (p. 159). Other researchers also support using compensatory approaches when providing services to adults with learning disabilities (e.g., Gray, 1981; Mangrum & Strichart, 1988; Vogel, 1987). The burnout that adults with LD experience as a result of years of remedial instruction that yielded little benefit, and the appeal of immediate solutions to particular problems, lend support to using a compensatory approach when using assistive technology with these adults (Raskind, 1994).

Current support for assistive technology also arises from a growing understanding of its positive effects. Greater independence and relief from anxiety are benefits noted by Barton and Fuhrmann (1994) for students with learning disabilities who use tools to free them from the drudgery imposed by their disability: "Sometimes a simple handheld spelling checker relieves more anxiety than hours of therapy" (p. 91). Other writers have noted a heightened sense of self-esteem in students with disabilities who gain competency with technology (Raskind, 1994), a reduction of reliance on others and a move toward independence (Brown, 1989), and a regaining of a sense of control leading to vocational success (Reiff, Gerber, & Ginsberg, 1992).

The advantages of using assistive technology are numerous, as outlined above. However, the current literature regarding assistive technology focuses on the technology itself (hardware and software). There is no empirical research demonstrating the effectiveness of specific technologies in compensating for specific types of disabilities.

LEGISLATION ADDRESSING ASSISTIVE TECHNOLOGY

Lawmakers recognize the need for assistive technology; this section provides an overview of federal assistive technology-related legislation that affects postsecondary students with disabilities.

Section 504

Legislation mandating access to adaptive computer technology systems and services includes Section 504 of the 1973 Rehabilitation Act. This law mandates accessibility to postsecondary education for "otherwise qualified" students with disabilities; however, Subpart E of the rules and regulations addressing postsecondary educational services was not in place until 1978. According to the Rehabilitation Act Regulations, postsecondary services are required to provide auxiliary aids, such as taped texts, to students with disabilities (Rothstein, 1993). These auxiliary aids are referred to in the educational literature as *ancillary equipment, adapted computer technology,* and *assistive technology.* Allowing students with disabilities to use such aids is considered making an academic adjustment or reasonable accommodation.

The Technology-Related Assistance for Individuals with Disabilities Act

More recent legislation addressing assistive technology includes the Technology-Related Assistance for Individuals with Disabilities Act of 1988 (Tech Act; P.L. 100-407; reauthorized in 1994). "This law along with others, has directly influenced the availability and utilization of specially designed devices and accommodations meant to empower persons with disabilities" (Chandler, Czerlinsky, & Wehman, 1993, p. 117). An assistive technology device (ATD) is defined by P.L. 100-407 as "any item, piece of furniture, or system used to increase, maintain, or improve the functional capabilities of individuals with disabilities." An ATD can be low-tech (mechanical) or high-tech (electro-mechanical or computerized). Under the Tech Act, states are awarded grants to develop assistive devices and to provide training and technical assistance; 52 states and territories have currently received systems change grants under the law (Button & Wobschall, 1994). Information and referral services, equipment loan libraries, loan-financing programs, and protection and advocacy assistance are some services of state projects. Agencies involved with the Tech Act and professionals providing technology-related services to postsecondary students with disabilities, particularly students with learning disabilities, need to ensure that the needs of these students are considered when planning assistive technology services.

The Americans with Disabilities Act

The Americans with Disabilities Act (ADA) does not specifically address assistive technology. It extends civil rights protection to postsecondary students with disabilities not previously protected by the Rehabilitation Act, and more fully protects students for whom coverage was limited. As Button and Wobschall (1994) stated, with the passage of ADA, "the message to our nation was clearly that the historical and often intentional segregation and exclusion of people with disabilities would no longer be tolerated" (p. 196). These authors concluded that technology services and devices will be critical in achieving the nondiscrimination provisions of ADA.

Wilson (1992) pointed out that even though the majority of colleges and universities say they are in compliance with Section 504 of the Rehabilitation Act, the publicity ADA is receiving may result in even better access to assistive technology for students with disabilities on campuses. If institutions are not in compliance with existing laws in terms of computer access (e.g., computerized card catalogs, physical access to facilities, computing networks), Wilson predicted that students will be more inclined to use the legal system to enforce rights. In describing differences between Section 504 and ADA, Jarrow (1993) stated, "ADA can be viewed as '504+'" (p. 21). Some individuals who experience difficulty in learning, for instance, persons with environmental disabilities or chemical sensitivity, are not covered under Section 504 but may be under ADA to the extent that the disability limits a major life activity.

POSTSECONDARY ISSUES INVOLVING ASSISTIVE TECHNOLOGY

This section discusses the issues of litigation, computerized testing, and access in relation to assistive technology at the postsecondary level.

Litigation

The responses by colleges and universities to Section 504 in regard to academic adjustments involving assistive technology for students with learning disabilities have not resulted in litigation. Two cases involving reasonable accommodation of exam format and what constitutes admissions discrimination were resolved by the courts; other litigation may have been initiated but was settled out of court (Rothstein, 1993).

A number of issues related to assistive technology could result in litigation. For example, difficulty could arise if colleges do not allow accommodations involving computers and word processors with spell checking programs for testing purposes. These arrangements might require monitoring of students to ensure that they do not access information stored in the computer's memory during testing, or that unapproved accommodations (e.g., grammar checkers) are not used. To deny this accommodation, the institution would have to prove that monitoring the computer exam would create an undue hardship.

Another source of difficulty may arise if faculty members refuse to allow accommodations requested for a student by the disabled student service office. This situation is more likely to lead to litigation when the institution has no grievance procedure in place. For example, if a student is not allowed to use a device recommended by the office of disabled student services, and no grievance procedure is in place, both the instructor and the institution may be liable (Rothstein, 1993).

Computerized Testing

Colleges and universities are currently responding to issues involving assistive technology and computerized educational testing. Advances by major testing companies in computerized versions of standardized admissions tests (e.g., American College Test, Graduate Record Exam) have led to issues of equitable access in the testing environment for students with learning disabilities. It is not known if the ability to perform well on computerized standardized tests is impaired or enhanced for students with learning disabilities. Given the heterogeneous nature of the population, it is likely that some individuals with learning disabilities will benefit from computerized testing and others will not. Research to determine whether barriers are created by technology must be conducted in the near future to ensure that access is not *decreased* by the introduction of technology (Hockley, 1990).

Access

As a result of the Rehabilitation Act and increased awareness of disability issues since the passage of ADA in 1990, services for students with learning disabilities have flourished. As services increase in the postsecondary setting, so too does the use of auxiliary aids, including assistive technology. Bursuck, Rose, Cowen, and Yahaya (1989), in their nationwide survey of postsecondary services for students with learning disabilities, reported that a majority of the schools they surveyed provided auxiliary aids, such as taped textbooks, tape recordings of lectures, calculators, and word processing programs. The same study concluded that small colleges and community colleges offer more personalized services, such as individualized tutoring and counseling, the use of Individualized Education Programs (IEPs), and progress monitoring of students with learning disabilities. It is unclear, however, whether access to assistive technology, and support in its use, vary according to the size of the institution. Major universities may employ more faculty for technology instruction and allocate more funds for technological purchases than 2-year or community colleges. Or, the personalized services characteristic of smaller colleges may result in assistive technology's having a greater impact on these students' successful completion of postsecondary education. This is a viable area for future study in the use of assistive technology.

Whether the setting is a large state university or a 2-year community college, educators agree that once a functional level of competency in using an assistive device is gained, the student with disabilities should move into the mainstream setting (Brinckerhoff, 1993; Brown, 1989). For example, the student with dysgraphia (for whom writing is an agonizing task) could learn how to use a word processor to organize, compose, edit, and print thoughts using computer adaptations in the support services lab. This student could then use the writing lab available for all students in completing his or her regular class writing assignments. Hilton-Chalfen (1991b), in his tips for starting an assistive technology program said, "Go campus-wide from the beginning. Become part of the larger computing picture" (p. 43). By accommodating students with learning disabilities in this way, existing services are not duplicated, and accommodations become an integral part of the academic support network available to all students (Shaw et al., 1994).

BARRIERS AND SOLUTIONS

This section describes two historic barriers to assistive technology use. Also described are solutions to these barriers.

Complexity

Early barriers to using assistive technologies are dissolving. Technology is now simpler, less expensive, and more widely available on campuses. Computer adaptations once involved mechanical devices that took hours to install and learn to use (Brown, 1989). Now, many specialized programs are software-based. Users may access technical support by either calling the manufacturer using a toll-free number or on screen by utilizing a "help command" option (Raskind & Scott, 1993). Furthermore, programs that rely on graphical user interface (pull-down menus and icons) are now available for most types of computers. Some students find these programs easier to operate and the commands easier to remember.

Availability

Assistive devices are present in virtually every postsecondary support services setting because federal legislation requires that postsecondary institutions receiving federal funds provide auxiliary aids to students with learning disabilities (e.g., Americans with Disabilities Act of 1990; Reha-bilitation Act of 1973). In the 1994 Florida Career and Information Deliv-ery System Report (Florida Bureau of Career Development, 1994), for instance, 90 of 91 community colleges and state universities surveyed indicated that they did provide learning aids for students with disabilities.

Additionally, innovative companies, recognizing the potential for a new market, have created technologies with new capabilities. Technolo-gies that did not exist only a few years ago (e.g., reading systems that scan books, convert the text to speech, and simultaneously highlight the text and read it out loud) are now available as compensatory tools for stu-dents with dyslexia or other learning disabilities. Also, the expansion of existing services that provide taped books for students with print disabili-ties has resulted in increased availability of assistive technology for postsecondary students with learning disabilities. For example, recent changes in policies and operating procedures by Recording for the Blind and the Library of Congress address the changing needs of students with learning disabilities and have resulted in more four-track tape recorders and taped texts being made available to students with learning disabilities (Wilkison, 1989).

POSTSECONDARY ASSISTIVE TECHNOLOGY PROGRAM COMPONENTS

This section provides a review of the literature describing assistive technology program components in colleges and universities across the country. An increase in the number of program descriptions should lead to the delineation of best practices in providing assistive technology ser-vices at the postsecondary level.

Currently, only California has introduced a statewide system of spe-cialized educational programming involving technology for students with disabilities in the postsecondary setting. In 1985, California established adapted computer technology centers in educational institutions across the state (Brown, 1989). These "High-Tech Centers for the Disabled" help students with disabilities, including individuals with learning dis-abilities, to successfully complete their postsecondary education. Special-ized courses in the use of adapted technologies are taught by the technology specialists and instructional aides at the High-Tech centers. One adaptation students with learning disabilities learn to make uses technology to change the focus in the writing environment from a visual to an auditory one (Brown, 1989), which involves a combination of word processor, real time spell checker (which monitors spelling as words are being typed), screen-reading system, and speech synthesizer. It is reported that individuals whose oral language abilities exceed their written language abilities find this adaptation very helpful. Once the student becomes comfortable using the appropriate adaptation, he or she is encouraged to use campus-wide computer facilities, such as computer centers or writing labs.

This California model provides one tested framework for examination by other university systems interested in establishing programs that emphasize assistive technology for students with disabilities in the postsecondary setting. Additional centers with similar missions are emerging in other states (Hilton-Chalfen, 1991a). The University of Missouri–Columbia established the Adaptive Computing Technology Center in 1986. One objective of that center is to identify and evaluate assistive technology. The Educational Center for Disabled Students at the University of Nebraska–Lincoln evolved from a 3-year demonstration project into an integral part of the Services for Students with Disabilities Office. Academic and technical support are integrated with the provision of services to help students with disabilities successfully compete in the postsecondary environment. At the University of North Texas, the office of Disabled Student Services helps students with disabilities access computer center and media library services. Accessibility to computer hardware is emphasized. A graduate student funded through the Disabled Student Services trains students to use centrally located assistive technology.

SELECTION AND TRAINING GUIDELINES

It is important for postsecondary service providers to be familiar with selection criteria and training concerning assistive technology. This section provides pertinent guidelines along with an overview of how secondary educators can prepare students with learning disabilities for using assistive technology at the postsecondary level.

Secondary Preparation

Since the passage of Public Law 94-142, children with disabilities have been assured access to education. Elementary and secondary schools are required to identify and serve students with disabilities; however, at the postsecondary level, according to Section 504 of the Rehabilitation Act of 1973, the responsibility for initiating provision of services and accommodations falls to the individual student. Educational preparation for assuming this role in the postsecondary setting should begin at the secondary level. During the middle school and high school years, students need to develop self-advocacy skills to prepare for this future role of initiator. Students also need to be confident of the strategies and accommodations that work for them so they will know what to request of service providers. Additionally, students need to be comfortable using computers, taped books, and calculators before entering college to bene-fit from those supports once there. Secondary educators, working as a multidisciplinary team, play an important role throughout the high school years in preparing students with learning disabilities for college by creating Individual Transition Plans that provide for the development of self-advocacy skills, compensatory techniques, and experience with appro-priate technologies.

Some students with learning disabilities reach the postsecondary level without being exposed to assistive technology and its benefits. Addi-tionally, some students with learning disabilities are not identified until they reach the postsecondary level. For these reasons, it is important that postsecondary service providers be familiar with selection criteria and training guidelines concerning assistive technology. Raskind and Scott (1993) pointed out the importance of choosing technologies relative to the individual, the functions to be performed, and the contexts in which the technologies will be used. Constraints limiting the use of technology across the contexts of home, school, workplace, and social settings may be physical (e.g., insufficient lighting, excessive noise, a lack of space) or psychosocial (e.g., reactions of others to use of the device) and should be considered in selecting technology. Purchasing a screen-reading program with a speech synthesizer for use in the campus writing center where other students work, for example, would not be wise unless earphones were included and used.

It is also important to consider future needs when purchasing tech-nology. When possible, select technology designed for use by the general public, rather than technology designed specifically for individuals with disabilities. This standard technology is usually less expensive and in many instances will better prepare the student for the workplace (Raskind & Scott, 1993). Also, consider the compatibility between new software or hardware and that already owned or being used. Some manufacturers allow buyers a trial period in which to evaluate new technology. If the technology meets the needs of the individual in bypassing the deficit, has the ability to perform necessary functions, and is appropriate for use across settings, it should improve the functional capabilities of the indi-vidual with disabilities.

Training

Once the appropriate technology has been selected, instruction in its use should include general strategies effective in teaching all students with learning disabilities. Effective training strategies include the following (Brown,1989; Raskind & Scott, 1993).

1. Using a multisensory approach to training, in which students are provided with visual instruction (including videotapes and diagrams), oral instruction, and written instruction. Related to this strategy is the notion of using technology to teach technology. Having students watch videotapes demonstrating how a device is used can be an effective training strategy that simultaneously teaches the use of other types of technology. Trainers should be cautioned, however, not to overload students with too much technology at one time.

2. Providing repetition by giving students numerous opportunities to practice what they have learned.

3. Modeling, whereby students watch others using the device and then attempt to do the same.

4. Having frequent concept reviews, that is, competency checks conducted frequently during each training session, in which students demonstrate what they know. Also, each training session should begin with a review of the previous day's session. This allows the trainer to assess whether the student retained previous information and is ready for additional information; if not, previously presented information must be retaught.

5. Providing meaningful instruction. Allow students to generate their own words for technical terms, based on what is meaningful to them. Assist students in developing mnemonics to foster information retention. This strategy includes the use of acronyms, visualization, and rhyme to help students remember functions or steps in operating a device.

6. Using concise, clear language in describing features and operations of the technology and presenting only the amount of information needed to complete the task at hand.

7. Instilling motivation. To be motivated to learn to use technology the student must accept that a disability exists and have an immediate need that can be met by the technology. The instruction should be meaningful. Develop the concept of need and the value of incorporating student experiences in their suggestions for training.

CONCLUSIONS

Assistive technology is a tool for making the learning environment more accessible and for enhancing individual productivity. Assistive technology that enables individuals with learning disabilities to compensate for reading, organization, memory, or math deficits are available and are increasingly more affordable. The use of assistive technology in postsecondary settings may enable students with learning disabilities to express themselves at levels commensurate with their intelligence. Federal legislation has been enacted regarding assistive technology use at the postsecondary level, and the advantages of assistive technology have been reported; however, the effectiveness of specific devices has not been empirically documented. Some barriers to the use of assistive technology are dissolving; however, educational service providers at the postsecondary level must be prepared to continue addressing issues related to assistive technology, such as making reasonable accommodations; providing grievance procedures to mediate conflicts among faculty members, students with disabilities, and assistive technology service providers; and ensuring equitable access in the testing environment for students with learning disabilities.

Students who have been identified as having a learning disability at the secondary level should come into the postsecondary setting fully aware of the strategies, accommodations, and devices that work for them. In addition to instructional accommodations, transition plans, written and implemented at the secondary level, should assist students with the development of self-advocacy skills, so that students can initiate services needed at the postsecondary level.

Some students with learning disabilities are identified after arrival at the postsecondary level. In addition to being knowledgeable about various types of devices, postsecondary service providers need to be familiar with issues related to device selection and to training guidelines.

Successful selection and use of assistive technology at the postsecondary level has implications for assistive technology use after college. It is acknowledged by those in the field that learning disabilities continue throughout the lifespan (Patton & Polloway, 1992). This implies that the need for assistive technology does not end with the fulfillment of the individual's educational aspirations, but persists in his or her employment, social, and leisure endeavors.

11. Multimedia: Enhancing Instruction for Students with Learning Disabilities

CHERYL A. WISSICK

Due to advances in computer technology and the availability of large storage devices such as CD-ROM drives, numerous educational programs are now published in a multimedia format—the nonlinear or non-sequential presentation of text, graphics, animation, voice, music, slides, movies, or motion video in a single system that involves the user as an active participant. Some multimedia programs serve as a multisensory database of information; others create realistic simulations for content learning. Students with learning disabilities will not benefit from these programs, even with the programs' options for multisensory input and output, without a knowledgeable teacher who can facilitate the instruction. Teachers are challenged to understand multimedia terminology, to become knowledgeable about multimedia technology demands related to the hardware and software, and to create uses for multimedia to enhance the learning environment.

Multimedia terminology is problematic because definitions often vary and the jargon is technical in nature. Multimedia programs have

Reprinted, with changes, from "Multimedia: Enhancing instruction for students with learning disabilities," by Cheryl A. Wissick, *Journal of Learning Disabilities,* Vol. 29, 1996, pp. 493–503. Copyright © 1996 by PRO-ED, Inc.

also been described as those that use interactive videodisc, hypertext, hypermedia, or integrated media. The Cognition and Technology Group at Vanderbilt University (1993b) prefers the term *integrated media* (IM) because IM stresses the need to integrate the media, not just present multiple media. Other researchers use *hypermedia* because it implies that the media can be accessed in a nonlinear manner. The term *hypertext* indicates the nonlinear access of text alone. *Interactive videodisc* programs use the combination of the computer for text and graphics with the videodisc to show high-quality photographs or motion video. The video-disc images are usually shown on a separate television monitor, with the text appearing on the computer screen. Some programs incorporate a small window on the computer screen to show the videodisc image. The majority of commercial programs are advertised as "multimedia," "in multimedia format," or having a "multimedia interface." In this article, the term *multimedia* will be used, emphasizing both the multiple use of media and nonlinear access by the user.

To learn the specifics of multimedia technology, teachers can seek out other multimedia users, attend conferences, contact computer coor-dinators, enroll in classes, or even ask for assistance on the Internet (see Note). Although this takes time and effort, teachers encounter an even greater challenge when adapting this technology for students with learn-ing disabilities. With few specific examples of multimedia use by students with learning disabilities found in the literature, teachers can have diffi-culty determining which multimedia programs and design aspects will assist or hinder their students.

The purpose of this chapter is to examine the literature for examples of multimedia use within specific classroom learning environments and relate those applications to students with learning disabilities. For each classroom situation, I will discuss opportunities for students with learning disabilities and the particular challenges teachers would encounter.

MULTIMEDIA APPLICATIONS WITHIN LEARNING ENVIRONMENTS

Teachers can select multimedia programs to apply in different learn-ing environments: as a teaching and demonstration tool, as an individual learning station or tutor, or as a small group creation station where multimedia becomes the tutee (Taylor, 1980). In developing lessons that use multimedia, the integration process can be facilitated if teachers envision in what part of the lesson they will use the technology. The use of multimedia in each of the three learning environments can also be asso-ciated with specific teaching events or parts of a lesson (see Figure 11.1).

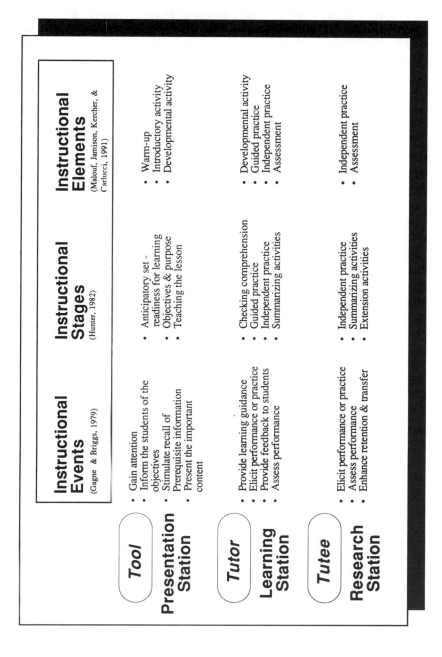

Figure 11.1 Instructional uses for multimedia.

By following a model such as Gagné and Briggs's (1979), the teacher could demonstrate or teach with multimedia to gain attention, inform students of the objectives, stimulate recall of prerequisite information, or present important content. Similarly, in applying Hunter's (1982) model of multimedia as an individual learning research station or tutor, the teacher checks student comprehension, provides guided or independent practice, or relates a summarizing activity. The choice to use multimedia as a creation station indicates that the teacher is in the final instructional stages of a lesson and is continuing independent practice, assessing the learning, and providing experiences for transfer.

Given the small amount of time teachers have to learn new programs and adapt the technology, they need to make choices regarding the most effective way to begin the process of technology integration and ways to expand. Teachers also need to envision ways that multimedia can change the way they teach and structure their classroom. Many multimedia projects begin with the student as creator, using multimedia as the tutee (D'Ignazio, 1994; M. L. Miller, personal communication, June 17, 1994; Snyder, 1993). The focus on student as creator and teacher as mediator assists in breaking the mode of traditional teaching. However, will that be the most advantageous way to begin multimedia if no teacher in the school knows how to author or create his or her own multimedia programs? Teachers without a technology background can opt to integrate multimedia as only a demonstration station or tool, later allowing students to use the tools in the learning and research station. As both teachers and students gain skills in the technology, the use of multimedia as a creation station will emerge.

Multimedia as a Tool

The use of multimedia as a tool can increase the teacher's productivity and effectiveness at demonstrating subject matter to the whole class or facilitating group interaction. Teachers and students alike can use multimedia presentations to enhance any subject matter demonstration, lecture, or report. Animation, still-frame video, full-motion video, and high-quality audio can supplement lesson materials to make learning situations realistic.

Teachers have been using multiple media (e.g., slides, films, videotape) to augment their lessons for years. Multimedia offers the capability for combining several media into one unit that can be used interactively, rather than a single-medium, preprogrammed manner, such as with slides or videotapes. In addition, videodisc technology gives the teacher rapid random access to the video-based material and provides high-quality still-frame presentation not generally available with videotape. Using multimedia as a tool, teachers can focus on gaining the students' attention, providing objectives or the anticipatory set, conducting warm-up introductory activities, and then presenting the important concepts (see Figure 11.1).

Instructional Opportunities.   Multimedia presentations using videodiscs or multimedia programs can motivate students by enlivening content material with dynamic visual representations of concepts or events. Previously seen and discussed concepts can be connected to new material, thereby stimulating recall of prerequisite knowledge. The connections may be programmed before class time by the teacher and then controlled by use of a computer attached to the videodisc player. If a teacher wants a less technical presentation format without worrying about computer controls or cables, a videodisc player can be accessed with a remote control. A bar code reader can also be used if commercial guides to the videodisc are available with the codes for each frame or motion sequence. The teacher can also develop and print specific bar codes with a special program. In either case, if a particular video segment is desired, the teacher simply scans the bar code that corresponds to that sequence. Each of these devices—bar code, remote control, or computer—provides both teachers and students with varying levels of control and interactivity for instruction.

Teachers can access videodisc-based courses for direct instruction of concepts in a particular content area. Research on math and science videodisc courses has indicated that students, both with and without learning disabilities, who received the videodisc instruction learned significantly more than the students in traditional programs (Engelmann & Carnine, 1989; Woodward & Gersten, 1992). Teachers found the programs manageable and accommodating to the instructional techniques they incorporated, such as frequent feedback, opportunities to answer, and high engaged time. In another study, measuring the Mastering Fractions (1985) videodisc program, Bottage and Hasselbring (1993a) indicated that remedial students' scores were comparable to those of their pre-algebra peers on a test of fractions computation. However, the pre-algebra peers were still significantly superior in their ability to complete word problems. The results indicate that the program is effective for basic skills but must be paired with contextual examples to assist students in transfer to real-life situations.

Powerful multimedia tools for presentation are ones that are based on stories (McLellan, 1993), because the story presents a familiar information structure. Using specially produced videodiscs, or videodisc versions of feature films, teachers can "anchor" the instruction by providing students with problem-rich situations in a story format. With multimedia comes the opportunity to go beyond direct instruction to provide generative learning environments in which students have a chance for an apprenticeship and to learn how to solve the type of multistep problems that occur in real life (Cognition and Technology Group, 1991). The possibilities multimedia affords to embed basic skill practice within realistic situations provides teachers the opportunity to improve their instruction by giving students with learning disabilities functional life skills. For example, the Cognition and Technology Group at Vanderbilt University produced a series of videodiscs that situate instruction in meaningful narrative contexts that allow students to explore and generate both problems and solutions. The Adventures of Jasper Woodbury (1992) series focuses on mathematical problem solving and provides an example of the interdisciplinary nature of multimedia. Situations that Jasper and his friends encounter, such as recycling cans, are related to activities in math, science, and social studies.

Research on the 1990–1991 implementation of the Jasper series in schools indicated that the Jasper groups performed better than the controls in areas of attitude, problem solving, math facts, and standardized test scores (Pellegrino et al., 1992). Only 16 students with learning disabilities participated in this research; individual data on these students are not available. However, Bottage and Hasselbring (1993a) compared the use of video or contextual-based instruction, similar to Jasper Woodbury, to specific instruction in word problems; remedial students were then tested in both contexts. Both groups did equally well on the word problems, but the video-context group scored significantly higher than the word-problem group on the video-context problem. Thus the video context seemed to facilitate the students' ability to interpret data in a video context and also in a word context. Many students with learning disabilities are placed in remedial classes and probably function at a level similar to that of the students in this study. Therefore, we could conclude that the use of the video context would assist in transferring knowledge to a variety of situations.

Teachers who do not have access to the Jasper series can adapt feature films, such as *Raiders of the Lost Ark* (1981) or *Star Wars* (1977), to provide motivating lessons for various subjects (Sherwood et al., 1987). Using video-based material, teachers mediate the instruction by arranging the environment so that learners are exposed to specific situations and experiences. Teachers use these visual demonstrations to help students with learning disabilities distinguish important information from incidental, and connect past experiences to the present situation (Hasselbring, Goin, & Wissick, 1989).

Teachers can also use the videodisc as a book with 50,000 pictures (Bull & Cochran, 1987). Any picture in the book can be accessed within about 3 seconds to provide visual images for the content material. Together the students and teacher work in the shared context defining language appropriate to the situation (Bull, Cochran, & Snell, 1988). For an interactive environment, students can take control by locating images they think are appropriate for the lesson or that they will then describe using appropriate language. The vivid visual nature of the activity may stimulate communication and language for students with learning disabilities.

The Windows on Science Programs (1993) have been marketed for teacher presentation and are now packaged with bar codes included in the teachers' manuals. Companies such as Josten's Learning that previously developed programs only for integrated learning labs are now developing teacher presentation stations. Teachers can also use examples from commercial programs to introduce a lesson. For example, in a social studies class studying the South and the Civil War, the teacher might use visuals of Charleston from the interactive program Hurricane Hugo (1990), whereby students could view videodisc-based photographs of Charleston and imagine how the city has changed since the Civil War. In addition, predictions could be made of the effects of the hurricane, then the video would reinforce any predictions.

Multimedia as a tool should not be viewed only as a large class-lecture situation but as any size group working with the teacher. Work has also been done with young children using video-based instruction (Sharp et al., 1993). In small-group settings, children at risk and not at risk worked in either a video context, watching a story on video, or a storybook context, listening to the story with still pictures. All students in the video context performed better than those in the storybook context in answering literal and inferential questions. However, the at-risk students in the video group did not spontaneously generalize the information to other related but nonvideo information. In a subsequent study, students did not achieve a high rate of comprehension from the video alone, emphasizing the need for continuous interaction with the environment.

Instructional Challenges.   In developing multimedia demonstrations, it is crucial that the teacher consider the format, anticipate students' responses, and plan for high rates of interaction. Multimedia can enhance a lesson by providing appropriate video to illustrate specific information. However, multimedia should not be viewed simply as a vehicle for delivering instruction that is based on current teaching models (Ulmer, 1990). We must use multimedia to progress beyond the lecture format. The developer of the presentation or group activity must anticipate reactions to the material in order to incorporate effective links between related topics that then provide the additional information.

Authoring, or presentation, systems—software that allows the creation of multimedia—provide teachers with the tools to create individual lessons without having to learn a complete programming language. Nevertheless, learning the authoring software and creating the application can take time. In addition to designing the initial concepts for instruction, the teacher is required to organize the information, create the text, design graphics, and create the final links. Teachers must balance the amount of time necessary for creating quality educational multimedia with the extent to which it will be used by students and other teachers. A solution to creating a completely new program from scratch is to use templates, or shells, which are frameworks for the organization of the material and that include all the essential programming. Templates allow teachers to create individual programs and modify the text or video for their students without performing the complex programming (Boone & Higgins, 1991; Cognition and Technology Group, 1994; Wissick, Foelber, & Berdel 1989).

Authoring systems also provide the teacher with the tools to "repurpose," or design a new purpose for, commercial video. Feature films and commercial videodiscs (e.g., A World Alive, 1991; BioSci, 1992; National Gallery of Art, 1983; Regard for the Planet [Garanger, 1989]; Salamandre: Chateaux of the Loire Valley, 1988) offer numerous possibilities for creating units that are viable in more than one curriculum area. As photographers and state libraries or archives continue to document their accumulation of slides on such technology formats as videodisc or CD-ROM, the possibilities for classroom use increase. Nevertheless, the video-context research conducted with young children (Sharp et al., 1993) indicates that teachers cannot show video without describing and discussing the context in a purposeful dialogue. The video context needs to be presented as a source of information that can be referred to again for a review of information.

Concerns about the hardware prompt teachers and administrators to create innovative solutions. Using a videodisc player with a large-screen monitor is usually sufficient for whole class teaching; however, when both a computer and a videodisc image must be displayed to a large group, then additional projection devices must be available. CD-ROM programs with motion video may need to be used with a high-quality large-screen projection device for students with learning disabilities to interpret the message in the video. Teachers who teach in several classrooms also need to consider the portability of their multimedia presentation equipment, because current costs prohibit equipping all classrooms with this technology.

In summary, the use of multimedia programs with vivid visual representations have shown to be an effective tool for presenting content and assisting transfer of learning to new situations. However, with students who are labeled at risk, remedial, or learning disabled, teacher-directed multimedia lessons on specific skills will not necessarily assist the transfer of learning to real-life situations without meaningful dialogue and activities related to that context. Teachers can assist students in making connections when facilitating large- or small-group interactions. When moving from the use of multimedia as a tool to its use as a tutor, teachers must consider the connections, or "misconnections," that students might make.

Multimedia as Tutor

After a teacher introduces the content of a lesson, she or he provides learning guidance by offering guided and independent practice, eliciting performance, and providing feedback on performance (see Figure 11.1). At this point in the instructional process, multimedia acts as a tutor or learning station. Programs that typically provide learning guidance (e.g., computer-based instruction, or CBI) are often categorized as (a) drill and practice, (b) tutorial, or (c) simulation. After conducting a meta-analysis on 63 studies that used interactive video instruction, McNeil and Nelson (1991) indicated that the use of multimedia with videotape or videodisc allowed the developers to simultaneously incorporate aspects of drill and practice, tutorial, simulation, and sensory motor skills guidance into one program. The average overall effect size for interactive video in their study was positive as well as slightly higher than those previously reported for computer-assisted instruction without the interactive video enhancements. The ability of multimedia or interactive video to depict real-life situations with applications for a variety of instructional outcomes (i.e., practice of facts, psychomotor skills, application of rules/ principles, problem solving) at varying levels might account for this difference between interactive video and computer-assisted instruction.

Instructional Opportunities.   Students are motivated by these realistic ("you are there") features of multimedia. Simulations based on fantasy or popular feature films provide students with continued enjoyment when they can view and interact with their favorite scenes (Wissick et al., 1989). Students also find incentive to interact if simulations are based on realistic situations that they might actually encounter. Students' attention is sustained because they can directly manipulate these materials to solve the problems. For students with learning disabilities, the teacher might suggest search strategies and ask specific questions, and then allow the students to explore different paths to locate their answers using multimedia's nonlinear capabilities.

Following teacher or program guidelines, students can explore the program and locate information. To help students record information immediately, teachers should look for programs that incorporate an electronic notepad. Using programs such as The Storyteller (1992) or Hurricane Hugo (1990), students can note any connections they make when they are investigating the programs. McLellan (1992) reported on the development of the Cheyanne Bottoms project, in which students interacted first with guided tours, then storytellers, and finally interactive scenarios. A notebook and toolbox were provided in both structured and unstructured real-world situations.

The Cognition and Technology Center at Vanderbilt (1994) has designed several projects that promote literacy and incorporate the important aspects of multimedia. Using the Peabody Literacy Program, students can speak to a tutor, view videos from a videodisc on important topics, and then read passages about the topic. The students practice reading using the repeated reading, choosing the correct passage from three examples. Students' reading is monitored through a voice recognition system (a component being incorporated into new multimedia computers). This capability allows students to practice independently yet be provided with corrective feedback.

In addition to programs that are specifically designed for learner guidance and practice, programs developed for large-group instruction can be modified for individual student use. Creating a learning or review center with multimedia presentation materials, such as the videodisc-based programs described previously, provides the teacher with additional means to individualize for students who require extra practice or who are absent and miss the introduction to the material. Although students who view a lesson individually might not gain the experience obtained from teacher direction and class interactions, they are nevertheless exposed to the original content presentation. When students are absent, teachers seldom have time to repeat the content presentation for just those students. In this situation, multimedia acts as a teacher's assistant.

Teachers can use multimedia to establish cooperative groups as an instructional strategy for helping students in life skills, such as social learning and group problem solving. Many multimedia programs have been developed that foster cooperative learning groups. For example, Tom Synder Productions develops computer and multimedia programs that provide each student or group of students with a role and specific tasks to accomplish in that role. In contrast, the Adventures of Jasper Woodbury Series creates a context for cooperative learning by allowing students to define their own subproblems and create their own roles in the solution (Cognition and Technology Group, 1993a).

Results of the comparison of cooperative groups versus individuals indicated that students working in groups of two to three attained higher scores than students working individually or in larger groups (Cockayne, 1991). However, students working in groups sometimes take longer to complete tasks than students working individually, due to time needed for discussion and reaching consensus on answers. Students working together can often help each other with program control and problem solving. An additional benefit of cooperative groups is that they lend themselves to students' working creatively to enhance retention and transfer. Research with cooperative groups of mixed ability levels, such as those including students with learning disabilities, provides insight for teachers on how to structure and manage groups when using multimedia to facilitate instruction.

Repman, Weller, and Lan (1993) indicated that high-ability eighth graders working in mixed ability groups scored dramatically lower than high-ability students working individually or those working in homogeneous pairs. Low-ability students working in either homogenous or mixed pairs scored higher than students working individually on a multimedia ethics program. Signer (1992) observed the use of an interactive video program with fourth and fifth graders. She noted that in dyads of high- and low-ability students, the high-ability students frequently took control of the keyboard. In studies such as these, although not specifically labeled, students with learning disabilities would have been considered part of the low-ability group. Apparently low-ability students benefit from either homogeneous or heterogeneous cooperative groups. Low-ability students may work better with another low-ability pair, rather than with a high-ability student who monopolizes the computer. The teacher would need to assign students to groups carefully, making sure that the achievement of the high-ability students does not decline as a result of a mixed pairing.

Multimedia that enhances regular basal text has had a positive impact on the reading progress of low-achieving students in kindergarten through third grade (Boone & Higgins, 1993). A 3-year study was conducted to analyze the effects (a) of each year and (b) longitudinally. The first year, significant improvement was noted for both the whole class and the low-ability groups. For the second year, although whole class differences between the control and experimental groups were not significant, the lower ability students outperformed their control counterparts. In the third year, significant improvement was noted only with low-ability students in groups for kindergarten. Unfortunately, in the third year of this project, the control classes were contaminated by students who had been in experimental groups the previous years. The multimedia enhancements assisted students' ability to gain reading comprehension and decoding skills independently.

Multimedia can also offer a large database of information from text, visual, motion video, and aural sources. After reviewing several multimedia programs, Wilson and Tally (1991) described the database as the basic component of multimedia discovery-oriented programs. Using this database, the student has different means of accessing the information and various tools for manipulating the data. Many programs on CD-ROM exploit the ability to mass large amounts of text via data links. Encyclopedias in text format have been used as a database of information for years, and now these tools are available in multimedia format. Edyburn (1991) studied the fact retrieval skills of students with and without learning handicaps using different database mediums and found that students performed better when they were assigned tasks as opposed to self-selecting tasks. They also used menu-driven programs more efficiently than those with the possibility of open searching. Thus, the format for searching the database is crucial if students with learning disabilities are required to access this type of learning and research station independently. To use databases that rely on the user to provide commands for searching, students with learning disabilities will need to have specific training on the prerequisite searching skills.

The use of learning stations is most prevalent in schools with integrated learning systems. D'Ignazio (1994) reported that students favor integrated learning systems because they are more interactive than a lecture setting with teachers. With computer-managed programs, teachers need to monitor program levels or activities so that students who have difficulty with the basic skills are not forced to remain on a level that hinders higher order thinking skills. These programs have management features that allow students to progress at their own pace. However, teachers of students with learning disabilities must, again, look carefully at the programs and match their students' learning styles to the appropriate levels or activities.

Instructional Challenges.   Students without prior knowledge, such as students with learning disabilities, will need to be guided by the teacher or the multimedia program or be given only small amounts of individual control in the use of multimedia (Gay, 1986; Hooper & Hannafin, 1988; Kinzie, Sullivan, & Berdel, 1988; Locatis, Letourneau, & Banvard, 1990; Morrison, Ross, & Baldwin, 1992), until they reach such a level of proficiency that they can access the options for navigation and assistance independently. Teachers also need to examine programs for the links that they allow or encourage. Teachers and designers should be consistent with screen design by using color or patterns to denote changes in levels, or using sound to cue links. Many programs use icons to depict the main menu selections. Teachers may need to teach some students with LD how to use the icons and offer strategies for remembering the icon representations.

When presenting content to a larger group, the teacher needs to have access to only one station; however, several stations might be needed if individual students are to use multimedia programs for learning guidance. Cooperative groups working at a station can reduce the need for equipment.

Assessment of student learning with multimedia is another concern. If students are accessing multimedia, with its rich audio and visual component, in a nonlinear manner, should they be evaluated with paper-

and-pencil memorization questions? Two questions are being asked by researchers and developers interested in authentic assessment: First, is student evaluation being conducted in the same format as learning is occurring? Second, are innovative evaluation techniques required if students are assessed on more than just factual knowledge? Without alternative assessments, teachers will not be aware of the related information that students are learning incidentally. If schools really want to prepare students for lifelong learning and help them acquire the ability to transfer skills to real situations, then assessment methods need to change (Bottage & Hasselbring, 1993b; Pellegrino et al., 1992).

In summary, teachers can employ multimedia when they want to guide students' learning and create social situations that promote lifelong learning. Teachers do have to examine programs carefully and structure the learning environment to maximize the use of multimedia by students with learning disabilities. Cooperative learning groups can assist students in learning group problem-solving skills only if teachers effectively monitor the groups, along with individual achievement and affect. Programs that incorporate verbal feedback to the students, allowing all portions of text found in the program to be read, will be more beneficial than programs that allow only direction screens to be read. With the expanding capabilities of computer hardware, it will be easier to incorporate voice recognition systems into multimedia programs, thus offering students with disabilities corrective feedback on their reading responses. Then, as students become proficient in using multimedia programs, they will probably want to create their own products rather than using commercial materials.

Multimedia as Tutee

As a creation station, multimedia becomes the tutee (Taylor, 1980), and the student is now in charge of the teaching and learning. In this way, the teacher gains valuable information about how the student has processed and synthesized information about a topic. Although the teacher can provide independent practice, assess performance, and promote activities that enhance retention and transfer (see Figure 11.1), unless students have the ability to transfer information to new situations, knowledge remains inert (Bransford, Sherwood, Hasselbring, Kinzer, & Williams, 1990). The students can use the computer to create their own reports, thus becoming the researcher, designer, developer, and, finally, the producer.

Instructional Opportunities. D'Ignazio (1989) described students and teachers as multimedia explorers, willing to take risks, make mistakes, and improvise. Students experience self-efficacy because they make personal choices about their projects and even act as producers and developers for teachers who have little time to devote to developing multimedia lectures. Students then learn how to interact with teachers as clients and develop products according to their client's outline or specifications.

When multimedia is used as a creation station, the *process*, rather than the product, becomes important (Bull & Cochran, 1991; D'Ignazio, 1994); this shift of focus forces the teacher to assess learning differently. Critical to the use of multimedia is the emphasis on the processes of creating, problem solving, and decision making. Students working together to coordinate video, audio, text, and presentation order are engaged in problem solving beyond just one solution to a problem. They must choose and create the links, pictures, or definitions for concepts that they consider important to the overall project. With CDs, videodiscs, slides, and tapes, students doing research have access to original information on events in history. If students want to relate past information with a relevant current situation, or with people in their community, they can produce their own photographs or videos to be added to the report. After students conduct in-depth research on specific topics and develop multimedia reports to present the material, they might become the experts in their class—and possibly the school—on that topic (Cognition and Technology Group, 1991, 1994). The implications for the self-esteem of students with learning disabilities, a group traditionally lacking in this area, are obvious.

Turner and Dipinto (1992) used descriptive data to document the creation of multimedia reports on mammals in science. Thirty-seven seventh graders in a kindergarten-through-eighth-grade university school worked in pairs for 35 minutes twice a week for 8 weeks. The researchers used observations, interviews, reflections, and analyses of student stacks for content and links to evaluate the overall project. All students were able to learn enough Hypercard (a multimedia authoring program) to complete a computer report within the 8 weeks. The teacher reported that she lost about 6 weeks in the curriculum completing the unit but that by spring was only 3 days behind the previous year. She felt that the work done with Hypercard allowed the students to synthesize the materials better so that subsequent units were covered more quickly than in previous years.

Technology projects with students as creators have been described in the literature and in popular technology magazines (Cognition and Technology Group, 1994; Snyder, 1993; Thorpe, 1993). Preliminary results from a similar technology integration project in process in the Rochester (NY) City Schools indicate that comparable results are possible with at-risk students (M. L. Miller, personal communication, June 17, 1994). The underlying goals for the project included getting the students to come to class, remain on task, and make connections in the curriculum. A group of at-risk 10th graders created multimedia presentations on global studies. The teachers worked together to create an integrated curriculum with a thematic unit focused on "Balance and Stability in a Changing World." They used a multimedia authoring program to combine information and report on facts gained in social studies, science, math, and English regarding a particular country. The students related their final projects to their global studies exam and accessed specific facts with the multimedia program MacGlobe (1992). The students worked on their reports during activity time, at lunch, and after school. They were held accountable to complete the project on time and present it to the class. Observations indicated that the students created connections between the factual information that they were learning in each of their content classes.

Instructional Challenges.   As with any learning activity, teachers must guide the learning and creative processes of students producing multimedia projects. The projects reported earlier indicate that students achieved academic success when teachers committed to integrating technology into their curriculum. The science teacher who worked with Turner and Dipinto (1992) demonstrated that the original time to work on the material provided advanced understanding later. Unfortunately, many teachers and administrators are not willing to consider the year's long-range goals, or even lifelong learning. In the Rochester Project, as with many projects, a facilitator was assigned to work with the teachers on curriculum and technology and with the students on learning the authoring package and completing the projects. Will a greater gap exist in our schools if some students are not provided opportunities for multimedia creation because their teachers do not have sufficient training to implement this type of project, or their school does not have a technology facilitator?

When multimedia projects are completed, teachers must remember to separate content from production quality and to value the students' information over the production effects. Huntley (1991) warned that the danger in multimedia is a heightened preoccupation with style, appearance, and effect at the expense of intellectual content and emotional depth. Both teachers and students should be aware of the glitz and fancy wrappings of a multimedia report. If teachers or students become absorbed by the media or the authoring system, then they frequently spend too much time on the graphic details or isolated parts of text. Students also have to learn to be ethical producers concerning copyright laws. For example, Truett (1994), reporting on the use of CD-ROM and videodisc technology among media specialists in North Carolina, cited an increase in plagiarism. With easy access to original sources and to capturing and copying data, students have to understand what constitutes ethical use and cite their sources accordingly.

Once students complete their multimedia projects, teachers must develop clearly defined criteria for evaluating the products. Multimedia projects and research do not lend themselves to simple assessments with right and wrong answers. Teachers have to gain expertise in evaluating projects that might have outstanding content but poor design and presentation quality, versus projects with fancy graphics, color, animation, and other effects but insubstantial content. In an effort to evaluate the outcomes of learning with multimedia, teachers can ask students to create portfolios of their work, which provide teachers with a progression of skills throughout the year. With the importance placed on process, then teachers can have students maintain logs, or journals, of their work in which they can record insights about the content material and comments about the process of working cooperatively with other students. Although portfolios and multimedia reports might not provide the exact scores that achievement tests do, they provide students with skills that they will use in lifelong learning.

CONCLUSIONS

Multimedia provides teachers and students with a powerful tool to access a combination of media for enhancement of instructional events and learning. Furthermore, multimedia provides the learner with a nonsequential means to interact with a combination of media, thereby increasing motivation, maintaining attention, stimulating cognition, and illustrating content or facts. With multimedia, teachers, students, administrators, and teacher educators have new potential to change the way schools are structured and the way they teach and learn.

How will multimedia affect or enhance instruction for students with learning disabilities?

- Multimedia has the potential to enhance instruction at all levels of instruction when sound instructional principles are applied to the selection of programs, but teachers must integrate it into instruction as a tool, instead of just a supplement to the curriculum.

- Instructional designers and developers must go beyond the traditional models for instruction that have driven technology development in the past. Developers should be encouraged to create templates for teachers, allowing them to incorporate their own text, graphics, and video into advanced programs without dealing with the details of programming.

- Multimedia programs need to be developed for use with different hardware configurations, allowing teachers who do not have all the hardware access to certain aspects of the programs as they build on their configurations.

- Teachers and students must be aware of the "big picture," or the overall goals of the lesson, so they are not swept away by the glitz and attend only to the production and not the content.

- Possibly the greatest potential of multimedia is that it allows teachers to create environments where students can be researchers and creators of products for reports, becoming experts in certain subjects.

The full potential of multimedia applications has not been realized. Teachers and students must continue to use multimedia to perform feats previously thought impossible, instead of applying multimedia to current traditions. Although the effects will not be noticed for several years, teachers and students must continue to use this new technology to reach new levels of invention and integration.

NOTE

A growing resource for multimedia can be found on the electronic highway. Some teachers have direct access to list services on the Internet. For others who need access to information on special education and multimedia, NCIPnet would a resource. NCIPnet is the network of the National Center to Improve Practice, a project funded by the Office of Special Education Programs, U.S. Department of Education. NCIP's mission is to expand and improve the ways in which technology is used with students with disabilities. Users of NCIPnet are those interested in conversing about issues related to technology and special education. With the support of a network facilitator, participants converse about effective practice, share information and resources, and help each other solve problems. Topics that have recently been explored online are multimedia, technology for visual impairment, and inclusion. For more information on NCIPnet, contact Denise Ethier, Network Coordinator, 617/969-7100, x2422, or 617/969-4529 (TTY).

12. A Federal Perspective on Special Education Technology

JANE HAUSER AND DAVID B. MALOUF

For more than two decades, the Office of Special Education Programs (OSEP) has been committed to using technology, educational media, and materials to help persons with disabilities discover new learning opportunities, communicate effectively, control their environment, and achieve greater mobility. During this time, there has been discussion of what constitutes an appropriate federal role in determining the evolution of technology in education. In a 1988 report, the congressional Office of Technology Assessment (OTA) concluded that the federal government must take an active role if technology was to realize its potential for improving education. The report encouraged flexibility, as "there is no single 'best use' of technology in schools to improve learning" (p. 5). OTA's view was that research efforts should study technology's educational effectiveness and at the same time study technology innovations. At the time of the OTA reports, OSEP already had an established history of such research efforts and a commitment that continues to this day to use the results of research to improve outcomes for students with disabilities.

In this chapter, we will discuss how the current federal program in special education technology reflects the ways in which patterns of

Reprinted, with changes, from "A federal perspective on special education technology," by Jane Hauser and David B. Malouf, *Journal of Learning Disabilities,* Vol. 29, 1996, pp. 504–511. Copyright © 1996 by PRO-ED, Inc.

research in technology have changed over the years and how the role of technology in instruction has changed and expanded. Some of the companion chapters in this book are indicative of such changes and expansions. We also will examine federally funded "futures" studies of technology, society, and the implications for students with learning disabilities. And, finally, we will discuss the recently formulated national agenda for special education technology (Division of Innovation and Development, 1992b) and its potential for providing an arena for OSEP and the field of special education to continue to collaborate and grow in our efforts to serve children with disabilities.

Our use of student population labels should be explained. Many of the special education technology research projects focus on learning difficulties, and many of them specify students with learning disabilities as a targeted group. However, these projects tend to use school-system identifications of learning disabilities rather than the more rigorous definitions and sample descriptions proposed for research (CLD Research Committee, 1993). Further, these projects often work with cross-categorical samples, such as "mild" or "educational" disabilities, which include but are not limited to learning disabilities. Thus, it is most accurate to say that the approaches, findings, and issues discussed in this chapter generally apply to a student population that includes but is not limited to learning disabilities.

The Changing Face of Research

It seems appropriate to begin this section on research by posing a key research question: Does technology teach students with learning disabilities better than other approaches? Research questions on comparative media effectiveness seem to arise with each successive wave of technological innovation ("Does instructional radio teach better than live instruction?" "Does instructional television teach better than live instruction?" "Does computerized instruction teach better than noncomputer instruction?"). A number of studies in general and special education have addressed these questions, and meta-analyses of media comparison studies (e.g., Kulik, Bangert, & Williams, 1983; Kulik, Kulik, & Bangert-Drowns, 1985) are among the most widely cited references in the literature on educational technology.

Comparisons among media are unavoidable. Certainly a school administrator contemplating spending millions of dollars for educational technology wants to have some evidence of its advantages over existing alternatives. However, research intended to compare the effectiveness of different media has been criticized for confounding media, methods, and content, and for being susceptible to novelty effects, experimenter bias, and editorial gatekeeping (Clark, 1985). In fact, questions of comparative media effectiveness often muddle so many factors that they may be "unanswerable, naive, or uninstructive" (Salomon & Gardner, 1986, p. 13). Thus, the question of technology effectiveness may be both unavoidable and unanswerable, essential and irrelevant.

Salomon (1991) suggested a way out of this dilemma by defining two complementary approaches to research—*analytic* and *systemic*. Analytic research investigates discrete variables and their effects, usually through controlled experimental designs. Systemic research investigates holistic systems of interdependent variables, such as those found in school settings. The assumptions underlying these two approaches are quite distinct, and each has strengths and weaknesses. Analytic research can establish functional links between specific treatment variables and outcomes, but its generalizability is sometimes questioned. Systemic research illuminates complex real-world processes and events, but is less strong at establishing specific functional links. Achieving the appropriate balance between these two orientations is one challenge facing a federal program of research.

Analytic Research

There is a long history of analytic research on special education technology, and this research orientation appears to be predominant in the literature. Possible reasons for this are not difficult to find: Analytic research is compatible with methodologies and research doctrine that are well established in special education; furthermore, analytic research is useful for studying the discrete factors and processes involved in the behavioral, task-analytic, and learning strategy models that have influenced technology-based instruction. Several good reviews of this research literature are available (see Ellis & Sabornie, 1986; Okolo, Bahr, & Rieth, 1993).

A number of projects listed in the appendix to this chapter involve analytic research using experimental or quasi-experimental designs to study the effects of technology-based interventions. These interventions vary greatly in complexity. Some current projects are studying relatively focused, uncomplicated interventions, such as captioning videos or providing the teacher with classroom information systems. Other projects are studying complex interventions with multiple technological, curricular, and instructional elements. These include multimedia, technology-based learning tools, and telecommunications. Several projects are analyzing components of complex interventions. For example, a project at the University of Delaware, entitled "Features That Support Learning by Secondary Students with Learning Disabilities," is studying the effects of several specific aspects of hypermedia textbooks, including speech synthesis, video, and graphic organizers. A project at the University of Idaho, entitled "Experimental Validation of the Effects of Assistive Writing Technologies on the Literacy of Students with Disabilities," is studying the effects of several specific assistive writing tools, such as voice recognition, word prediction, and alternative keyboard systems.

Systemic Research

Analytic research tells us what effects *can* occur when technology is applied in special education. However, it is less able to tell us is what effects *will* occur under natural conditions, where "clouds" of factors associated with technology, students, teachers, and context interact to determine outcomes (Salomon, Perkins, & Globerson, 1991). Systemic research is therefore needed to complete the picture. A report prepared by the Division of Innovation and Development (1992a) describes eight projects that received federal funds between 1982 and 1992 to conduct systemic studies of administrative, implementation, and instructional aspects of technology in special education.

Systemic research does not necessarily mean qualitative research, because several quantitative methodologies are available (e.g., path analysis, structural modeling). However, qualitative methodology has become the standard approach for a number of reasons. Qualitative methodology can be used to study numerous interrelated variables in context. Moreover, many important variables in technology research are difficult to quantify, and qualitative methods provide a rigorous means for studying such factors. Finally, special education technology studies are often exploratory in nature, and qualitative methods allow the researcher to expect the unexpected.

Many of the projects listed in the appendix are conducting systemic, qualitative research, often in combination with analytic research. Systemic research in these projects is intended to study contextual factors that influence the implementation and effectiveness of technology interventions. Obviously, contextual factors are important for technologies that involve dramatic changes in curriculum and instruction, such as multimedia or other technologies used to support inquiry-based learning. A good example of this is Make It Happen, a product under study at Education Development Center in Newton, MA. Make It Happen originated in a project funded in 1986 to study technology integration. After considerable systemic research, this project concluded that technology could not be isolated from context, and it developed Make It Happen as a package that merges technology, teacher collaboration, curriculum innovation, and inquiry-based learning. The importance of context is not limited to complex technological interventions. The projects in the appendix are finding that even such seemingly simple, circumscribed interventions as adding captions to videos can interact with context in complex ways.

The Emergence of Constructivism

Research on technology in special education has been influenced in recent years by the emergence of a new instructional paradigm. Terms such as *constructivism, situated instruction, anchored instruction,* and *cognitive apprenticeship* have proliferated in the literature, and a growing number of federally funded technology projects are based on these ideas. For the sake of discussion, we will use the term *constructivism* as a general designation of these models.

From a constructivist perspective, technology is not primarily a means for imparting information and skills. It is instead one supportive element of a learning context that includes student exploration and problem solving, authentic instructional tasks, cooperative learning, and teacher facilitation (Means et al., 1993; Merrill, 1991; Poplin, 1988). Instead of the technology acting on the student to deliver instruction, the student uses the technology and other contextual resources to act on information and thereby learn. The technology can be seen as a cognitive tool, or "partner," that supports the cognitive processes of learning (Salomon, Perkins, & Globerson, 1991).

The application of constructivist principles to special education technology raises some challenging issues of research methodology. Process and outcome variables are extended into multiple new domains, such as generalized problem-solving skills, strategies, motivation, social skills, "authentic" learning, and teacher and context factors. For many of these constructs, no direct measurement instruments are available. Further, specific processes and outcomes are likely to differ for different students and situations.

Several projects conducted at Vanderbilt University (see the appendix) exemplify technology research based on constructivist principles. These projects employ multimedia technology to present visual and auditory information in flexible and adaptable ways. Students in these projects range in grade level from early elementary through high school, and curricular areas include mathematics, reading, and functional living skills. Common to all of these projects is the concept of "anchored instruction," whereby issues or situations presented via multimedia are used as anchors for student learning.

THE CHANGING FACE OF TECHNOLOGY

As early as the 1960s, general research efforts by OSEP (then the Bureau of Education for the Handicapped) were laying the groundwork for what in the 1980s would become closed-captioned television. In the 1970s, research and development efforts were yielding such results as the Kurzweil reading machine.

More systematic efforts began in the mid-1980s when, for the first time, OSEP earmarked certain competitions specifically for research in technology. Early projects often concentrated on research and development of technologies to improve access or compensate for physical difficulties. The technology programs begun in the 1980s soon expanded into more specific research in how technology could be used to deliver instruction. In due course, the manner in which technology was viewed and used began to change, and research on technology changed accordingly. As indicated earlier, some of the projects in the appendix are illustrative of current research methodology. Many of them combine research with the use of evolving technologies. Such combinations have the potential to expand both theory and practice.

As Congress came to recognize the potential of technology, important changes became evident in patterns of federal legislation. The late 1980s and early 1990s saw a number of statutes strengthening the delivery of services through technology for persons with disabilities. One significant piece of legislation was the enactment of Part G of the Education for all Handicapped Children Act of 1986, P.L. 99-457, which authorized the Technology, Educational Media, and Materials Program for Individuals with Disabilities and budgeted $4.7 million for fiscal year 1987. Since then, the program has invested more than $35 million in research and development of technology tools for students with disabilities.

How will technology continue to change? We can make certain inferences by examining technology research conducted by other disciplines and considering the impact such work is likely to have. For example, many technologies designed for business, science, medicine, and the military, when adapted to special education, have the potential to benefit persons with disabilities (Hauser, 1991).

Learning From "Futures" Studies

OSEP conducted its first "futures" study in 1984 to investigate technologies that might be adapted to benefit students with disabilities. The project examined research on and applications of simulation, artificial intelligence, and robotics technologies in business, medicine, and the military. The study found that, at that time, computer simulation appeared to present the fewest technical barriers to adaptation (Moore, Yin, & Lahm, 1985). As a result, OSEP funded projects to use simulation (software and videotape) to teach work-related social competence skills; it also continued to support basic research using robotics and artificial intelligence technologies with persons with disabilities.

The next "futures" study began in 1989 (Middleton & Means, 1991) and examined business and military applications of technology that had the potential to be adapted for special education. Using the results of the study, the project developed a series of scenarios based on the needs of youth with disabilities. The group then discussed the potential matchup between students' needs and the developing technologies (ranging from hand-held computers to virtual reality). For example, such technologies as individualized learning systems, word retrievers, telecommunications networks, and databases all fuel our imagination about the potential of far-reaching new technologies. It becomes tempting to think of children with learning disabilities using integrated multimedia technology routinely to call up historical images from other times and cultures, to write collaborative short stories with friends, and to take an active involvement in their own education.

However, special education research studies of future workplaces and of the outlook for special education students have raised concerns that go far deeper than how present and future technologies will affect students with disabilities (Howell, 1991; Woodward, 1992). Recent studies generally agree about the kinds of skills the future workforce will need as society shifts from a manufacturing to a service orientation and from an industrial to an information-based society. Elements constituting the foundation of success in the workplace are basic skills, higher order thinking skills, and interpersonal skills. Workers will need to apply fundamental mathematical concepts, write brief communications, and be able to work effectively as part of a team (U.S. Department of Labor, 1991). Beyond basic skills, those who succeed will need to possess broader intellectual abilities in abstraction, experimentation, and collaboration (Reich, 1991; Woodward, 1992).

Many students with learning disabilities already acquire jobs of low social status, and the problem is likely to worsen. Woodward (1992) argued that the cognitive abilities demanded by the new work environments are in direct contrast to those defining the typical special education student. We might question whether the way we are currently educating children with disabilities is preparing them for the changes occurring in society and for the work environment of their future. What changes must we make in our thinking and in education to inculcate skills that are realistic for emerging employment fields, such as electronics, aerospace, and pharmaceuticals?

Planning for the Future

As we have seen, major advances in rehabilitation and multimedia technologies have clear benefits for children and youth with disabilities. At the same time, the new technologies will demand that a large number of students with disabilities and their teachers become proficient in computers and other high-technology instructional systems. The challenge is for educators not only to make some fundamental changes in how they think about instruction, but also to deliver more diverse special educa-tion and related services. Embedded in a sound instructional program, technology has the potential to bridge what Johnston and Packer (1987) described as the gap between the low education skills of new workers and the advancing skill requirements of the work world.

Meeting that challenge requires a realistic look at what is really happening in an average educational setting. It should be recognized that the value of research in special education technology is diminished if the research findings do not find their way into practice. There are a number of general impediments to the application of research in practice, including disparate knowledge types, teacher attitudes and beliefs, and organizational barriers (Malouf & Schiller, in press). There are also barriers unique to the area of technology. Specialized teacher competencies are needed to apply technology in a meaningful way, and developing such competencies takes time and effort (Sheingold & Hadley, 1990). Also to be considered are the expense of making up-to-date technologies available for widespread educational use, and the disparity between the cutting-edge technologies favored by researchers and developers and the some-what dated technologies typically found in schools (Hanley, 1993; Means et al., 1993). In truth, most schools have neither the quantity of systems nor the upgrades necessary to make technology an integral part of the instructional program. Typically, there is one computer for every 30 stu-dents, or little more than 1 hour a week per student (Hasselbring, 1991).

Computer technology, grounded in a sound program of instruction, has the potential to enhance students' work and to perform routine basic-skills tasks. This frees students to learn to operate at the higher cognitive levels that will be required in the workplace. Growth of installed bases of technology in schools, and access to them by students with dis-abilities and trained teachers, are elements critical to the future of stu-dents and teachers alike.

CONCLUSIONS

The past two decades have been marked by continuing exami-nations of how we think about research, technology, instructional prac-tice, and the future. Any federal program intended to advance the use of technology with students with disabilities faces certain questions: What do we really know about how students learn and technology's relationship with that process? How can technology enhance learning? As technologies advance in fields beyond education, can we adapt them to the teaching of children with disabilities? How can we get powerful tools into the hands of our teachers and give them the training and support they need? What do we need to know to guide future research?

Research not only is driven by questions but also builds on the knowledge it amasses to frame new questions. How then, can we advance the use of research on technology to improve outcomes for children with disabilities? In the past, OSEP's planning efforts have relied on a combination of existing knowledge from (a) researchers in the field; (b) funded projects, particularly those in field-initiated competitions; and (c) staff expertise. Thus, the groundwork had already been laid when the Individuals with Disabilities Education Act Amendments of 1990, P.L. 101-476, required that programs initiate a systematic process for developing program goals and priorities. In October 1991, OSEP's Division of Innovation and Development began a national agenda-building process for the Technology, Educational Media, and Materials Program for Individuals with Disabilities. Wide participation was invited from the professional, advocacy, parent, and disability communities. Using a variety of formats, including focus groups and electronic conferences, the Division solicited the views of parents, researchers, administrators, association representatives, consumers, and OSEP staff. The result was a national agenda that will drive future plannning and priorities regarding the use of technology, media, and materials to improve outcomes for individuals with disabilities.

This agenda sets forth four program commitments by which the use of technology will be advanced for all categories of disability, including students with learning disabilities: (a) *Enable the learner across environments* by fostering the creation of state-of-the-art instructional environments; (b) *promote effective policy* at all levels in government, schools, and business; (c) *foster use through professional development* by training and supporting teachers, administrators, parents, and related service personnel; and (d) *create innovative tools* by encouraging the development of varied and integrated technologies, media, and materials. It is believed that this agenda will foster lifelong learning; encourage inclusion in diverse educational, domestic, work, and community environments; promote equity in opportunity for individuals with disabilities; and enable those with disabilities to be productive and independent. The agenda will be flexible and responsive to developments in the field, the growing body of research findings, the state of the art in technology, and the needs of children and youth with disabilities.

Authors' Note

The opinions expressed in this chapter are those of the authors and do not necesssarily reflect the position or policy of the U.S. Department of Education; official endorsement neither is implied nor should be inferred.

APPENDIX: SELECTED PROJECTS FUNDED UNDER THE TECHNOLOGY, EDUCATIONAL MEDIA, AND MATERIALS FOR INDIVIDUALS WITH DISABILITIES PROGRAM

Project title	*Make It Happen! The Impact of Innovative Technologies to Support Inquiry-Based Instruction on Adolescents with Disabilities*
Organization	Education Development Center, Inc.
Project director	Judith Zorfass

Project title	*Project SUCCESS: Students Using Cognitively Based Computer-Enhanced Study Strategies*
Organization	University of Oregon
Project director	Lynne Anderson-Inman

Project title	*Demonstrating and Evaluating the Benefits of Captioned Instructional Television*
Organization	National Captioning Institute
Project director	Eric Kirkland

Project title	*Literacy for Life: MOST Environments for Accelerating Literacy Development in High School Special Education Students*
Organization	Vanderbilt University
Principal investigators	Ted Hasselbring and Herbert Rieth

Project title	*Improving Management, Planning, and Achievement Through Computer Technology: Project IMPACT*
Organization	Vanderbilt University
Principal investigators	Lynn Fuchs and Doug Fuchs

Project title	*Telecommunications in Literacy Intervention for Inner-City Learning Disabled and At-Risk Students*
Organization	Lin, Bierstedt & Associates
Principal investigators	Agnes Lin

Project title	*Demonstration and Evaluation of Interactive Video Instruction: Increasing Teacher Instructional Effectiveness in the Inclusive Classroom*
Organization	University of Kansas
Project directors	Jerry Chaffin, Robert Campbell, and Patti Campbell

Project title	*An Integrated Curriculum and Life-Style Knowledge Approach to Literacy and Social Studies Instruction for Students with Mild Disabilities*
Organization	Vanderbilt University
Principal investigators	Herbert Rieth, Charles Kinzer, and Marcy Singer-Gabella

Project title	*Personal Captioning for Students with Language-Related Learning Needs: A Study of Effectiveness and Implementation*
Organization	CPB/WGBH National Center for Accessible Media
Project director	Mardi Loeterman

Project title	*Computer-Enhanced Inclusion: A Model for Computer-Based Instructional Management in Mainstream Classrooms*
Organization	University of Minnesota
Principal investigators	Steve Robinson and Stanley Deno

Project title	*Effects of Individualized Closed-Captioned Video Prompt Rate on Reading Skills of Disabled and Nondisabled Elementary Students in Inclusive and Noninclusive Classrooms*
Organization	Valdosta State College
Project directors	Martha Meyer and Yung-bin Lee

Project title	*Learning by Design: Multimedia Projects for Students with Disabilities*
Organization	University of Delaware
Principal investigators	Ralph Ferretti and Cynthia Okolo

Project title	*Integrating Captioning Technology with Mainstreamed Social Studies Instruction*
Organization	National Captioning Institute
Project director	Eric Kirkland

Project title	*Linking Text-Processing Tools to Student Needs*
Organization	Western Michigan University
Project directors	Christine Bahr and Nickola Nelson

Project title	*Project WRITE: Writing and Reading Instruction Through Technology, Educational Media, and Materials*
Organization	University of North Carolina at Chapel Hill
Principal investigator	David Koppenhaver

Project title	*Informed Instruction in Mathematics*
Organization	University of Puget Sound
Project director	John Woodward

Project title	*MOST Environments for Accelerating Literacy Development in Young Children At Risk of School Failure*
Organization	Vanderbilt University
Project directors	Ted Hasselbring and Diana Sharp

Project title	*Features that Support Learning by Secondary Students with Learning Disabilities*
Organization	University of Delaware
Project director	Charles MacArthur

Project title	*Teaching Workplace Literacy*
Organization	University of Puget Sound
Project directors	John Woodward and Juliet Baxter

Project title	*The Early Childhood Emergent Literacy Technology Project*
Organization	Western Illinois University
Project director	Patricia Hutinger

Project title	*Developing Mathematical Literacy Through the Use of Contextualized Learning Environments*
Organization	Vanderbilt University
Principal investigators	Ted Hasselbring and Prisca Moore

Project title	*Enhancing the Writing Skills of Students with Learning Disabilities Through Technology: An Investigation of the Effects of Text Entry Tools, Editing Tools, and Speech Synthesis*
Organization	San Diego State University
Project director	Rena Lewis

Project title	*Project CONNECT: Content-Area-Literacy via Networked Notetaking for Exceptional Children and Teachers*
Organization	University of Oregon
Principal investigator	Lynne Anderson-Inman

Project title	*Experimental Validation of the Effects of Assistive-Writing Technologies on the Literacy of Students with Disabilities*
Organization	University of Idaho
Project director	Bryce Fifield

Project title	*Literacy in an Innovative, Technology-Enriched Science Context for Students with Learning Disabilities*
Organization	Technical Education Research Centers
Project director	Sylvia Weir

Project title	*National Center to Improve the Tools of Educators*
Organization	University of Oregon
Project director	Douglas Carnine

Project title	*National Center to Improve Practice in Special Education Through Technology, Media and Materials*
Organization	Education Development Center, Inc.
Project director	Judith Zorfass

References

Chapter 1

Division of Innovation and Development, Office of Special Education Programs. (1992). *The technology, educational media, and materials strategic program agenda for individuals with disabilities*. Washington, DC: U.S. Department of Education.

Horn, R. E. (1989). *Mapping hypertext*. Lexington, MA: The Lexington Institute.

Negroponte, N. (1995). *Being digital*. New York: Alfred A. Knopf.

Office of Technology Assessment, U.S. Congress. (1995). *Teachers and technology: Making the connection* (S/N 052-003-01409-2). Washington, DC: U.S. Government Printing Office.

Sivin-Kachala, J., & Bialo, E. R. (1995). *Report on the effectiveness of technology in schools 1990–1994*. Washington, DC: Software Publishers Association.

Thornburg, D. (1994). *Education in the communication age*. San Carlos, CA: Starsong.

Chapter 2

Bahr, C. M., Nelson, N. W., & Van Meter, A. (1994). Planning to write: Comparison of a text-based versus a graphics-based tool. Manuscript submitted for publication.

Bangert-Drowns, R. L. (1993). The word processor as an instructional tool: A meta-analysis of word processing in writing instruction. *Review of Educational Research, 63*, 69–93.

Becker, H. J. (1993). Teaching with and about computers in secondary schools. *Communications of the ACM, 36*(5), 69–72.

Borgh, K., & Dickson, W. P. (1992). The effects on children's writing of adding speech synthesis to a word processor. *Journal of Research on Computing in Education, 24*, 533–544.

Calkins, L. M. (1991). *Living between the lines*. Portsmouth, NH: Heinemann.

Cochran-Smith, M. (1991). Word processing and writing in elementary classrooms: A critical review of related literature. *Review of Educational Research, 61*, 107–155.

Cognition and Technology Group at Vanderbilt Learning Technology Center. (1993). Integrated media: Toward a theoretical framework for utilizing their potential. *Journal of Special Education Technology, 12*(2), 71–85.

Cohen, M., & Riel, M. M. (1989). The effect of distant audiences on students' writing. *American Educational Research Journal, 26*, 143–159.

Co:Writer [Computer program]. (1992). Wauconda, IL: Don Johnston Developmental Equipment.

Daiute, C. (1986a). Physical and cognitive factors in revising: Insights from studies with computers. *Research in the Teaching of English, 20,* 141–159.

Daiute, C. (1986b). Do 1 and 1 make 2? Patterns of influence by collaborative authors. *Written Communication, 3,* 382–408.

Daiute, C. (1992). Multimedia composing: Extending the resources of kindergarten to writers across the grades. *Language Arts, 69,* 250–260.

Dalton, B. M. (1988). A comparative study of five spell checkers' analyses of learning disabled and normally achieving fourth grade students' written compositions. Unpublished manuscript, Harvard Graduate School of Education, Cambridge, MA.

Dalton, B., Winbury, N., & Morocco, C. C. (1990). "If you could just push a button": Two fourth-grade boys with learning disabilities learn to use a computer spelling checker. *Journal of Special Education Technology, 10,* 177–191.

DECtalk [Computer hardware]. (no date). Maynard, MA: Digital Equipment Corp.

Emerson & Stern Associates. (1992). Write This Way [Computer program]. Petaluma, CA: Interactive Learning Materials.

Englert, C. S., Raphael, T. E., Anderson, L. M., Anthony, H. M., & Stevens, D. D. (1991). Making writing strategies and self-talk visible: Cognitive strategy instruction in writing in regular and special education classrooms. *American Educational Research Journal, 28,* 337–372.

Englert, C. S., Raphael, T. E., Anderson, L. M., Gregg, S. L., & Anthony, H. M. (1989). Exposition: Reading, writing, and the metacognitive knowledge of learning disabled students. *Learning Disabilities Research, 5,* 5–24.

Explore-a-Science [Computer program]. (1993). Acton, MA: Bradford.

Fitzgerald, J. (1987). Research on revision in writing. *Review of Educational Research, 57,* 481–506.

Flower, L., & Hayes, J. R. (1981). A cognitive process theory of writing. *College Composition and Communication, 32,* 365–387.

Garner, R., Alexander, P. A., & Hare, V. C. (1991). Reading comprehension failure in children. In B. Y. L. Wong (Ed.), *Learning about learning disabilities* (pp. 284–307). San Diego: Academic Press.

Graham, S. (1990). The role of production factors in learning disabled students' compositions. *Journal of Educational Psychology, 82,* 781–791.

Graham, S., Harris, K., MacArthur, C. A., & Schwartz, S. S. (1991). Writing and writing instruction with students with learning disabilities: A review of a program of research. *Learning Disability Quarterly, 14,* 89–114.

Graham, S., & MacArthur, C. (1988). Improving learning disabled students' skills at revising essays produced on a word processor: Self-instructional strategy training. *The Journal of Special Education, 22,* 133–152.

Hasselbring, T., & Goin, L. (1991). Enhancing writing through integrated media. *The Writing Notebook, 9(1),* 27–29.

Hidi, S., & Hildyard, A. (1983). The comparison of oral and written productions of two discourse types. *Discourse Processes, 6,* 91–105.

Inspiration (Version 4.0) [Computer program]. (1994). Inspiration Software.

Kid Pix [Computer program]. (1992). Novato, CA: Broderbund.

Kid Works 2 [Computer program]. (1992). Torrance, CA: Davidson & Associates.

King, M. L., & Rentel, V. M. (1981). Research update: Conveying meaning in written texts. *Language Arts, 58,* 721–728.

Kinzer, C. K., Hasselbring, T. S., Schmidt, C. A., & Meltzer, L. (1990, April). *Effects of multimedia to enhance writing ability.* Paper presented at the annual conference of the American Educational Research Association, Boston.

MacArthur, C. A. (1988). The impact of computers on the writing process. *Exceptional Children, 54,* 536–542.

MacArthur, C. A. (1994). *[Review of a grammar checker designed for students with learning disabilities].* Unpublished raw data.

MacArthur, C. A., & Graham, S. (1987). Learning disabled students' composing under three methods of text production: Handwriting, word processing, and dictation. *The Journal of Special Education, 21(3),* 22–42.

MacArthur, C. A., Graham, S., Haynes, J. A., & De La Paz, S. (in press). Spelling checkers and students with learning disabilities: Performance comparisons and impact on spelling. *The Journal of Special Education.*

MacArthur, C. A., Graham, S., & Schwartz, S. (1991). Knowledge of revision and revising behavior among learning disabled students. *Learning Disability Quarterly, 14,* 61–73.

MacArthur, C. A., Graham, S., & Schwartz, S. S. (1993). Integrating word processing and strategy instruction into a process approach to writing. *School Psychology Review, 22,* 671–681.

MacArthur, C. A., Schwartz, S. S., & Graham, S. (1991). Effects of a reciprocal peer revision strategy in special education classrooms. *Learning Disabilities Research & Practice, 6,* 201–210.

Mirenda, P., & Beukelman, D. R. (1987). Comparison of speech synthesis intelligibility with listeners from three age groups. *Augmentative and Alternative Communication, 3,* 120–128.

Mitton, R. (1987). Spelling checkers, spelling correctors and the misspellings of poor spellers. *Information Processing and Management, 23,* 495–505.

Montague, M., Graves, A., & Leavell, A. (1991). Planning, procedural facilitation, and narrative composition of junior high students with learning disabilities. *Learning Disabilities Research & Practice, 6,* 219–224.

Morocco, C., Dalton, B., & Tivnan, T. (1990, April). *The impact of computer-supported writing instruction on the writing quality of 4th grade students with learning disabilities.* Paper presented at the annual meeting of the American Educational Research Association, Boston.

Morocco, C. C., & Neuman, S. B. (1986). Word processors and the acquisition of writing strategies. *Journal of Learning Disabilities, 19,* 243–247.

My Words [Computer program]. (1993). Dimondale, MI: Hartley.

Peyton, J. K., & Batson, T. (1986). Computer networking: Making connections between speech and writing. *ERIC/CLL News Bulletin, 10(1),* 1, 5–7.

Riel, M. M. (1985). The computer chronicles newswire: A functional learning environment for acquiring literacy skills. *Journal of Educational Computing Research, 1,* 317–337.

Rosegrant, T. J. (1986, April). *It doesn't sound right: The role of speech output as a primary form of feedback for beginning text revision.* Paper presented at the annual meeting of the American Educational Research Association, San Francisco.

Salomon, G. (1992, February). *Metacognitive facilitation and cultivation during essay writing: The case of the "Writing Partner."* Paper presented at the Third International Conference on Cognitive Education, Riverside, CA.

Scardamalia, M., Bereiter, C., & Goelman, H. (1982). The role of production factors in writing ability. In M. Nystrand (Ed.), What writers know: The language, process, and structure of written discourse (pp. 173–210). New York: Academic Press.

Stoddard, B., & MacArthur, C. A. (1993). A peer editor strategy: Guiding learning disabled students in response and revision. Research in the Teaching of English, 27, 76–103.

Storybook Weaver [Computer program]. (1992). Minneapolis, MN: MECC.

Talking Textwriter [Computer program]. (no date). New York: Scholastic.

Write:Outloud [Computer program]. (1993). Wauconda, IL: Don Johnston Developmental Equipment.

Writer's Helper [Computer program]. (1990). Iowa City, IO: CONDUIT, University of Iowa.

CHAPTER 3

Applebee, A. N., & Langer, J. A. (1983). Instructional scaffolding: Reading and writing as natural language activities. Language Arts, 60, 168–175.

Atwell, N. (1987). In the middle: Writing, reading, and learning with adolescents. Portsmouth, NH: Heinemann.

Bahr, C. M., & Nelson, N. W. (1993). Linking text-processing tools to student needs. Unpublished manuscript, Western Michigan University, Kalamazoo.

Bangert-Drowns, R. L. (1993). The word processor as an instructional tool: A meta-analysis of word processing in writing instruction. Review of Educational Research, 63, 69–93.

Barenbaum, E. M., Newcomer, P. L., & Nodine, B. F. (1987). Children's ability to write stories as a function of variation in task, age, and developmental level. Learning Disability Quarterly, 10, 175–188.

Bereiter, C., & Scardamalia, M. (1985). Cognitive coping strategies and the problem of "inert knowledge." In S. Chipman, J. Segal, & R. Glaser (Eds.), Thinking and learning skills: Current research and open questions (Vol. 2, pp. 65–80). Hillsdale, NJ: Erlbaum.

Bereiter, C., & Scardamalia, M. (1987). The psychology of written expression. Hillsdale, NJ: Erlbaum.

Bing, J., Swicegood, P., Delaney, E., & Hallum, C. (1993). Technology and whole language for students with learning disabilities. LD Forum, 19(1), 6–12.

Boder, E., & Jarrico, S. (1982). Boder test of reading–spelling patterns. San Antonio, TX: Psychological Corp.

Bruner, J. S. (1978). The role of dialogue in language acquisition. In A. Sinclair, R. J. Jarvella, & W. J. M. Levelt (Eds.), The child's conception of language: Springer series in language and communication (pp. 242–256). New York: Springer-Verlag.

Calkins, L. M. (1983). Lessons from a child: On the teaching and learning of writing. Portsmouth, NH: Heinemann.

Calkins, L. M. (1991). Living between the lines. Portsmouth, NH: Heinemann.

Cazden, C. B. (1983). Adult assistance to language development: Scaffolds, models, and direct instruction. In R. Parker & F. Davis (Eds.), Developing literacy: Young children's use of language (pp. 3–18). Newark, DE: International Reading Association.

Cochran, P. S., & Bull, G. L. (1991). Integrating word processing into language intervention. Topics in Language Disorders, 11(2), 31–49.

Cochran-Smith, M. (1991). Word processing and writing in elementary classrooms: A critical review of related literature. Review of Educational Research, 61, 107–155.

Daiute, C. (1992). Multimedia composing: Extending the resources of kindergarten to writers across the grades. Language Arts, 69, 250–260.

Dwyer, D. (1994). Apple classrooms of tomorrow: What we've learned. Educational Leadership, 51(7), 4–10.

Englert, C. S. (1992). Writing instruction from a sociocultural perspective: The holistic, dialogic, and social enterprise of writing. Journal of Learning Disabilities, 25, 153–172.

Englert, C. S., & Palincsar, A. S. (1991). Reconsidering instructional research in literacy from a sociocultural perspective. Learning Disabilities Research & Practice, 6, 225–229.

Entwisle, D. R., & Astone, N. M. (1994). Some practical guidelines for measuring youths' race/ethnicity and socioeconomic status. Child Development, 65, 1521–1540.

Gardner, J. E., & Bates, P. (1991). Attitudes and attributions on use of microcomputers in school by students who are mentally handicapped. Education and Training in Mental Retardation, 26(1), 98–107.

Golub, L. S., & Frederick, W. C. (1970). An analysis of children's writing under different stimulus conditions. Research in the Teaching of English, 4, 168–180.

Graham, S., & Harris, K. R. (1989). Component analysis of cognitive strategy instruction: Effects on learning disabled students' compositions and self-efficacy. Journal of Educational Psychology, 81, 353–361.

Graham, S., & Harris, K. R. (1994). Implications of constructivism for teaching writing to students with special needs. The Journal of Special Education, 28, 275–289.

Graham, S., Harris, K. R., MacArthur, C. A., & Schwartz, S. (1991). Writing and writing instruction for students with learning disabilities: Review of a research program. Learning Disability Quarterly, 14, 89–114.

Graves, A., & Montague, M. (1991). Using story grammar cueing to improve the writing of students with learning disabilities. Learning Disabilities Research & Practice, 6, 246–250.

Graves, A., Montague, M., & Wong, Y. (1990). The effects of procedural facilitation on story composition of learning disabled students. Learning Disabilities Research, 5, 88–93.

Graves, D. H. (1983). Writing: Teachers and children at work. Portsmouth, NH: Heinemann.

Hammill, D. D., & Larsen, S. C. (1988). Test of written language–2. Austin, TX: PRO-ED.

Hedberg, N. L., & Stoel-Gammon, C. (1986). Narrative analysis: Clinical procedures. Topics in Language Disorders, 7(1), 58–69.

Hedberg, N. L., & Westby, C. E. (1993). Analyzing storytelling skills: Theory to practice. Tucson, AZ: Communication Skill Builders.

Hermann, M. (1991). Type to learn [Computer program]. Pleasantville, NY: Sunburst Communications.

Hunt, K. W. (1970). Syntactic maturity in school children and adults. Society for Research in Child Development Monographs, No. 134, 35(1).

Hunt-Berg, M., Rankin, J., & Beukelman, D. (1994). Ponder the possibilities: Computer-supported writing for struggling writers. Learning Disabilities Research & Practice, 9, 169–178.

MacArthur, C. A. (1988). The impact of computers on the writing process. Exceptional Children, 54, 536–542.

MacArthur, C. A. (1993). Beyond word processing: Computer support for writing processes. LD Forum, 19(1), 22-27.

MacArthur, C. A., & Graham, S. (1987). Learning disabled students' composing under three methods of text production: Handwriting, word processing, and dictation. The Journal of Special Education, 21, 22–42.

MacArthur, C. A., Graham, S., & Schwartz, S. (1993). Integrating strategy instruction and word processing into a process approach to writing instruction. School Psychology Review, 22, 671–681.

MacArthur, C. A., Schwartz, S. S., & Graham, S. (1991). A model for writing instruction: Integrating word processing and strategy instruction into a process approach to writing. Learning Disabilities Research & Practice, 6, 230–236.

Malouf, D. B. (1987-88). The effects of instructional computer games on continuing student motivation. The Journal of Special Education, 21(4), 27–38.

Miller, J. F., & Chapman, R. (1986). Systematic analysis of language transcripts [Computer program]. Madison, WI: Language Analysis Laboratory, Waisman Center on Mental Retardation and Human Development.

Montague, M., Graves, A., & Leavell, A. (1991). Planning, procedural facilitation, and narrative composition of junior high students with learning disabilities. Learning Disabilities Research & Practice, 6, 219–224.

Montague, M., Maddux, C. D., & Dereshiwsky, M. I. (1990). Story grammar and comprehension and production of narrative prose by students with learning disabilities. Journal of Learning Disabilities, 23, 190–197.

Nelson, N. W. (1995). Scaffolding in the secondary school: A tool for curriculum-based language intervention. In D. F. Tibbits (Ed.), Language disabilities beyond the primary grades (pp. 377–421). Austin, TX: PRO-ED.

Newcomer, P. L., Barenbaum, E. M., & Nodine, B. F. (1988). Comparison of the story production of LD, normal-achieving, and low-achieving children under two modes of production. Learning Disability Quarterly, 11, 82–96.

Nodine, B. F., Barenbaum, E. M., & Newcomer, P. L. (1985). Story composition by learning disabled, reading disabled, and normal children. Learning Disability Quarterly, 8, 167–179.

Roblyer, M. D., Castine, W. H., & King, F. J. (1988). Assessing the impact of computer-based instruction: A review of recent research. Computers in the Schools, 5(3/4), 11–149.

Rogers, A. (1985). FrEdWriter [Computer program]. Santa Clara, CA: Computer Using Educators Softswap.

Scardamalia, M., & Bereiter, C. (1986). Research on written composition. In M. Wittrock (Ed.), Handbook of research on teaching (3rd ed., pp. 778–803). New York: Macmillan.

Stein, N. L., & Glenn, C. G. (1979). An analysis of story comprehension in elementary school children. In R. O. Freedle (Ed.), New directions in discourse processing (Vol. 2, pp. 53–120). Norwood, NJ: Ablex.

Stein, N. L., & Glenn, C. G. (1982). Children's concept of time: The development of a story schema. In W. Freeman (Ed.), The developmental psychology of time (pp. 255–282). New York: Academic Press.

Storeygard, J., Simmons, R., Stumpf, M., & Pavloglou, E. (1993). Making computers work for students with special needs. Teaching Exceptional Children, 26(1), 22–24.

Teale, W. H., & Sulzby, E. (1986). (Eds.). Emergent literacy: Writing and reading. Norwood, NJ: Ablex.

Tharp, R. G., & Gallimore, R. (1988). Rousing minds to life: Teaching, learning, and schooling in social context. New York: Cambridge University Press.

Thomas, C., Englert, C., & Gregg, S. (1987). An analysis of errors and strategies in the expository writing of learning disabled students. Remedial and Special Education, 8, 21–30.

Tolman, M. N., & Allred, R. A. (1991). The computer and education. Washington, DC: National Education Association.

Urban, D., Rushing, L., & Star, J. (1990). Once upon a time [Computer program]. New Haven, CT: Compu-Teach Corp.

Vacc, N. N. (1987). Word processor versus handwriting: A comparative study of writing samples produced by mildly mentally handicapped students. Exceptional Children, 54, 156–165.

Vallecorsa, A. L., & Garriss, E. (1990). Story composition skills of middle-grade students with learning disabilities. Exceptional Children, 57, 48–54.

Warden, M. R., & Hutchinson, T. A. (1992). Writing process test. Chicago: Riverside.

Weaver, C. (1982). Welcoming errors as signs of growth. Language Arts, 59, 438–444.

Westby, C. E., Van Dongen, R., & Maggart, Z. (1989). Assessing narrative competence. Seminars in Speech and Language, 10(1), 63–76.

Yang, Y. (1992). The effects of media on motivation and content recall: Comparison of computer- and print-based instruction. Journal of Educational Technology Systems, 20(2), 95–105.

CHAPTER 4

Allen, R. V., & Allen, C. (1968). Language experience in reading. Chicago: Encyclopedia Britannica.

Ashton-Warner, S. (1986). Teacher (rev. ed.). New York: Simon & Schuster.

Bereiter, C., & Scardamalia, M. (1987). The psychology of written composition. Hillsdale, NJ: Erlbaum.

California State Department of Education. (1986). Handbook for planning an effective writing program (rev. ed.). Sacramento: California State Department of Education.

Englert, C., Anthony, H., Fear, K., & Gregg, S. (1988). A case for writing intervention: Strategies for writing informational text. Learning Disability Focus, 3, 98–113.

Graham, S., & Harris, K. (1988). Instructional recommendations for teaching writing to exceptional students. Exceptional Children, 54, 506–512.

Graham, S., & Harris, K. (1989). Improving learning disabled students' skills at composing essays: Self-instructional strategy training. Exceptional Children, 56, 201–214.

Jacobson, S. (1994). Voice activated word processing: An application of computers for enhancing the learning of students with learning disabilities [summary]. In Proceedings of the Annual Technology and Media Conference (pp. 43–44).

MacArthur, C., & Graham, S. (1987). Learning disabled students' composing under three methods of text production: Handwriting, word processing and dictation. The Journal of Special Education, 21(3), 22–42.

Newcomer, P., & Barenbaum, E. (1991). The written composing ability of children with learning disabilities: A review of the literature from 1980 to 1990. Journal of Learning Disabilities, 24, 578–592.

Stauffer, R. (1970). The language experience approach to teaching reading. New York: Harper & Row.

VoiceType. (1992). IBM Direct, PC Software Dept., One Culver Road, Dayton, NJ 08810.

Wechsler, D. (1974). Wechsler intelligence scale for children–Revised. San Antonio, TX: Psychological Corp.

Wetzel, K. (1992). Computers and the writing process. Eugene, OR: ISTE.

Woodcock, R. W. (1989). Woodcock-Johnson tests of achievement: Standard and supplementary batteries. Allen, TX: DLM Teaching Resources.

CHAPTER 5

Becker, H. J. (1991). How computers are used in United States schools: Basic data from the 1989 I.E.A. computers in education survey. Journal of Educational Computing Research, 7, 385–406.

Carroll, J. B. (1963). A model for school learning. Teachers College Record, 64, 723–733.

Chiang, B. (1986). Initial learning and transfer effects of microcomputer drills on LD students' multiplication skills. Learning Disability Quarterly, 9, 118–123.

Collins, M., Carnine, D., & Gersten, R. (1987). Elaborated corrective feedback and the acquisition of reasoning skills: A study of computer assisted instruction. Exceptional Children, 54, 254–262.

Cosden, M. A. (1988). Microcomputer instruction and perceptions of effectiveness by special and general education elementary school teachers. The Journal of Special Education, 22, 242–253.

Cosden, M. A., & Abernathy, T. V. (1990). Microcomputer use in the schools: Teacher roles and instructional options. Remedial and Special Education, 11(5), 31–38.

Eckert, R., & Davidson, J. (1987). Math blaster plus [Computer software]. Torrance, CA: Davidson & Associates.

Fuchs, D., & Fuchs, L. (1994). Inclusive schools movement and the radicalization of special education reform. Exceptional Children, 60, 294–309.

Harris, K., Graham, S., Reid, R., McElroy, K., & Hamby, R. S. (1994). Self-monitoring of attention versus self-monitoring of performance: Replication and cross-task comparison studies. Learning Disability Quarterly, 17, 121–139.

Hasselbring, T., Goin, L., & Bransford, J. (1988). Developing math automaticity in learning handicapped children: The role of computerized drill and practice. Focus on Exceptional Children, 20(6), 1–7.

Haynes, M. C., & Jenkins, J. (1986). *Reading instruction in special education resource rooms. American Educational Research Journal, 23,* 161–190.

Kaufman, A., & Kaufman, N. (1985). *Kaufman test of educational achievement. Circle Pines, MN: American Guidance Service.*

Kulik, C. C., & Kulik, J. A. (1991). *Effectiveness of computer-based instruction: An updated analysis. Computers in Human Behavior, 7,* 75–94.

Kulik, J., & Kulik, C. (1987). *Review of recent research literature on computer-based instruction. Contemporary Educational Psychology, 12,* 222–230.

Majsterek, D., & Wilson, R. (1989). *Computer-assisted instruction for students with learning disabilities: Considerations for practitioners. Learning Disabilities Focus, 5,* 18–27.

Majsterek, D., & Wilson, R. (1993). *Computer-assisted instruction (CAI): An update on applications for students with learning disabilities. LD Forum, 19(1),* 19–21.

Miller, J. H., & Milam, C. P. (1987). *Multiplication and division errors committed by learning disabled students. Learning Disabilities Research, 2,* 119–122.

Pellegrino, J. W., & Goldman, S. R. (1987). *Information processing and elementary mathematics. Journal of Learning Disabilities, 20,* 23–32, 57.

Rosenshine, B. (1983). *Teaching functions in instructional programs. The Elementary School Journal, 83,* 335–351.

Salisbury, D. G. (1990). *Cognitive psychology and its implications for designing drill and practice activities for the computer. Journal of Computer-Based Instruction, 17,* 22–30.

Schmidt, M., Weinstein, T., Niemic, R., & Walberg, H. J. (1985-86). *Computer-assisted instruction with exceptional children. The Journal of Special Education, 19,* 493–501.

Sindelar, P., Rosenberg, M., & Wilson, R. (1989). *An adapted alternating treatments design for instructional purposes. Education and Treatment of Children, 8,* 67–76.

Trifiletti, J. J., Frith, G. H., & Armstrong, S. (1984). *Microcomputers versus resource rooms for LD students: A preliminary investigation of the effects on math skills. Learning Disability Quarterly, 7,* 69–76.

U.S. Department of Education, Office of Special Education and Rehabilitative Services. (1992). *Fourteenth annual report to Congress on the implementation of the Individuals with Disabilities Education Act. Washington, DC: Author.*

Watkins, M. W., & Webb, C. (1981). *Computer assisted instruction with learning disabled students. Educational Computer Magazine, 1(3),* 24–27.

Wechsler, D. (1974). *Wechsler intelligence scale for children–Revised. San Antonio, TX: Psychological Corp.*

Wilson, R., Majsterek, D., & Simmons, D. (1994). *Teaching math facts purposefully. Unpublished manuscript.*

Wilson, R., & Wesson, C. (1986). *Making every minute count: Academic learning time in LD classrooms. Learning Disabilities Focus, 2,* 13–19.

Woodward, J., Carnine, D., Gersten, R., Gleason, M., Johnson, G., & Collins, M. (1986). *Applying instructional design principles to CAI for mildly handicapped students: Four recently conducted studies. Journal of Special Education Technology, 8,* 13–26.

CHAPTER 6

Apple Computer, Inc. (1995). Hypercard (Version 2.3) [Computer software]. Santa Clara, CA: Claris Corp.

Babbitt, B. C. (1993). Hypermedia: Making the mathematics connection. Intervention in School and Clinic, 28, 294–301.

Babbitt, B. C., & Kubala, D. (1991). Mathematics Assistant Program (MAP) [Hypercard software]. Las Vegas, NV: Authors.

Babbitt, B. C., & Usnick, V. (1993). Hypermedia: A vehicle for connections. Arithmetic Teacher, 40, 430–432.

Bahr, C. M., & Rieth, H. J. (1989). The effects of instructional computer games and drill and practice software on learning disabled students' mathematics achievement. Computers in the Schools, 6, 87–101.

Bennett, K. (1982). The effects of syntax and verbal mediation on learning disabled students' verbal mathematical problem scores. Dissertation Abstracts International, 42, 1093A.

Berthold, H. C., & Sachs, R. H. (1974). Education of the minimally brain damaged child by computer and by teacher. Programmed Learning and Educational Technology, 11(3), 121–124.

Blankenship, C. S., & Lovitt, T. C. (1976). Story problems: Merely confusing or downright befuddling? Journal for Research in Mathematics Education, 7, 290–298.

Bley, M. S., & Thornton, C. A. (1989). Teaching mathematics to the learning disabled. Austin, TX: PRO-ED.

Bos, C. S., & Anders, P. L. (1990). Interactive teaching and learning: Instructional practices for teaching content and strategic knowledge. In T. E. Scruggs & B. Y. L. Wong (Eds.), Intervention research in learning disabilities (pp. 166–185). New York: Spring-Verlag.

Bottge, B. A., & Hasselbring, T. S. (1993). A comparison of two approaches for teaching complex, authentic mathematics problems to adolescents in remedial math classes. Exceptional Children, 59, 556–566.

Bransford, J. D., Sherwood, R. D., Hasselbring, T. S., Kinzer, C. K., & Williams, S. M. (1990). Anchored instruction: Why we need it and how technology can help. In D. Nix & R. Spiro (Eds.), Cognition, education, multimedia (pp. 115–141). Hillsdale, NJ: Erlbaum.

Carnine, D. W. (1980a). Two letter discrimination sequences: High-confusion alternatives first versus low-confusion alternatives first. Journal of Reading Behavior, 12(1), 41–47.

Carnine, D. W. (1980b). Relationships between stimulus variation and the formation of misconceptions. Journal of Educational Research, 74, 106–110.

Case, L. P., Harris, K. R., & Graham, S. (1992). Improving the mathematical problem-solving skills of students with learning disabilities: Self-regulated strategy development. The Journal of Special Education, 26, 1–19.

Cawley, J. F., & Miller, J. H. (1989). Cross-sectional comparisons of the mathematical performance of children with learning disabilities: Are we on the right track toward comprehensive programming? Journal of Learning Disabilities, 23, 250–254, 259.

Cawley, J. F., Miller, J. H., & School, B. A. (1987). A brief inquiry of arithmetic word-problem solving among learning disabled secondary students. Learning Disabilities Focus, 2, 87–93.

Christensen, C. A., & Gerber, M. M. (1990). Effectiveness of computerized drill and practice games in teaching basic math facts. Exceptionality, 1, 149–165.

Cognition and Technology Group at Vanderbilt University. (1991). Technology and design of generative learning environments. Educational Technology, 31(5), 34–40.

Cognition and Technology Group at Vanderbilt University. (1992). The adventures of Jasper Woodbury: Assessment of instructional outcomes. Nashville, TN: Vanderbilt University.

Darch, C., Carnine, S., & Gersten, R. (1984). Explicit instruction in mathematics problem solving. Journal of Educational Research, 77, 351–359.

Dunlap, W. P., & Strope, G. J. (1982). Reading mathematics: Review of literature. Focus on Learning Problems in Mathematics, 4, 39–50.

Englert, C. S., Culatta, B. E., & Horn, D. G. (1987). Influence of irrelevant information in addition word problems on problem solving. Learning Disability Quarterly, 10, 29–36.

Fafard, M. (1976). The effects of instruction on verbal problem solving in learning disabled children. Dissertation Abstracts International, 37, 5741A.

Fleischner, J. E., Nuzum, M. B., & Marzola, E. S. (1987). Devising an instructional program to teach arithmetic problem-solving skills to students with learning disabilities. Journal of Learning Disabilities, 20, 214–217.

Gleason, M., Carnine, D., & Boriero, D. (1990). Improving CAI effectiveness with attention to instructional design in teaching story problems to mildly handicapped students. Journal of Special Education Technology, 10, 130–136.

Goldman, S. R., & Pellegrino, J. W. (1987). Information processing and educational microcomputer technology: Where do we go from here? Journal of Learning Disabilities, 20, 144–154.

Greenstein, J., & Strains, P. S. (1977). The utility of the Keymath diagnostic arithmetic test for adolescent learning disabled students. Psychology in the Schools, 14, 275–282.

Hasselbring, T., Sherwood, R., Bransford, J., Fleenor, K., Griffith, D., & Goin, L. (1987–1988). An evaluation of a level-one instructional videodisc program. Journal of Educational Technology Systems, 16, 151–169.

Havertape, J., & Kass, C. (1978). Examination of problem solving in learning disabled adolescents through verbalized self-instruction. Learning Disability Quarterly, 1, 94–100.

Howell, R., Sidorenko, E., & Jurica, J. (1987). The effects of computer use on the acquisition of multiplication facts by a student with learning disabilities. Journal of Learning Disabilities, 20, 336–340.

Hutchinson, N. L. (1993). Effects of cognitive strategy instruction on algebra problem solving of adolescents with learning disabilities. Learning Disability Quarterly, 16, 34–63.

IBM Corp. (1992). Linkway (Version 2.01) [Computer software]. Armonk, NY: Author.

Kameenui, E. J., & Simmons, D. C. (1990). Designing instructional strategies: The prevention of academic learning problems. Columbus, OH: Merrill.

Kolich, E. M. (1985). Microcomputer technology with the learning disabled: A review of the literature. Journal of Learning Disabilities, 18, 428–431.

Kramer, K. (1970). The teaching of elementary school mathematics. Boston: Allyn & Bacon.

Lee, W. M., & Hudson, F. G. (1981). A comparison of verbal problem-solving in arithmetic of learning disabled and non–learning disabled seventh grade males (Research Rep. No. 43). Lawrence: Institute for Research in Learning Disabilities, University of Kansas.

Lerner, J. (1993). Learning disabilities (6th ed.). Boston: Houghton Mifflin.

Lynch, P. (1991). Multimedia: Getting started. Sunnyvale, CA: Publix Information Products.

Mahlios, J. (1988). Word problems: Do I add or subtract? Arithmetic Teacher, 36, 48–52.

Mastropieri, M. A., Scruggs, T. E., & Shiah, S. (1991). Mathematics instruction for learning disabled students: A review of research. Learning Disabilities Research & Practice, 6, 89–98.

Mellard, D., & Alley, G. (1981). Production deficiency vs. processing dysfunction: An experimental assessment of LD adolescents (Research Rep. No. 40). Lawrence: Institute for Research in Learning Disabilities, University of Kansas.

Mercer, C. D. (1992). Students with learning disabilities (4th ed.). New York: Macmillan.

Miller, S. P., & Mercer, C. D. (1993a). Using a graduated word problem sequence to promote problem-solving skills. Learning Disabilities Research & Practice, 8, 169–174.

Miller, S. P., & Mercer, C. D. (1993b). Mnemonics: Enhancing the math performance of students with learning difficulties. Intervention in School and Clinic, 29, 78–82.

Montague, M., & Applegate, B. (1993). Middle school students' mathematical problem solving: An analysis of think-aloud protocols. Learning Disability Quarterly, 16, 19–32.

Montague, M., Applegate, B., & Marquard, K. (1993). Cognitive strategy instruction and mathematical problem-solving performance of students with learning disabilities. Learning Disabilities Research & Practice, 8, 223–232.

Montague, M., & Bos, C. S. (1986). Verbal mathematical problem solving and learning disabilities: A review. Focus on Learning Problems in Mathematics, 8(2), 7–21.

Montague, M., & Bos, C. S. (1992). Cognitive and metacognitive characteristics of eighth grade students' mathematical problem solving. Unpublished manuscript.

Moore, L. J., & Carnine, D. (1989). Evaluating curriculum design in the context of active teaching. Remedial and Special Education, 10(4), 28–37.

National Council of Teachers of Mathematics. (1980). An agenda for action: Recommendations for school mathematics of the 1980s. Reston, VA: Author.

National Council of Teachers of Mathematics. (1989). Curriculum and evaluation standards for school mathematics. Reston, VA: Author.

Nuzum, M. (1987). Teaching the arithmetic story problem process. Reading, Writing, and Learning Disabilities, 3, 53–61.

Okolo, C. M. (1992). The effect of computer-assisted instruction format and initial attitude on the arithmetic facts proficiency and continuing motivation of students with learning disabilities. Exceptionality, 3, 195–211.

Paivio, A. (1971). Imagery and verbal processes. New York: Holt, Rinehart & Winston.

Polloway, E. A., & Patton, J. R. (1993). Strategies for teaching learners with special needs. New York: Macmillan.

Polya, G. (1957). How to solve it (2nd ed.). Garden City, NY: Doubleday.

Robinson, S. L., DePascale, C., & Roberts, F. C. (1989). Computer-delivered feedback in group-based instruction: Effects for learning disabled students in mathematics. Learning Disabilities Focus, 5, 28–35.

Roger Wagner Publishing, Inc. (1993). Hyperstudio (Version 3.0) [Computer software]. El Cajon, CA: Author.

Smith, C. R. (1985). Learning disabilities: The interaction of learner, task, and setting. Boston: Little, Brown.

Snyder, K. (1988). RIDGES: A problem-solving math strategy. Academic Therapy, 23, 262–263.

Sowder, L. (1989). Story problems and students' strategies. Arithmetic Teacher, 36(9), 25–26.

Trifiletti, J. J., Frith, G. H., & Armstrong, S. (1984). Microcomputers versus resource rooms for LD students: A preliminary investigation of the effects on math skills. Learning Disability Quarterly, 7, 69–76.

U.S. Department of Education. (1991). America 2000: An education strategy. Washington, DC: U. S. Government Printing Office.

U.S. Department of Labor. (1991). What work requires of schools. Washington, DC: The Secretary's Commission on Achieving Necessary Skills.

Wager, W. (1992). Educational technology: A broader vision. Education and Urban Society, 24, 454–465.

Watanabe, A. (1991). The effects of a mathematical word problem solving strategy on problem solving performance by middle school students with mild disabilities. Unpublished doctoral dissertation, University of Florida, Gainesville.

Willoughby, S. S. (1990). Mathematics education for a changing world. Alexandria, VA: Association for Supervision and Curriculum Development.

Zentall, S. S. (1990). Fact-retrieval automatization and math problem-solving: Learning disabled, attention disordered, and normal adolescents. Journal of Educational Psychology, 82, 856–865.

CHAPTER 7

Alexander, P. A., Kulikowich, J. M., & Jetton, T. L. (1994). The role of subject-matter knowledge and interest in the processing of linear and nonlinear texts. Review of Educational Research, 64(2), 201–252.

Anderson, T. H., & Armbruster, B. B. (1984). Content area textbooks. In R. C. Anderson, J. Osborn, & R. J. Tierney (Eds.), Learning to read in American schools (pp. 193–226). Hillsdale, NJ: Erlbaum.

Apple Computer. (1989). HyperCard 2.0 for the Macintosh computer [Computer program]. Cupertino, CA: Author.

Armbruster, B. B., & Anderson, T. H. (1988). On selecting "considerate" content area textbooks. Remedial and Special Education, 9, 47–52.

Becker, D. A., & Dwyer, M. M. (1994). Using hypermedia to provide learner control. Journal of Educational Multimedia and Hypermedia, 3(2), 155–171.

Boone, R., Higgins, K., Falba, C., & Langley, W. (1993). Cooperative text: Reading and writing in a hypermedia environment. LD Forum, 19(1), 28–37.

Carnine, D., Kameenui, E., & Dixon, B. (1993). NCITE's role in informing publishers and developers. The NCITE Network, 1(1), 1–8.

Chapman, W. (1993). Color coding and the interactivity of multimedia. Journal of Educational Multimedia and Hypermedia, 2(1), 3–23.

Cohen, R. (1993, October). Browsers get BookWorm for Mac. MacWeek.

Gillet, J. W., & Temple, C. (1994). Understanding reading problems: Assessment and instruction. New York: HarperCollins.

Grimm, P. (1983). Attention, perception, and memory: Screen design for CBT. Data Training, 3(1), 41–42.

Harris, J. B., & Grandgenett, N. F. (1993). A developmental sequence of children's semantic relationships: Implications for the design of interactive hypermedia materials. Journal of Educational Multimedia and Hypermedia, 2(1), 83–101.

Heines, J. M. (1983). Screen design strategies for computer aided instruction. Bedford, MA: Digital Press.

Lee, Y. B., & Lehman, J. D. (1993). Instructional cuing in hypermedia: A study with active and passive learners. Journal of Educational Multimedia and Hypermedia, 2(1), 25–37.

Lorch, R. F., & Lorch, E. P. (1986). On-line processing of summary and importance signals in reading. Discourse Processes, 9, 489–496.

Lovitt, T. C., & Horton, S. V. (1994). Strategies for adapting science textbooks for youth with learning disabilities. Remedial and Special Education, 15, 105–116.

Macmillan/McGraw-Hill. (1994). Interactive multimedia literature program. New York: Author.

Mastropieri, M. A., & Scruggs, T. E. (1994). Effective instruction for special education. Austin, TX: PRO-ED.

Mayer, M. (1992). Just grandma and me [Computer program]. Novato, CA: Broderbund Software.

Meyer, B. J. F. (1979). A selected review and discussion of basic research on prose comprehension (Prose Learning Series: Research Report No. 4). Tempe: Arizona State University.

Nagy, W. (1988). Teaching vocabulary to improve reading comprehension. Unpublished manuscript.

Owl International. (1987). Guide: Hypertext for the Macintosh [Computer program]. Seattle, WA: Author.

Pelz, R. (1979). The Washington story: A history of our state. Seattle, WA: Seattle Public Schools.

Potter, B. (1990). The tale of Peter Rabbit [Computer program]. Toronto, Canada: Discis Knowledge Research.

Prescott G. A., Balow, I. H., Hogan, T. P., & Farr, R. C. (1984). The metropolitan achievement test. San Antonio, TX: Psychological Corp.

Prickett, E. M., Higgins, K., & Boone, R. (1994). Technology for learning . . . not learning about technology. Teaching Exceptional Children, 26(4), 56–60.

Sarnacki, R. E. (1979). An examination of test-wiseness in the cognitive test domain. Review of Educational Research, 49(2), 252–279.

Shimmerlik, S. M. (1978). Organization theory and memory for prose: A review of the literature. Review of Educational Research, 48, 103–120.

Tyree, R. B., Fiore, T. A., & Cook, R. A. (1994). Instructional materials for diverse learners. Remedial and Special Education, 15, 363–376.

Wagner, R. (1990). Hyperstudio [Computer program]. Los Angeles: Roger Wagner Publishing.

CHAPTER 8

Adams, M. (1990). Beginning to read: Thinking and learning about print. Cambridge, MA: MIT Press.

Anderson, J. R. (1987). Skill acquisition: Compilation of weak-method problem solutions. Psychological Review, 94, 192–210.

Apple Computer and LIST Services, Inc. (1991). Exemplary writing projects. The Computing Teacher, 18(5), 30–33.

Barnes, D., & Todd, F. (1977). Communication and learning in small groups. London: Routledge & Kegan Paul.

Beck, I. L., & McKeown, M. G. (1991). Substantive and methodological considerations for productive textbook analysis. In J. P. Shaver (Ed.), Handbook of research on social studies teaching and learning (pp. 496–512). New York: Macmillan.

Blumenfeld, P. C., Krajcik, J. S., Marx, R. W., & Soloway, E. (1994). Lessons learned: How collaboration helped middle grade science teachers learn project-based instruction. Elementary School Journal, 94, 539–551.

Blumenfeld, P. C., Soloway, E., Marx, R. W., Krajcik, J. S., Guzdial, M., & Palincsar, A. (1991). Motivating project-based learning: Sustaining the doing, supporting the learning. Educational Psychologist, 26, 369–398.

Bransford, J. D., Goldman, S. R., & Vye, N. J. (in press). Making a difference in people's abilities to think: Reflections on a decade of work and some hopes for the future. In R. J. Sternberg & L. Okagaki (Eds.), Directors of development: Influences on children (pp. 147–180). Hillsdale, NJ: Erlbaum.

Bransford, J., Kinzer, C., Risko, V., Rowe, D., & Vye, N. (1989). Designing invitations to thinking: Some initial thoughts. In S. McCormick & J. Zutell (Eds.), Cognitive and social perspectives for literacy research and instruction (pp. 35–54). Chicago: National Reading Conference.

Bransford, J. D., & Stein, B. S. (1984). The IDEAL problem solver. New York: W. H. Freeman.

Brophy, J. (1988). Teaching for conceptual understanding and higher order applications of social studies content. East Lansing: Institute for research on Teaching, Michigan State University.

Brophy, J. (1990). Teaching social studies for understanding and higher-order applications. The Elementary School Journal, 90, 351–417.

Brown, A. S. (1994). The advancement of learning. Educational Researcher, 23, 4–12.

Brown, J. S., Collins, A., & Duguid, P. (1989). Situated cognition and the culture of learning. Educational Researcher, 17, 32–41.

Carver, S. M. (1992, April). A researcher's approach to assessing interdisciplinary design tasks. Paper presented at the annual meeting of the American Educational Research Association, San Francisco.

Carver, S. M. (in press). The Discover Rochester Design Experiment: Collaborative change through five designs. In J. Hawkins & A. Collins (Eds.), Design experiments: Integrating technology into schools. Cambridge: Cambridge University Press.

Carver, S. M., Lehrer, R., Connell, T., & Erickson, J. (1992). Learning by design: Issues of assessment and implementation. Educational Psychologist, 27, 385–404.

Cherryholmes, C. (1990). Social studies for what century? Social Education, 54, 438–442.

Chi, M. T. H., Glaser, R., & Farr, M. (1988). The nature of expertise. Hillsdale, NJ: Erlbaum.

Chomyn, M. (1992, April). A teacher's approach to assessing interdisciplinary design tasks. Paper presented at the annual meeting of the American Educational Research Association, San Francisco.

Cognition and Technology Group at Vanderbilt. (1990). Anchored instruction and its relationship to situated cognition. Educational Researcher, 19, 2–10.

Cohen, E. G. (1994). Restructuring the classroom: Conditions for productive small groups. Review of Educational Research, 64, 1–35.

Collins, A., Brown, J. S., & Newman, S. E. (1989). Cognitive apprenticeship: Teaching the craft of reading, writing, and mathematics. In L. B. Resnick (Ed.), Knowing and learning: Issues for a cognitive science of instruction. Hillsdale, NJ: Erlbaum.

Cooper, L., Johnson, D., Johnson, R., & Wilderson, F. (1980). Effects of cooperative, competitive, and individualistic experiences on interpersonal attraction among heterogeneous peers. Journal of Social Psychology, 111, 243–252.

Cornbleth, C. (1985). Critical thinking and cognitive process. In W. B. Stanley (Ed.), Review of research in social education 1976–1983 (pp. 11–63). Boulder, CO: ERIC Clearinghouse for Social Studies Education.

Cosden, M. A., Goldman, S. R., & Hine, M. S. (1990). Learning handicapped students' interactions during a microcomputer-based group writing activity. Journal of Special Education Technology, 10, 220–232.

Curtis, C. K. (1991). Social studies for syudents at-risk and with disabilities. In J. P. Shaver (Ed.), Handbook of research on social studies teaching and learning (pp. 157–174). New York: Macmillan.

Dewey, J. (1916). Democracy and education. New York: The Free Press.

Dewey, J. (1933). How we think. Boston: D. C. Heath.

Engle, S. H. (1990). The commission report and citizenship education. Social Education, 54, 431–434.

Epstein, T. L., & Evans, R. W. (December/November, 1990). Special section: Reactions to Charting a course: Social studies for the 21st century. Social Education, 427–429.

Ferretti, R. P., & Cavalier, A. R. (1991). Constraints on the problem solving of persons with mental retardation. In N. W. Bray (Ed.), International review of research in mental retardation (Vol. 17, pp. 153–192). New York: Academic Press.

Ferretti, R. P., & Okolo, C. (1993, February). Children and knowledge design: Perspectives on multimedia design projects in the social studies. Paper presented at Technology and Media Division's (TAM) Annual Conference on Special Education Technology, Cromwell, CT.

Feuerstein, R., Rand, Y., Hoffman, M., Hoffman, R., & Miller, R. (1980). Instrumental enrichment. Baltimore: University Park Press.

Gentile, C. (1992). Exploring new methods for collecting students' school-based writing: NAEP's 1990 portfolio study. Washington, DC: U.S. Government Printing Office.

Harris, K. R., & Graham, S. (1994). Constructivism: Principles, paradigms, and integration. The Journal of Special Education, 28, 233–247.

Hidi, S. (1990). Interest and its contribution as a mental resource for learning. Review of Educational Research, 60, 549–571.

Hidi, S., Renninger, K. A., & Krapp, A. (1992). The present state of interest research. In K. A. Renninger, S. Hidi, & A. Krapp (Eds.), The role of interest in learning and development (pp. 433–446). Hillsdale, NJ: Erlbaum.

Johnson, D. W. (1979). *Educational psychology*. Englewood Cliffs, NJ: Prentice-Hall.

Johnson, D. W., & Johnson, R. (1979). Conflict in the classroom: Controversy and learning. *Review of Educational Research, 49*, 51–70.

Johnson, D. W., & Johnson, R. T. (1981). The integration of the handicapped into the regular classroom: Effects of cooperative and individualistic instruction. *Contemporary Educational Psychology, 6*, 344–355.

Johnson, D. W., & Johnson, R. T. (1982). *Joining together: Group theory and group skills (2nd ed.)*. Englewood Cliffs, NJ: Prentice-Hall.

Johnson, D. W., & Johnson, R. T. (1983). The socialization and achievement crisis: Are cooperative learning experiences the solution? *Applied Social Psychology Annual, 4*, 119–164.

Johnson, D. W., & Johnson, R. T. (1984). Building acceptance of differences between handicapped and nonhandicapped students: The effects of cooperative and individualistic instruction. *Contemporary Educational Psychology, 6*, 344–353.

Johnson, D. W., & Johnson, R. T. (1985). The internal dynamics of cooperative learning groups. In R. Slavin, S. Sharan, S. Kagan, R. H. Lazarowitz, C. Webb, & R. Schmuck (Eds.), *Learning to cooperate, cooperating to learn* (pp. 103–124). New York: Plenum.

Kinder, D., & Bursuck, W. (1991). The search for a unified social studies curriculum: Does history really repeat itself? *Journal of Learning Disabilities, 24*, 270–275, 320.

Krajcik, J. S., Blumenfeld, P. C., Marx, R. W., & Soloway, E. (1994). A collaborative model for helping middle school science teachers learn project-based learning. *The Elementary School Journal, 94*, 483–497.

Kuhn, D. (1991). *The skills of argument*. Cambridge: Cambridge University Press.

Kuhn, D. (in press). Thinking as argument. *Harvard Educational Review*.

Learning with Hypermedia Group. (1989–1991). *HyperAuthor: A users' guide*. Madison: University of Wisconsin.

Lehrer, R. (1993). Authors of knowledge: Patterns of hypermedia design. In S. Lajoie & S. Derry (Eds.), *Computers as cognitive tools* (pp. 197–227). Hillsdale, NJ: Erlbaum.

Lehrer, R., Erickson, J., & Connell, T. (1993, April). *The restless text: Student authoring with hypermedia tools*. Paper presented at the annual meeting of the American Educational Research Association, Atlanta, GA.

Lehrer, R., Erickson, J., & Connell, T. (in press). Learning by designing hypermedia documents. *Computers in the Schools*.

Lundberg, M. A., Coballes-Vega, C., Standiford, S., Langer, L., & Dibble, K. (1992, April). *A study of project-based computer learning*. Paper presented at the annual meeting of the American Educational Research Association, San Francisco.

Marx, R. W., Blumenfeld, P. C., Krajcik, J. S., Blunk, M., Crawford, B., Kelly, B., & Meyer, K. M. (1994). Enacting project-based science: Experiences of four middle grade teachers. *The Elementary School Journal, 94*, 517–538.

McMillan, G. (1990). Multimedia: An educator's link to the 90s. *The Computing Teacher, 18*(3), 7–9.

McNamara, T. P., Miller, D. L., & Bransford, J. D. (1991). Mental models and reading comprehension. In R. Barr, M. Kamil, P. Mosenthal, & T. D. Pearson (Eds.), *Handbook of reading research* (Vol. 2, pp. 490–511). New York: Longman.

Muir, M. (1992). How do you run HyperCard projects? *The Computing Teacher, 20*(2), 10–12.

Nastasi, B. K., & Clements, D. H. (1991). Research on cooperative learning: Implications for practice. School Psychology Review, 20(1), 110–131.

National Assessment of Educational Progress. (1981). Reading, thinking, and writing: Results from the 1979–1980 national assessment of reading and literature (Report No. 11-L-01). Denver: Education Commission of the States.

National Commission on Excellence in Education. (1983). A nation at risk: The imperative for educational reform. Washington, DC: U.S. Government Printing Office.

National Commission on Social Studies in the Schools. (1989). Charting a course: Social studies for the 21st century. Washington, DC: National Commission on the Social Studies in the Schools.

Nelson, J. L. (December/November, 1990). Charting a course backwards: A response to the National Commission's nineteenth century social studies program. Social Education, pp. 434–437.

Newmann, F. M. (1990). Higher order thinking in teaching social studies: A rationale for the assessment of classroom thoughtfulness. Journal of Curriculum Studies, 22, 41–56.

Newmann, F. M. (1991). Classroom thoughtfulness and students' higher order thinking: Common indicators and diverse social studies courses. Theory and Research in Social Education, 19, 410–433.

Nickerson, R. S., Perkins, D. N., & Smith, E. E. (1985). The teaching of thinking. Hillsdale, NJ: Erlbaum.

Okolo, C. M., & Ferretti, R. P. (1994, February). Multimedia project-based learning in social studies classrooms for students with mild disabilities. Paper presented at the TAM Annual Conference on Special Education Technology, St. Paul, MN.

Okolo, C. M., & Ferretti, R. P. (in press). The impact of multimedia design projects on the knowledge, attitudes, and collaboration of students in inclusive classrooms. Journal of Computers in Childhood Education.

Oliver, D. W., & Shaver, J. P. (1966). Teaching public issues in the high school. Boston: Houghton Mifflin.

Palincsar, A. S., & Brown, A. L. (1984). Reciprocal teaching of comprehension-fostering and monitoring activities. Cognition and Instruction, 1, 117–175.

Palincsar, A. S. (1986). The role of dialogue in providing scaffolded instruction. Educational Psychologist, 21, 73–98.

Parker, W. C. (1991). Achieving thinking and decision-making objectives. In J. P. Shaver (Ed.), Handbook of research on social studies teaching and learning (pp. 345–356). New York: Macmillan.

Patton, J., Polloway, E., & Cronin, M. (1987). Social studies instruction for handicapped students: A review of current practices. The Social Studies, 78, 131–135.

Perkins, D. N. (1986). Knowledge as design. Hillsdale, NJ: Erlbaum.

Perlbachs, K. (1992). Envisioning, acquiring, and running a multimedia lab in your classroom. In R. Boone & K. Higgins (Eds.), Multimedia: TAM Topical Guide No. 1 (pp. 25–29). Reston, VA: Council for Exceptional Children.

Pintrich, P. R. (1989). The dynamic interplay of student motivation and cognition in the college classroom. In C. Ames & M. Maehr (Eds.), Advances in motivation and achievement: Motivation-enhancing environment (Vol. 6, pp. 117–160). Greenwich, CT: JAI Press.

Pintrich, P. R., & Garcia, T. (1991). Student goal orientation and self-regulation in the college classroom. In M. Maehr & P. R. Pintrich (Eds.), Advances in motivation and achievement: Goals and self-regulatory processes (Vol. 7, pp. 371–402). Greenwich, CT: JAI Press.

Prickett, E. M. (1992). The multimedia classroom. In R. Boone & K. Higgins (Eds.), Multimedia: TAM Topical Guide No. 1 (pp. 56–65). Reston, VA: Council for Exceptional Children.

Resnick, L. B. (1987). Education and learning to think. Washington, DC: National Academy Press.

Salomon, G., & Globerson, T. (1989). When teams do not function the way they ought to. International Journal of Educational Research, 13, 89–99.

Saloman, G., Perkins, D., & Globerson, T. (1991). Partners in cognition: Extending human intelligence with intelligent technologies. Educational Researcher, 20, 2–9.

Schmalhofer, F., & Kähn, O. (1988). Acquiring computer skills by exploration versus demonstration (Tech. Rep. No. 83.3). Montreal, Quebec: Laboratory of Applied Cognitive Science, McGill University.

Sharan, Y., & Sharan, S. (1992). Expanding cooperative learning through group investigation. New York: Teachers College Press.

Sherwood, R., Kinzer, C., Hasselbring, T., & Bransford, J. (1987). Macro-contexts for learning: Initial findings and issues. Journal of Applied Cognition, 1, 93–108.

Simon, H. A. (1980). Problem solving and education. In D. T. Tuma & R. Reif (Eds.), Problem solving and education: Issues in teaching and research (pp. 81–96). Hillsdale, NJ: Erlbaum.

Slavin, R. E. (1990). Cooperative learning: Theory, research and practice. Englewood Cliffs, NJ: Prentice-Hall.

Smith, K. J. (1992). Using multimedia with Navajo children: An effort to alleviate problems of cultural learning style, background of experience, and motivation. Reading and Writing: Overcoming Learning Difficulties, 8, 287–294.

Smith, K., Johnson, D. W., & Johnson, R. T. (1982). Effects of cooperative and individualistic instruction on the achievement of handicapped, regular, and gifted students. The Journal of Social Psychology, 116, 277–283.

Tobias, S. (1994). Interest, prior knowledge, and learning. Review of Educational Research, 64, 37–54.

Torgesen, J. K., Kistner, J. A., & Morgan, S. (1987). Component processes in working memory. In J. G. Borkowski & J. D. Day (Eds.), Cognition in special children: Comparative approaches to retardation, learning disabilities, and giftedness (pp.49–85). Norwood, NJ: Ablex.

Toulmin, S. E. (1958). The uses of argument. Cambridge: Cambridge University Press.

Turner, S. V., & Dipinto, V. M. (1992). Students as hypermedia authors: Themes emerging from a qualitative study. Journal of Research on Computing in Education, 25, 187–199.

VanSledright, B., & Brophy, J. (1992). Storytelling, imagination, and fanciful elaboration in children's historical reconstructions. American Educational Research Journal, 29, 837–859.

Voss, J. F. (1991). Informal reasoning and international relations. In J. F. Voss, D. N. Perkins, & J. W. Segal (Eds.), Informal reasoning and education (pp. 37–58). Hillsdale, NJ: Erlbaum.

Voss, J. F., Greene, T. R., Post, T. A., & Penner, B. C. (1983). Problem solving skill in the social sciences. In G. H. Bower (Ed.), The psychology of learning and motivation: Advances in research and theory (Vol. 17, pp. 165–213). New York: Academic Press.

Voss, J. F., & Post, T. A. (1988). On the solving of ill-structured problems. In M. T. H. Chi, R. Glaser, & M. J. Farr (Eds.), The nature of expertise (pp. 261–285). Hillsdale, NJ: Erlbaum.

Voss, J. F., Tyler, S. W., & Yengo, L. A. (1983). Individual differences in the solving of social science problems. In R. F. Dillon & R. R. Schmeck (Eds.), Individual differences in cognition (pp. 205–232). New York: Academic Press.

Vygotsky, L. S. (1978). Mind in society. Cambridge, MA: Harvard University Press.

Wiggins, G. P. (1993). Assessing student performance. San Francisco: Jossey-Bass.

Yager, S., Johnson, R. T., Johnson, D. W., & Snider, B. (1985). The impact of group processing on achievement in cooperative learning groups. The Journal of Social Psychology, 126, 389–397.

CHAPTER 9

Adams, A., & Anderson-Inman, L. (1991). Electronic outlining: A computer-based study strategy for handicapped students in regular classrooms. In J. Marr & G. Tindal (Eds.) Oregon conference monograph 1991 (pp. 86–92). Eugene, OR: University of Oregon.

Adams, V. (1992). Comparing paper based and electronic outlining as a study strategy for mainstreamed students with learning disabilities. Unpublished doctoral dissertation, University of Oregon.

Anderson-Inman, L. (1991, April). Computer-based outlining programs: Tools for academic studying and educational change. Paper presented at the annual conference of the American Educational Research Association, Chicago.

Anderson-Inman, L. (1992a). Computer-supported studying for students with reading and writing difficulties. Reading and Writing Quarterly, 8, 317–319.

Anderson-Inman, L. (1992b). Electronic studying: Computer-based information organizers as tools for lifelong learning. In N. Estes & M. Thomas (Eds.), Education "sans frontiers": Proceedings of the ninth annual International Conference on Technology and Education, (pp. 1104–1106). Austin, TX: The University of Texas at Austin.

Anderson-Inman, L. (1995/1996). Computer-assisted outlining: Information organization made easy. Journal of Adolescent & Adult Literacy, 39, 316–320.

Anderson-Inman, L., Horney, M. A., Chen, D., & Lewin, L. (1994). Hypertext literacy: Observations from the ElectroText project. Language Arts, 71(4), 37-45.

Anderson-Inman, L., & Knox-Quinn, C. (1996). Spell checking strategies for successful students. Journal of Adolescent & Adult Literacy, 39, 500–503.

Anderson-Inman, L., Redekopp, R., & Adams, V. (1992). Electronic studying: Using computer-based outlining programs as study tools. Reading and Writing Quarterly: Overcoming Learning Difficulties, 8, 337–358.

Anderson-Inman, L., & Tenny, J. (1989). Electronic studying: Information organizers to help students study "better," not "harder"—Part 1. The Computing Teacher, 16(8), 33–36.

Anderson-Inman, L., & Zeitz, L. (1994). Beyond notecards: Synthesizing information with electronic study tools. The Computing Teacher, 21(8), 21–25.

Armbruster, B. B., Echols, C. H., & Brown, A. L. (1983). The role of metacognition in reading to learn: A developmental perspective (Reading Education Report No. 40). Champaign: University of Illinois at Urbana-Champaign. (ERIC Document Reproduction Service No. ED 228 617)

Arms, V. M. (1984). A dyslexic can compose on a computer. In A. Lane (Ed.), Readings in microcomputers and special education (pp. 64–66). Guilford, CT: Special Learning Corporation.

Aweiss, S. (1994–95). Situating learning in technology: The case of computer-mediated reading supports. Journal of Educational Technology Systems, 23(1), 63–74.

Bianco, L., & McCormick, S. (1989). Analysis of effects of a reading study skill program for high school learning-disabled students. Journal of Educational Research, 82(5), 282–288.

Borkowski, J. G., Schneider, W., & Pressley, M. (1989). The challenges of teaching good information processing to learning disabled students. International Journal of Disability, Development and Education, 36(3), 169–185.

Brown, A. L., Campione, J. C., & Day, J. D. (1981). Learning to learn: On training students to learn from texts. Educational Researcher, 10, 14–21.

Dansereau, D. (1985). Learning strategy research. In J. Segal, S. Chipman, & R. Glaser (Eds.), Thinking and learning skills (pp. 42–64). Hillsdale, NJ: Erlbaum.

Deshler, D. D., & Lenz, B. K. (1989). The strategies instructional approach. International Journal of Disability, Development and Education, 36, 203–224.

Deshler, D. D., & Schumaker, J. B. (1986). Learning strategies: An instructional alternative for low-achieving adolescents. Exceptional Children, 53, 583–590.

Ekvall, E. E. (1986). Ekvall reading inventory (2nd ed.). Boston: Allyn & Bacon.

Fais, L., & Wanderman, R. (1987). A computer-aided writing program for learning disabled adolescents. Litchfield, CT: Forman School.

Graham, S., & MacArthur, C. A. (1988). Improving learning disabled students' skills at revising essays produced on a word processor: Self-instructional strategy training. The Journal of Special Education, 22, 133–152.

Haller, E. P., Child, D. A., & Walberg, H. J. (1988). Can comprehension be taught? A quan-titative synthesis of "metacognitive" studies. Educational Researcher, 17(9), 5–8.

Higgins, K., & Boone, R. (1990). Hypertext computer study guides and the social studies achievement of students with learning disabilities, remedial students, and regular education students. Journal of Learning Disabilities, 23, 529–540.

Horney, M. A., & Anderson-Inman, L. (in press). Hypermedia for readers with hearing impairments: Promoting literacy with electronic text enhancements. In C. K. Kinzer, K. Hinchman, & D. J. Leu (Eds.), Forty-third yearbook—National reading conference.

Horney, M., Zeitz, L., & Anderson-Inman, L. (1991). Electronic outlining promotes thinking and writing across the curriculum. The Writing Notebook, 1(2), 29–33.

Horton, S. V., Lovitt, T. C., Givens, A., & Nelson, R. (1989). Teaching social studies to high school students with academic handicaps in a mainstreamed setting: Effects of a computerized study guide. Journal of Learning Disabilities, 22, 102–107.

Inspiration Software, Inc. (1994). Inspiration 4.0 [Computer software]. Portland, OR: Author.

Jacobi, C. (1986). Word processing for special needs students: Is there really a gain? Educational Technology, 26, 36–39.

Kaufman, A. S., & Kaufman, N. L. (1985). *Kaufman test of educational achievement.* Circle Pines, MN: American Guidance Services.

Kaufman, A. S., & Kaufman, N. L. (1987). *Kaufman brief intelligence test.* Circle Pines, MN: American Guidance Services.

Kerchner, L. B., & Kistinger, B. J. (1984). Language processing/word processing: Written expression, computers and learning disabled students. *Learning Disability Quarterly, 7,* 329–335.

Lajoie, S. P. (1993). Computer environments as cognitive tools for enhancing learning. In S. P. Lajoie & S. J. Derry (Eds.), *Computers as cognitive tools* (pp. 261–288). Hillsdale, NJ: Erlbaum.

Lessen, E., Dudzinski, M., Karsh, K., & Van Acker, R. (1989). A survey of ten years of academic intervention research with learning disabled students: Implications for research and practice. *Learning Disabilities Focus, 4(2),* 106–122.

Loranger, L. A. (1994). The study strategies of successful and unsuccessful high school students. *Journal of Reading Behavior, 26(4),* 347–360.

MacArthur, C. A., & Haynes, J. A. (1995). Student assistant for learning from text (SALT): A hypermedia reading aid. *Journal of Learning Disabilities, 28(3),* 150–159.

MacArthur, C. A., Haynes, J. A., Malouf, D. B., Harris, K., & Owings, M. (1990). Computer assisted instruction with learning disabled students: Achievement, engagement, and other factors that influence achievement. *Journal of Educational Computing Research, 6,* 311–328.

Malouf, D. B., Wizer, D. R., Pilato, V. H., & Grogan, M. M. (1990). Computer-assisted instruction with small groups of mildly handicapped students. *Journal of Special Education, 24,* 51–68.

McCrady, W. (1982). *Listening and the learning disabled student.* (ERIC Document Reproduction Service No. ED 261 440)

McGuire, J. M., & O'Donnell, J. M. (1989). Helping learning disabled students to achieve: Collaboration between faculty and support services. *College Teaching, 37(1),* 29–32.

Newcomer, P. L., & Bryant, B. R. (1993). *Diagnostic achievement test for adolescents* (2nd ed.). Austin, TX: PRO-ED.

Novak, J. D., & Gowin, D. B. (1984). *Learning how to learn.* New York: Cambridge University Press.

Oregon Department of Education. (1994, July). *Oregon administrative rules: Chapter 581, Division 15–Department of Education.* Salem, OR: Office of the Secretary of State.

Outhred, L. (1989). Word processing: Its impact on children's writing. *Journal of Learning Disabilities, 22,* 262–264.

Pea, R. D. (1985). Beyond amplification: Using the computer to reorganize mental functioning. *Educational Psychologist, 20(4),* 167–182.

Perkins, D. N. (1985). The fingertip effect: How information-processing technology shapes thinking. *Educational Researcher, 14(7),* 11–17.

Reid, D. K. (1988). *Teaching the learning disabled.* Boston: Allyn & Bacon.

Reith, H. J., & Polsgrove, L. (1994). Curriculum and instructional issues in teaching secondary students with learning disabilities. *Learning Disabilities Research & Practice, 9(2),* 118–126.

Reyes, E. I., Gallego, M. A., Duran, G. Z., & Scanlon, D. J. (1989). Integration of internal concepts and external factors: Extending the knowledge of learning disabled adolescents. Journal of Early Adolescence, 9(1-2), 112–124.

Salomon, G. (1993). On the nature of pedagogic computer tools: The case of the writing partner. In S. P. Lajoie & S. J. Derry (Eds.), Computers as cognitive tools (pp. 179-196). Hillsdale, NJ: Erlbaum.

Salomon, G., Perkins, D. N., & Globerson, T. (1991). Partners in cognition: Extending human intelligence with intelligent technologies. Educational Researcher, 20, 10–16.

Saski, J., Swicegood, P., & Carter, J. (1983). Notetaking formats for learning disabled adolescents. Learning Disability Quarterly, 6, 265–272.

Schwartz, S. S., & MacArthur, C. A. (1990). Creating a community of writers: The Computers and Writing Instruction Project. Preventing School Failure, 34(4), 9–13.

Seidenberg, P. L. (1985). A framework for curriculum development for secondary learning disabled students. Brooklyn, NY: Long Island University Press. (ERIC Document Reproduction Service No. ED 274112)

Sizer, T. R. (1984). Horace's compromise: The dilemma of the American high school. Boston: Houghton Mifflin.

Sullivan, P. (1991). Taking control of the page: Electronic writing and word publishing. In G. E. Hawisher & C. L. Selfe (Eds.), Evolving perspectives on computers and composition studies: Questions for the 1990s (pp. 43–64). Urbana, IL: National Council of Teachers of English.

Tenny, J. L. (1988). A study of the effectiveness of computer mediated and rereading study procedures. Unpublished doctoral dissertation, University of Oregon.

Tenny, J. L. (1990). Inspiration: The thought processor. The Computing Teacher, 18(2), 46–49.

Thomas, J. W., & Rohwer, W. D., Jr. (1986). Academic studying: The role of learning strategies. Educational Psychologist, 21(1&2), 19–41.

Torgeson, J. K., & Licht, B. (1983). The disabled child as an inactive learner: Retrospect and prospects. In J. D. McKinney & L. Feagans (Eds.), Current topics in learning disabilities (Volume 1, pp. 3–31). Norwood, NJ: Ablex.

Wechsler, D. (1974). Wechsler intelligence scale for children. San Antonio, TX: Psychological Corp.

Wechsler, D. (1981). Wechsler adult intelligence scale–Revised. San Antonio, TX: Psychological Corp.

Wechsler, D. (1991). Wechsler intelligence scale for children–Third edition. San Antonio, TX: Psychological Corp.

Weinstein, C. E., & Palmer, D. R. (1990). Learning and study strategies inventory–High school version. Clearwater, FL: H & H Publishing.

Wise, W. B., & Olson, K. R. (1994). Computer speech and the remediation of reading and spelling problems. Journal of Special Education Technology, 12(3), 207–220.

Woodcock, R. (1987). Woodcock reading mastery tests–Revised. Circle Pines, MN: American Guidance Service.

Woodcock, R. W. (Ed.). (1989). Woodcock-Johnson psycho-educational battery–Revised. Allen, TX: DLM.

Woodcock, R. W., & Johnson, M. B. (Eds.). (1977). Woodcock-Johnson psycho-educational battery/tests of cognitive ability. Allen, TX: DLM.

Yankelovich, N., Meyrowitz, N., & Van Dam, A. (1985). Reading and writing the electronic book. Computer, 18, 15–30.

Zeitz, L., & Anderson-Inman, L. (1992). The effects of computer-based formative concept mapping on learning high school science. Paper presented at the annual meeting of the American Educational Research Association, San Francisco, CA.

Zigmond, N. (1990). Preview. Special Issue: Enhancing the education of difficult-to-teach students—Federally sponsored research in the mainstream. Exceptional Children, 57, 100.

Zigmond, N., Vallecorsa, A., & Leinhardt, G. (1980). Reading instruction for students with learning disabilities. Topics in Language Disorders, 1, 89–98.

CHAPTER 10

Adelman, P. B., & Vogel, S. A. (1992). Issues in program evaluation. In S. A. Vogel & P. B. Adelman (Eds.), Success for college students with learning disabilities (pp. 323–343). New York: Springer-Verlag.

Barton, R. S., & Fuhrmann, B. S. (1994). Counseling and psychotherapy for adults with learning disabilities. In P. J. Gerber & H. B. Reiff (Eds.), Learning disabilities in adulthood: Persisting problems and evolving issues (pp. 82–92). Stoneham, MA: Andover Medical.

Blalock, J. (1981). Persistent problems and concerns of young adults with learning disabilities. In W. Cruickshank & A. Silvers (Eds.), Bridges to tomorrow: The best of ACLD (Vol. 2, pp. 31–45). Syracuse, NY: Syracuse University Press.

Brinckerhoff, L. C. (1993). Establishing support services with minimal resources for college students with learning disabilities. In M. L. Farrell (Ed.), Support services for students with learning disabilities in higher education: A compendium of readings (Vol. 3, pp. 54–63). Columbus, OH: Association on Higher Education and Disability.

Brown, C. (1989). Computer access in higher education for students with disabilities: A practical guide to the selection and use of adapted computer technology (2nd ed.). Washington, DC: Fund for the Improvement of Postsecondary Education, U.S. Department of Education.

Bursuck, W. D., Rose, E., Cowen, S., & Yahaya, M. A. (1989). Nationwide survey of postsecondary education services for students with learning disabilities. Exceptional Children, 56, 236–245.

Button, C., & Wobschall, R. (1994). The Americans with Disabilities Act and assistive technology. Journal of Vocational Rehabilitation, 4, 196–201.

Chandler, S., Czerlinsky, T., & Wehman, P. (1993). Provisions of assistive technology: Bridging the gap of accessibility. In P. Wehman (Ed.), The ADA mandate for social change (pp. 117–134). Baltimore: Brookes.

Collins, T. (1990). The impact of microcomputer word processing on the performance of learning disabled students in a required first year writing course. Computers and Composition, 8, 49–68.

Cutler, E. (1990). Evaluating spell checkers, thesauruses, dictionaries, and grammar editors for the community college student with learning disabilities. In H. J. Murphy (Ed.), Proceedings of the Fifth Annual Conference on Technology and Persons with Disabilities (pp. 163–175).

Fairweather, J. ., & Shaver, D. M. (1991). Making the transition to postsecondary education and training. Exceptional Children, 34, 264–270.

Florida Bureau of Career Development. (1994). Career and information delivery system report. Tallahassee, FL: Author.

Garner, J., & Campbell, P. (1987). Technology for persons with severe disabilities: Practical and ethical considerations. The Journal of Special Education, 21, 24–32.

Gray, R. A. (1981). Services for the adult LD: A working paper. Journal of Learning Disabilities, 4, 426–431.

Henderson, C. (1992). College freshmen with disabilities: A statistical profile. Washington, DC: American Council on Education, HEATH Resource Center (ERIC Document Reproduction No. ED 354 792)

Hilton-Chalfen, L. (1991a). Computers and students with disabilities: New challenges for higher education. (Available from Educational Uses of Information Technology, 1112 16th St. NW, Suite 600, Washington, DC 20036)

Hilton-Chalfen, D. (1991b). Starting an assistive technology program. In H. J. Murphy (Ed.), The impact of exemplary technology-support programs on students with disabilities (pp 42–59). Washington, DC: National Council on Disability. (ERIC Document Reproduction Service No. ED 361 950)

Hockley, D. (1990). Planning adaptive computing services in post-secondary education: An integrated approach. In Proceedings of Beyond Ramps: A disabilities services conference for higher education (pp. 25–33). St. Paul, MN: (ERIC Document Reproduction Service No. ED 322 693)

Jarrow, J. E. (1993). A quick refresher course. In M. L. Farrell (Ed.), Support services for students with learning disabilities in higher education: A compendium of readings (Vol. 3, pp. 54–63). Columbus, OH: Association on Higher Education and Disability.

Mangrum, C. T., & Strichart, S. S. (1988). College and the learning disabled student. Philadelphia: Grune & Stratton.

Patton, J. R., & Polloway, E. A. (1992). Learning disabilities: The challenge of adulthood. Journal of Learning Disabilities, 25, 410–416.

P.L. 100–407, The Technology-Related Assistance for Individuals with Disabilities Act, 1988.

Primus, C. (1990). Computer assistance model for learning disabled (Grant # GOO 8630152-88). Washington, DC: Office of Special Education and Rehabilitation Services, U.S. Department of Education.

Raskind, M. H. (1994). Assistive technology for adults with learning disabilities: A rationale for use. In P. J. Gerber & H. B. Reiff (Eds.), Learning disabilities in adulthood: Persisting problems and evolving issues (pp. 152–162). Stoneham, MA: Andover Medical.

Raskind, M. H., & Scott, N. (1993). Technology for postsecondary students with learning disabilities. In S. A. Vogel & P. B. Adelman (Eds.), Success for college students with learning disabilities (pp. 240–280). New York: Springer-Verlag.

Reiff, H. B., Gerber, P. J., & Ginsberg, R. (1992). Learning to achieve: Suggestions from adults with learning disabilities. In M. L. Farrell (Ed.), Support services for students with learning disabilities in higher education: A compendium of readings (Vol. 3, pp. 135–144). Columbus, OH: Association on Higher Education and Disability.

Rothstein, L. F. (1993). Legal issues. In S. A. Vogel & P. B. Adelman (Eds.), Success for college students with learning disabilities (pp. 21–35). New York: Springer-Verlag.

Shaw, S., McGuire, J., & Brinckerhoff, L. (1994). College and university programming. In P. J. Gerber & H. B. Reiff (Eds.), Learning disabilities in adulthood: Persisting problems and evolving issues (pp. 141–151). Stoneham, MA: Andover Medical.

Vogel, S. A. (1987). Issues and concerns in LD college programming. In D. J. Johnson & J. W. Blalock (Eds.), Adults with learning disabilities: Clinical studies (pp. 239–275). Orlando, FL: Grune & Stratton.

Vogel, S. A. (1993). The continuum of responses to Section 504 for students with learning disabilities. In S. A. Vogel & P. B. Adelman (Eds.), Success for college students with learning disabilities (pp. 83–113). New York: Springer-Verlag.

Wilkison, P. (1989, January). [Interview with Loring Brinckerhoff, director of Learning Disabilities Support Services at Boston University]. RFB News, p. 8.

Wilson, D. L. (1992). New federal regulations on rights of the handicapped may force colleges to provide better access to technology. The Chronicle of Higher Education, 38(21), 1, 21–22.

CHAPTER 11

A World Alive [computer software]. (1991). Santa Monica, CA: Voyager Co.

Adventures of Jasper Woodbury [computer software]. (1992). Warren, NJ: Optical Data.

BioSci [computer software]. (1992) Seattle, WA: Videodiscovery.

Boone, R., & Higgins, K. (1991). Hypertext/hypermedia information presentation: Developing a hypercard template. Educational Technology, 31(2), 21–30.

Boone, R., & Higgins, K. (1993). Hypermedia basal readers: Three years of school-based research. Journal of Special Education Technology, 12, 86–106.

Bottage, B. A., & Hasselbring, T. S. (1993a). A comparison of two approaches for teaching complex, authentic mathematics problems to adolescents in remedial math classes. Exceptional Children, 59, 556–566.

Bottage, B. A., & Hasselbring, T. S. (1993b). Taking word problems off the page. Educational Leadership, 50(7), 36–38.

Bransford, J. D., Sherwood, R. D., Hasselbring, T. S., Kinzer, C. K., & Williams, S. M. (1990). Anchored instruction: Why we need it and how technology can help. In D. Nix & R. Spiro (Eds.), Cognition, education, and multimedia: Exploring ideas in high technology (pp. 115–141). Hillsdale, NJ: Erlbaum.

Bull, G. L., & Cochran, P. S. (1987). A book with 50,000 pictures: Logo and videodiscs. In T. Lough & G. Bull (Eds.), Conference proceedings East Coast Logo exchange (pp. 34–38). Arlington, VA: Meckler.

Bull, G. L., & Cochran, P. S. (1991). Learner-based tools. The Computing Teacher, 18(7), 50–53.

Bull, G. L., Cochran, P. S., & Snell, M. E. (1988). Beyond CAI: Computers, language, and persons with mental retardation. Topics in Language Disorders, 8(4), 55–76.

Cockayne, S. (1991). Effects of small group sizes on learning with interactive videodisc. Educational Technology, 31(3), 43–45.

Cognition and Technology Group at Vanderbilt University. (1991). Technology and the design of generative learning environments. Educational Technology, 31(5), 34–40.

Cognition and Technology Group at Vanderbilt University. (1993a). Designing learning environments that support thinking: The Jasper series as a case study. In T. M. Duffy, J. Lowyck, & D. H. Jonassen (Eds.), Designing environments for constructive learning (pp. 9–36). Washington, DC: Nato ASI Series.

Cognition and Technology Group at Vanderbilt University. (1993b). Integrated media: Toward a theoretical framework for utilizing their potential. Journal of Special Education Technology, 12, 71–85.

Cognition and Technology Group at Vanderbilt University. (1994). Multimedia environments for developing literacy in at-risk students. In B. Means (Ed.), Technology and education reform: The reality behind the promise (pp. 23–56). San Francisco: Jossey-Bass.

D'Ignazio, F. (1989). Welcome to the multimedia sandbox. The Computing Teacher, 17(1), 27–28.

D'Ignazio, F. (1994). Teachers' jobs: Opportunities for change and growth. The Computing Teacher, 21, 52–53.

Edyburn, D. L. (1991). Fact retrieval by students with and without learning handicaps using print and electronic encyclopedias. Journal of Special Education Technology, 11, 75–90.

Engelmann, S., & Carnine, D. (1989). Supporting teachers and students in math and science education through videodisc courses. Educational Technology, 29(8), 46–50.

Gagné, R. M., & Briggs, L. J. (1979). Principles of instructional design (2nd ed.). New York: Holt, Rinehart & Winston.

Garanger, M. (1989). Regard for the Planet [computer software]. Santa Monica, CA: Voyager.

Gay, G. (1986). Interaction of learner control and prior understanding in computer-assisted video instruction. Journal of Educational Psychology, 78, 225–227.

Hasselbring, T. S., Goin, L. I., & Wissick, C. A. (1989). Making knowledge meaningful: Applications of hypermedia. Journal of Special Education Technology, 10, 61–72.

Hooper, S., & Hannafin, M. J. (1988). Cooperative CBI: The effects of heterogenous versus homogeneous grouping on the learning of progressively complex concepts. Journal of Educational Computing Research, 4, 413–424.

Hunter, M. (1982). Mastery teaching. El Segundo, CA: Tip.

Huntley, M. (1991). The danger of style. ISTE Update, 3(8), 2–3.

Hurricane Hugo [computer software]. (1990). Atlanta, GA: Turner Educational Services.

Kinzie, M. B., Sullivan, H. J., & Berdel, R. L. (1988). Learner control and achievement in science computer-assisted instruction. Journal of Educational Psychology, 80, 299–303.

Locatis, C., Letourneau, G., & Banvard, R. (1990). Hypermedia and instruction. Educational Technology Research and Development, 37(4), 65–77.

MacGlobe [computer software]. (1992). Novato, CA: Broderbund.

Malouf, D. B., Jamison, P. J., Kercher, M. H., & Carlucci, C. M. (1991). Computer software aids effective instruction. Teaching Exceptional Children, 23(2), 56–57.

Mastering Fractions [computer software]. (1985). Washington, DC: Systems Impact.

McLellan, H. (1992). Hyper stories: Some guidelines for instructional designers. *Journal of Research on Computing in Education, 25,* 28–49.

McLellan, H. (1993). Hypertextual tales: Story models for hypertext design. *Journal of Educational Multimedia and Hypermedia, 2,* 239–260.

McNeil, B. J., & Nelson, K. R. (1991). Meta-analysis of interactive video instruction: A 10 year review of achievement effects. *Journal of Computer-Based Instruction, 18(1),* 1–6.

Morrison, G. R., Ross, S. M., & Baldwin, W. (1992). Learner control of context and instructional support in learning and elementary school mathematics. *Educational Technology Research and Development, 40,* 5–13.

National Gallery of Art [computer software]. (1983). New York, NY: Videodisc.

Pellegrino, J. W., Hickey, D., Heath, A., Rewey, K., Vye, N. J., & Cognition and Technology Group at Vanderbilt University. (1992). *Assessing the outcomes of an innovative instructional program: The 1990–1991 implementation of the "Adventures of Jasper Woodbury."* Nashville, TN: Learning Technology Center, Vanderbilt University.

Raiders of the lost ark [Film]. (1981). New York: Paramount Home Video.

Repman, J., Weller, H. G., & Lan, W. (1993). The impact of social context on learning in hypermedia-based instruction. *Journal of Educational Multimedia and Hypermedia, 2,* 283–298.

Salamandre: Chateaux of the Loire Valley [computer software]. (1988). Santa Monica, CA: Voyager Co.

Sharp, D. L., Goldman, S. R., Bransford, J. D., Hasselbring, T. S., Moore, P., Brophy, S., & Vye, N. (1993, April). *Developing strategic approaches to narrative structures with integrated media environments for young, at-risk children.* Paper presented at the annual meeting of the American Educational Research Association, Atlanta, GA.

Sherwood, R. D., Kinzer, C. K., Hasselbring, T. S., Bransford, J. D., Williams, S. M., & Goin, L. I. (1987). New directions for videodiscs. *The Computing Teacher, 14(6),* 10–13.

Signer, B. R. (1992). A model of cooperative learning with intergroup competition and findings when applied to an interactive video reading software. *Journal of Research on Computing in Education, 25,* 141–158.

Snyder, J. (1993). Hooking them with hypermedia—In any subject! *Hypernexus, 4(2),* 17-19.

Star wars [Film]. (1977). New York: CBS Fox Video.

The Storyteller [Computer software]. (1992). Columbia, SC: Star Express.

Taylor, R. (Ed.). (1980). *The computer in the school: Tutor, tool, tutee.* New York: Teachers College Press.

Thorpe, B. (1993). Kids can create videodisc reports. *The Computing Teacher, 20(5),* 22–23.

Truett, C. (1994). CD-rom, videodiscs, and new ways of teaching information and research skills. *The Computing Teacher, 21(6),* 42–45.

Turner, S. V., & Dipinto, V. M. (1992). Students as hypermedia authors: Themes emerging from a qualitative study. *Journal of Research on Computing in Education, 25,* 187–199.

Ulmer, E. J. (1990). High-tech instructional development: It's the thought that counts. Educational Technology Research and Development, 37(3), 95–101.

Wilson, K., & Tally, W. (1991). Looking at multimedia: Design issues in several discovery-oriented programs (Tech. Rep. No. 13). New York: Bank Street College of Education.

Windows on Science, Updated Version [Computer software]. (1993). Warren, NJ: Optical Data.

Wissick, C., Foelber, M., & Berdel, R. (1989). The repurposing of Raiders of the Lost Ark: Hypercard design and research on classroom use. In R. Fox (Ed.), Proceedings of the Society for Applied Learning Technology Eleventh Conference on Interactive Videodisc in Education and Training (pp. 8–10). Warrenton, VA: Society for Applied Learning Technology.

Woodward, J., & Gersten, R. (1992). Innovative technology for secondary students with learning disabilities. Exceptional Children, 58, 407–421.

CHAPTER 12

Clark, R. E. (1985). Confounding in educational computing research. Journal of Educational Computing Research, 1(2), 137–148.

CLD Research Committee: Rosenberg, M. S., Bott, D., Majsterek, D., Chiang, B., Gartland, D., Wesson, C., Graham, S., Smith-Myles, B., Miller, M., Swanson, H. L., Bender, W., Rivera, D., & Wilson, R. (1993). Minimum standards for the description of participants in learning disabilities research. Journal of Learning Disabilities, 26, 210–213.

Division of Innovation and Development, Office of Special Education Programs. (1992a). Administrative aspects of technology implementation in special education: A synthesis of information from eight federally-funded projects. Washington, DC: U.S. Department of Education. (ERIC Document Reproduction Service No. ED 349 752)

Division of Innovation and Development, Office of Special Education Programs. (1992b). The technology, educational media and materials strategic program agenda for individuals with disabilities. Washington, DC: U.S. Department of Education.

Ellis, E. S., & Sabornie, E. J. (1986). Effective instruction with microcomputers: Promises, practices, and preliminary findings. Focus on Exceptional Children, 19(4), 1–16.

Hanley, T. V. (1993). The future has been a disappointment: A response to Woodward and Noell's article on software development in special education. Journal of Special Education Technology, 12(2), 168–176.

Hasselbring, T. S. (1991). Improving education through technology: Barriers and recommendations. Preventing School Failure, 35(3), 33–37.

Hauser, J. (1991). From computers to virtual reality: A world of change for persons with disabilities. In T. Middleton (Ed.), Virtual worlds: Real challenges. Westport, CT: Meckler.

Howell, R. (1991). Working in the 21st Century: New Challenges for Special Education Students. Commissioned paper to the COSMOS Corporation, Washington, DC.

Johnston, W., & Packer, A. (1987). Workforce 2000. Indianapolis, IN: Hudson Institute.

Kulik, J. A., Banger, R. L., & Williams, G. W. (1983). Effects of computer-based teaching on secondary school students. Journal of Educational Psychology, 75(1), 19–26.

Kulik, J. A., Kulik, C. C., & Bangert-Drowns, R. L. (1985). Effectiveness of computer-based education in elementary schools. Computers in Human Behavior, 1(1), 59–74.

Malouf, D. B., & Schiller, E. P. (in press). Practice and research in special education. Exceptional Children.

Means, B., Blando, J., Olson, K., Middleton, T., Morocco, C. C., Remz, A. R., & Zorfass, J. (1993). Using technology to support education reform. Washington, DC: U.S. Government Printing Office.

Merrill, M. D. (1991). Constructivism and instructional design. Educational Technology, 31(5), 45–53.

Middleton, T., & Means, B. (1991). Exploring technologies for the education of children with disabilities (Final Report, Contract No. HS 89-027001). Washinton, DC: U.S. Department of Education.

Moore, G. B., Yin, R. K., & Lahm, E. A. (1985) Robotics, artificial intelligence, computer simulation: Future applications in special education (Final Report, Contract No. 300-84-0135). Washington, DC.: Department of Education.

Office of Technology Assessment. (1988). Power on! New tools for teaching and learning. Washington, DC: U. S. Government Printing Office.

Okolo, C. M., Bahr, C. M., & Rieth, H. J. (1993). A retrospective view of computer-based instruction. Journal of Special Education Technology, 12(1), 1–27.

Poplin, M. S. (1988). Holistic/constructivist principles of the teaching/learning process: Implications for the field of learning disabilities. Journal of Learning Disabilities, 21, 401–416.

Reich, R. (1991). The wealth of nations. New York: Knopf.

Salomon, G. (1991). Transcending the qualitative–quantitative debate: The analytic and systemic approaches to educational research. Educational Researcher, 20(6), 10–18.

Salomon, G., & Gardner, H. (1986). The computer as educator: Lessons from television research. Educational Researcher, 15(1), 13–19.

Salomon, G., Perkins, D. N., & Globerson, T. (1991). Partners in cognition: Extending human intelligence with intelligent technologies. Educational Researcher, 20(3), 2–9.

Sheingold, K., & Hadley, M. (1990). Accomplished teachers integrating computers into classroom practice. New York: Bank Street College of Education, Center for Children and Technology.

U.S. Department of Labor. (1991). What work requires of schools. Washington, DC: U.S. Government Printing Office.

Woodward, J. (1992). Workforce 2000 and the mildly handicapped. Commissioned paper to the COSMOS Corporation, Washington, DC. (ERIC Document Reproduction Service No. 350 765)

Contributors

Lynne Anderson-Inman, associate professor, education, University of Oregon

Beatrice C. Babbit, director of teacher education, and associate professor, special education, University of Nevada–Las Vegas

Christine M. Bahr associate professor, special education, Western Michigan University

Randall Boone, associate professor, computer education, University of Nevada–Las Vegas

Sheryl L. Day, doctoral candidate, special education, Florida State University

Barbara J. Edwards, assistant professor, special education, Florida State University

Ralph P. Ferretti, associate professor, educational studies and psychology, University of Delaware

Jane Hauser, dissemination specialist, Division of Innovation and Development, Office of Special Education Programs, Office of Special Education and Rehabilitative Services, U.S. Department of Education, Washington, DC

Kyle Higgins, associate professor, special education, University of Nevada–Las Vegas

Mark A. Horney, research associate, Center for Electronic Studying, University of Oregon

Carolyn Knox-Quinn, research associate, Center for Electronic Studying, University of Oregon

Thomas C. Lovitt, professor, special education, University of Washington–Seattle

Charles A. MacArthur, associate professor, educational studies, University of Delaware

David Majsterek, associate professor, special education and early childhood education, Central Washington University

David B. Malouf, education research analyst, Division of Innovation and Development, Office of Special Education Programs, Office of Special Education and Rehabilitative Services, U.S. Department of Education, Washington, DC

Susan Peterson Miller, associate professor, special education, University of Nevada–Las Vegas

Nickola W. Nelson, professor, speech pathology and audiology, Western Michigan University

Cynthia M. Okolo, associate professor, educational studies, University of Delaware

Deborah Simmons, assistant professor, learning and instructional leadership, University of Oregon

Adelia M. Van Meter, instructor, speech pathology and audiology, Western Michigan University

Keith Wetzel, assistant professor, educational media and computers, Arizona State University West Campus

Rich Wilson, associate professor and chair, special education, Bowling Green State University, Ohio

Cheryl A. Wissick, associate professor, special education, University of South Carolina

Author Index